THE CRAZY GANG

THE INSIDE STORY OF
VINNIE, HARRY, FASH & WIMBLEDON FC

THE CRAZY GANG

THE INSIDE STORY OF
VINNIE, HARRY, FASH & WIMBLEDON FC

MATT ALLEN

Published in 2005 by Highdown,
an imprint of Raceform Ltd
Compton, Newbury, Berkshire, RG20 6NL
Raceform Ltd is a wholly owned subsidiary of Trinity Mirror plc

A catalogue record for this book is available from the British Library.

ISBN 1-905156-01-4

Cover designed by Tracey Scarlett

Designed by Fiona Pike

Printed by Creative Print & Design, Wales

CONTENTS

ACKNOWLEDGEMENTS

Firstly, I'd like to extend a big thanks to Jonathan Taylor, who dug me out of a hole and allowed me to continue with an idea that seemed lost.

Many thanks as well to all at *FourFourTwo* for their endless help and the use of their library and newspaper cuttings. And big thanks to a long list of people who have helped me over the past year, probably without their ever realising it: Mooro, Susie Ember, James Bass, Dan Abrahams, Michael South, Phoebe Sinclair, Johnny Sharp, Richard Knott, Nick Caley, Lou Sanders, Dave Simmons, Richard Lonsdale, Warren Jackson, Paul Stokes, Kerry Potter, Richard Scott, Andy Fyfe, Dave Linley (for the *Match* magazines!), Louis Massarella, Dave Croghan, Katherine Green, Michael Hann, Griff, the Dodds, the Hiltons, Ron Humm, Sid Freeman, Craig Biscoe, Kev Liffen, the Tuesday Night Crazy Gang and Mum, Dad, Katie and Joanna.

And then, of course, there are the stars of the book: the Crazy Gang members who were interviewed along the way, and their adversaries and associates. Some were interviewed for *FourFourTwo* and the now sadly defunct *Total Sport* magazine, but in the main these interviews were conducted for the book itself. In no order, then, my thanks to Dave Bassett, John Fashanu, Don Howe, Warren Barton, John Hartson, Ron Atkinson, Tony Cottee, Chris Waddle, Robbie Earle, Paul Parker, Steve McMahon, Glen Cockerill, Steve Lovell, Tony Daley, Gordon Holmes, John Bond, Joe Royle, Neil Redfearn, Eric Hall, Les Brierly, Ronnie Brooks, Viv Anderson, Katrina McCreadie at Fulham, Rob Wilson at Crewe Alexandra, Debbie Williams-Wood at the League Managers Association, Trevor Williams at AFC Wimbledon, Julian Jenkins at Cardiff City, Katrina Bond at Cardiff City, Ron Noades, Kris Stewart, the FAI, the Brentford FC Press Office, Bobby Gould and Lawrie Sanchez.

INTRODUCTION

A FIGHT... ONE OF MANY

On the training ground, Fash wanted to kick Sanch into next week. He wanted to hurt him so badly that buckling his legs with a sharp blow to the calves seemed like a fair deal. But Lawrie Sanchez, his Wimbledon team-mate and adversary, wanted to hurt John Fashanu too. He'd had enough of the swaggering attitude that had accompanied Fash's arrival from Millwall earlier that year. There had been an immediate clash between the pair, and a battle of wills had simmered. This time, however, as practice started one soggy April morning in 1986, Fash had pushed Sanch too far.

In the temporary absence of the management team, Fash – who else? – had taken it upon himself to begin the morning's warm-up session. To everyone's annoyance he ordered the squad to jog around their Roehampton training ground, a public park in South London frequented by joggers and dog walkers. Standing in the mud and grass, Sanch began to seethe. This command seemed even more unbelievable given Fash's usually lethargic attitude towards practice sessions. He wore fancy suits to training as if he was finalising some bank-busting business deal rather than working for the team. He carried a briefcase around with him too, and it was only Second Division Wimbledon – hardly the height of financial wheeler-dealing.

Sanch had suffered enough. He was determined to end the bragging and the swaggering for good. Defiantly, he stood his ground in protest.

But Fash was eager to flex his authority too. He pointed and gestured at Sanch that he move in line with the others. *Cheeky.* His finger was slapped away, and Fash, who never shirked from a physical challenge, took the bait greedily. At Millwall Fash's team-mate Steven Lowndes had once issued a threat just like Sanch. He ended up sucking on hospital food for six weeks as payback.

This unfolding spat didn't surprise anybody in the Wimbledon team. The clash of personalities had been apparent from day one. Now both players were battling for territory, but it was Fash, not Sanch, who commanded the £125,000 fee (a so-called gift to the team from chairman Sam Hammam) and was a certified hotshot both on and off the pitch. The club expected much from their new investment, but Fash was expecting a lot from Wimbledon too. And now he believed his team-mates should fall in line behind him – even Sanch, one of the club's more senior players.

The others waited for the fists and teeth to fly. Up front, the mob leaders: keeper Dave Beasant (or Lurch as he had been nicknamed), striker Alan 'Corky' Cork and defender Nigel Winterburn. Even senior pro Wally Downes was there, the only other guy brave enough to challenge Fash during his short time at the club. When Fash arrived a month earlier, Wally had set fire to his favourite silk socks in the changing rooms. This was part of the traditional initiation ceremony that greeted every new face rather than a malicious act. Fash was lucky too: some players were stripped naked and beaten; others watched as their favourite shirts were cut to ribbons; but Fash hadn't seen the funny side of his induction. That incident and several other practical jokes wouldn't be forgotten. There had been a set-to with Wally and his new team-mates afterwards; Fash stood up to the others and proved his place. *Punched his weight.* After the smouldering silk socks, after his tea was laced with salt, Fash decided nobody was big enough to challenge him. His colleagues agreed and backed down. This was partly why he would wear a fancy suit on his way into Wimbledon's distinctly down-at-heel training ground: he wasn't turning up in a pair of jeans or a tracksuit like his team-mates, because Fash was there to do the business. In some strange way the suit represented a test to the others, a challenge.

Go on, are you brave enough?

Sure, Wally had been brave enough before, but this new spat was a clash of the titans. Sanch had stepped up to have a crack at the title, and in his own unique way he was also an individual like Fash. He rarely took part in the training-ground high jinks the others seemed to thrive on. He didn't enjoy dragging his butt-naked team-mates through the snow. He didn't agree with the hotel trashing, the mauling of journalists or the regular fist fights that seemed to accompany every training session and away match. Occasionally, though, there had been times when Sanch allowed himself a little chaotic fun. His team-mates would incredulously recall the moment when, during a team break one December, Sanch had body-slammed a Christmas tree to the ground in a hotel lobby before running into the street covered head to foot in fairy lights. But generally he was pretty strait-laced (he had thirteen O Levels and four A Levels; in one interview he claimed his favourite item of clothing was his black 501s because 'they were so practical'), and these moments of madness were few and far between. Nevertheless, Sanch was an important part of the Wimbledon team. He was a passionate and hard-working pro. He was also a dedicated trainer, which was where Fash seemed to be his very opposite. This angered Sanch most of all. He'd grumble when Fash dropped out of training on a Monday morning – yet again. He'd watch as Fash relaxed on the treatment table for a few days before declaring himself fit for the big game by Friday afternoon. And all the while, Sanch was working his arse off for Wimbledon, training in the rain and the mud and Roehampton's dog shit.

Who the hell does he think he is?

'This has been going on too long,' said Fash, eyeballing his adversary. 'We're two men, let's sort it. Let's take a walk. Lads, carry on jogging.'

And the pair walked away.

On paper, the odds were stacked in Fash's favour. At over six feet three inches he was one of the biggest in the squad, and his body was taut with muscle. The bulk was finely chiselled, and he regularly supplemented his football training with an intensive martial arts programme. Like his older brother Justin, Fash had once considered a career in heavyweight boxing before signing professional forms with Norwich City, and according to trainers at Watton Boys' Club in Norwich, Fash was no slouch in the ring. He once slugged out the English amateur schoolboys champion in a 'friendly' bout, and his coach, Gordon Holmes, noted an impressive technical prowess. 'John was a thinker [in the ring],' he said. 'He wouldn't tear your head off like the others, but he was a good fighter.' Wimbledon team-mate Warren Barton later issued a more direct assessment: 'You wouldn't want to upset Fash,' he warned.

Shoulder to shoulder, then, Sanch couldn't have expected anything less than a battering. But Fash knew the dogged fighter in Sanch wouldn't allow him to back down either, although he was aware of the odds in his favour. 'For Sanch this was the Walk of Death,' he told a reporter later, describing the incident as if it were something from a movie – two leading characters preparing for their final battle.

The pair walked behind a hedgerow. This would obscure their showdown from the eyes of the management. And it was going to be bloody. Fash was weighing up which karate chops and kicks to use. He knew striking Sanch across the face was out of the question, because any marks would alert their manager, Dave Bassett. The press boys would probably hear about it too, and they'd love a training-ground punch-up to sink their teeth into. Instead, Fash decided to employ a style used by a New York martial artist who had once taken on Muhammad Ali in a showcase fight in the 1970s. During the bout, Ali had issued a series of savage blows, but the smaller, quicker fighter relied on an attack of kicks to the back of the boxer's calves. The relentless assault pounded Ali's tissues into submission.

But before Fash had time to set himself, Sanch threw the first shot. The blow wasn't particularly painful, but its timing caught Fash off guard. Quickly, he struck back. 'I thought I'd teach Sanch a lesson and give him a sweep of the legs, but Sanch has calves like most people have thighs and he didn't move. So I gave him another couple, but Sanch came back at me. So I thought, "I'm gonna take this guy out," and I hit him with one of the best shots I'd been training with. Bam! Take that, Sanch! Right in the solar plexus – a shot that's supposedly capable of knocking a horse down.

'Sanch still stood there. Then youth-team coach Terry Burton came over to break the fight up'.

It was just another day on the Wimbledon training ground.

*

Everybody in football understood that crossing John Fashanu was a bad idea. But then, everybody knew that crossing Wimbledon during those few lawless years in the 1980s held even greater consequences. They cracked skulls, smashed teeth and bundled balls into nets with elbows, knees and foreheads. They bit journalists, trashed hotels and dropped their trousers in public. And no matter how many fights erupted, no matter how many red or yellow cards were brandished, no matter how often authority intervened or a so-called 'hard man' stepped in the way, nothing was going to stop them.

Galvanised by the management of Dave 'Harry' Bassett, an affable Londoner with a keen understanding of inspirational man-management, the Dons embarked on an incredible journey unrivalled by any team in football history, before or since. Somehow, in just under ten years, they climbed from a lowly position in the Southern Leagues (the semi-professional divisions) through the Football League to reach the old First Division. The feat was made even more remarkable by the fact that Harry, a former Wimbledon player, had little in the way of financial resources with which to strengthen his team. Wimbledon were a poor relation in comparison to football's bigger, wealthier brothers and their manager relied on a mixture of young talent and seasoned professionals to grab success. And Wimbledon's success could certainly be described as a grab. In fact, on occasions, their progression to Division One resembled an armed robbery at a 24-hour petrol station.

Under Harry's stewardship, the squad bonded through a series of vicious pranks off the pitch and a propensity for physical violence and intimidation on it. Their football was ugly, often based on long balls from defence to a burly front line that would resort to grievous bodily harm in order to get that ball into the back of the net. Short passing and mazy dribbles through midfield were eschewed in favour of high crosses and long clearances. The press and the fans hated it: they couldn't see the skill in it at all. Everybody criticised their style of football.

Meanwhile, red and yellow cards were shown to the Crazy Gang with a worrying regularity, even at a time when football was a man's game and the two-footed sweeping and reducer tackle (a challenge former Manchester United manager Ron Atkinson described as 'being intended to reduce the playing capacities of an opponent') was still an acceptable facet of the game. Wimbledon didn't care. It was all part of their strategy. In training, scraps like the one between Fash and Sanch were actively encouraged.

To the outside world, it looked like a nuthouse. In 1985 Wimbledon were nicknamed the Crazy Gang by *Daily Mirror* journalist Tony Stenson. During the run-in to an FA Cup fifth-round game against West Ham, he preceded an introductory feature on the team with the words: 'Meet Dave Bassett's barmy army, meet the ragtag and bobtail, the team that is so skint they nick towels from hotels. Let me introduce soccer's Crazy Gang.' It captured the public's imagination overnight, but their peers despised the scruffy image and bloodthirsty tactics. It seemed like a stupid joke. From the moment Division One status was secured in 1986, Wimbledon were viewed with derision. 'It would be fair to say that most of the other clubs in the league had a snotty attitude towards Wimbledon when they came up,' said West Ham's Tony Cottee, one of the leading strikers in Division One at the time. 'Sure, we appreciated what they had achieved, but that didn't mean we had to admire it.'

Off the pitch, the papers knew the deal. They knew the Crazy

Gang spirit was ugly and went against everything the game stood for, but the brawling and the thuggery made for good copy. Initially, the Football Association knew the deal too: here was a team that represented the pantomime villain, a counter punch to the beautiful football played by the top flight's connoisseurs and money movers. Who cared about a few bruises among the fancy Dans and poseurs? Their enthusiasm diminished as the complaints increased however, and suspensions and fines were later dished out like matchday programmes.

But it was the fans who really understood the Crazy Gang. Wimbledon were the team they loved to hate, to criticise, to boo. They represented everything that was wrong with professional football – the violence, the route one philosophy, the mob mentality – but at the same time they encompassed everything that was reassuring about the English game: the idea that an everyman team full of everyday players could scrap and battle their way from the mucky depths of non-league football to English football's pinnacle within a decade. It epitomised the nation's affection for an underdog, no matter how flea-bitten. To the regular fans, the Crazy Gang were just like them. They were hod carriers, brickies, plumbers, pub footballers, kids from broken families and end-of-the-earth housing estates. *Real people*, not prima donnas who swanned around in tight perms and even tighter shorts. They didn't make pop singles like Glenn and Chris, they didn't advertise shampoo products, and they certainly didn't make for teenage pin-up material. They were scum, everybody looked down on them, and the Crazy Gang loved it.

'The snotty attitude wound the players up, but it helped us,' said Harry Bassett. 'It motivated us. We knew the big teams didn't fancy coming to play us at our home ground, Plough Lane. And we didn't care about that, or the fact that people didn't like our style of football, because we liked it. We didn't care what people said about us.'

And if the Crazy Gang were crazy, their owner was worse. Far worse. Sam Hammam was an administrative oddball who pulled Wimbledon's strings behind the bloody noses and mob law. He'd arrived in London from Lebanon in 1977 and had grown to love the capital city, so much so that he decided to buy a large chunk of Wimbledon Football Club on a whim, as a 'souvenir', despite never having taken an interest in the game before.

But Sam, as he would prove throughout his career, was no business tourist. He was born to be a big hitter. As he settled in the capital and into his new role at Wimbledon, football chairmen soon became wary of him. Those witnessing his negotiation skills at first hand always walked away rattled. Even his close associates suffered as a result of his freewheeling techniques: Harry was once persuaded to bankroll his house as capital against a £100,000 loan; the money was later used to buy a handful of new players for the club as Harry's wife went bananas.

Sam's motivational techniques were unique too. As his team crawled up league tables and the noses of officialdom, he would often interrupt Wimbledon's half-time talks to deliver his own footballing monologue. More often than not players were ordered to win at all costs or face the prospect of eating camel's brains and sheep's testicles – those well-known Lebanese delicacies – for dinner. In order to keep the club's secrets in-house, he even ordered players to sign a non-disclosure agreement preventing them from recalling their manic escapades during and after their employment at the club. In 1993 he publicly challenged striker Dean Holdsworth to break the twenty-goal mark, a deal that carried a grisly sub-clause. 'If he scores twenty this season,' promised Sam, 'I will kiss his backside and take him for dinner at [London restaurant] Quaglino's. If he doesn't, he can kiss my backside.' Clearly the challenge worked: Holdsworth racked up 24 goals. More impressively, Sam remained true to his word and planted a smacker on Holdsworth's butt.

Bizarrely, he also once sent midfielder Vinnie Jones to ballet lessons as punishment for a poor performance. In 1999 journalists were warned they'd be eating horse manure if Wimbledon defied predictions and stayed in the Premiership. Former Dons coach Ray Harford was once paid a £10,000 bonus in pound coins, while Wimbledon manager Bobby Gould had a clause in his contract allowing the owner to make team changes until five minutes before kick-off. The clause was never exploited, but clearly Sam was not a man happy with a faceless boardroom existence. 'Sam is Sam,' said Gould. 'He's an exuberant character, yes, but he'd never step outside the law. Sam wants to be a winner, and he's a very clever man.' Larger-than-life football agent Eric Hall added, 'Sam Hammam is the loveliest man in the football world. He is slightly mad, but he's very shrewd. The man has got heart. We want more Sam Hammams, not fewer.'

At times, however, Sam did appear to overstep the mark. Witness his bold statement on Wimbledon's promotion to the First Division in 1986, only four years after he had taken full control: this was his greatest triumph, an achievement to be celebrated, a never-done-before, unbelievable rise from the slums of non-league football. And still Sam couldn't curb his battling spirit. 'We have to remain the British Bulldog SAS club,' he warned. 'We have to sustain ourselves with sheer power and the attitude that we will kick ass. Before we go down, we'll have a stream of blood from here to Timbuktu.' He even compared being a football fan to heroin addiction. Chairmen in the First Division shivered. And at other times he seemed just to plain old lose his mind. In 1997 he was physically manhandled from the Old Trafford touchline by security staff after attempting to sit in the Wimbledon dugout. Clearly, the whispers that dogged his Wimbledon career had been proved true. *Sam was a loose cannon.*

It certainly seemed that way as he embarked on his charge in the early 1980s. But to look at him you wouldn't have believed it. His gentle features – a shock of white hair perched above bushy eyebrows, warm eyes and a generous smile – were almost grandfatherly, though they belied a ruthless business streak, as Harry could testify. Whenever refereeing decisions went against the Dons' muscular game plan during their spats with the big guns of football few escaped the friendly fire. Sam punched his weight and battled through an eleven-man class war. Everybody looked down on Wimbledon and their aggressive attitude to the game, but Sam wasn't going to accept the criticism. He viewed the harsh decisions and sneering comments as a warped football snobbery. 'We're being raped by trigger-happy referees,' he spat in 1995. 'The fact of life is that the dice is loaded against the poorer people. Big clubs in football get away with murder. Referees believe we are macho thugs and seem to act accordingly. It doesn't happen to other clubs.'

To the public at large, Sam was just another crank in a club riddled with them. But over and above that, the outside world understood that Wimbledon's tale was a unique phenomenon, an unrepeatable rags-to-modest-riches nightmare. Later, once the dust had settled and the scars had healed, the authorities responsible for enhancing the Premiership's elite status with Sky TV's cash made sure it would never happen again. It was as if they wanted Wimbledon out of the picture altogether. Sadly, they succeeded.

But for a short while in the late 1980s Wimbledon's dream was a simple shakedown. Everybody knew the Crazy Gang were bad news, but everybody knew they were the best thing to have happened to English football for a long time. They were unique. Sure, it was ugly, but in a strange way it was romantic too.

PART ONE

IN THE MIXER

CHAPTER ONE

Harry Bassett cooked the madness at every turn. For a club that battled against the odds on an almost daily basis, the Crazy Gang needed a manager moulded in his kamikaze style. Like Fash, Sanch and Sam, Harry was a wildcard character, an individual who wouldn't take heat from any player or team that stood in his way. And because he appeared to be as anarchic as they were, his players quickly fell in line behind him.

The mad streak that cut through Wimbledon was cut through Harry too. He was a joker who regularly instigated the training-ground beatings that took place on a daily basis. He would also organise the practical jokes and rile his players before, during and after games – though he wasn't foolish enough to hang around once the fists began to fly. Once a stunt was pulled and the chaos unravelled around his club, Harry would walk away. The team could enjoy their own violent madness without him. He could take a joke too. His underpants were once sprayed with Deep Heat in the dressing room, and he was forced to run into the showers as his groin began to burn.

But like everything Harry did, the pranks were taken with a smile. He figured his players worked hard, so they were allowed to play hard too, even if on occasions it was achieved at his expense. Harry, after all, had been responsible for instilling the madness that twisted the Crazy Gang into public enemies and tabloid villains in the first place. When he signed for Wimbledon as a player in 1974, he caused mayhem behind the scenes. 'The Crazy Gang was Bassett's thing,' agreed one-time Wimbledon chairman Ron Noades. 'One morning they were on the M4 motorway travelling back from an evening game and one of the players was left stranded naked on a central reservation. It was reported on Radio Five news in the morning: somebody had seen a naked man on the motorway and had called the show.' Later, as a manager, he allowed staff to pour buckets of water over physios as they treated injured players. After one game, a member of the team was shocked to find that somebody had used his shoe as a toilet bowl – only after he'd slipped his foot in with a squelch. Harry laughed as hard as everybody else, just as he did when Dave Beasant's motorcycle helmet was filled with flour.

But when it came to organising his teams, he was no joker. Harry's peers dismissed him as a one-trick pony when Wimbledon arrived in the First Division in 1986. Fans marked him down as a tactician reliant on the long ball from defence and a brute physicality all over the park to win games. The media figured his teams battered their opponents into submission rather than outwitting them with guile and skill. All of this was true to a certain extent, but Harry always felt slighted by the stereotyping forced upon him. He'd developed a team on a shoestring budget, picking up skilled bargain-basement players, including Nigel Winterburn, Dave Beasant, Dennis Wise, John Fashanu and Vinnie Jones, and taken them to the First Division. All of these players were sold at huge mark-up prices. Meanwhile, many of his greatest victories had come after analysing a team's weaknesses and exploiting them rather than simply crushing them with a relentless barrage of long balls. There was much more to his game than everyone seemed to think.

Harry's problem was that he didn't come from the football aristocracy. Had he played for a professional side during his career, maybe more credit would have been handed to him. As a player, however, his football was played with the same sense of reckless abandon as the Crazy Gang. Harry was just your typical amateur footballer, and the achievements in his career were few and far between. As a midfielder with non-League Walton & Hersham, and later Wimbledon in the 1970s, he played with a quick mind, was strong in front of goal and remained a determined tackler. But deep down Harry knew he was never going to match the achievements of Bobby Moore or Martin Peters, and it frustrated him. He was still passionate, however, and throughout his life he loved playing football. It was never a job to him, so when Wimbledon initially handed him only a weekly semi-professional salary of £14, it didn't matter because he was a battler, prone to challenging adversity and therefore fantastic raw material for a team of the Crazy Gang's perennial underdog status. A small wage was just another obstacle for him to hurdle.

Harry was committed and focused. Certainly, anyone looking for evidence of his suitability for the manager's job at Wimbledon when it arose in 1981 needed only to glance at a lengthy CV. As a kid he had battled against the poor grades and the boring rigmarole of education. He'd hassled officials at professional clubs just to get a trial as a schoolboy player. Later, as an amateur footballer, he'd battled harder than anyone just to chase a throw-in or win every loose pass. Harry seemed determined to beat the bigger guys in everything he did. Off the field the work rate was even more strenuous. His football career at a string of middling non-League clubs (a spell that lasted from 1961 to 1981) had been supplemented with a vocation as an inspector for a London firm called Scottish Life Assurance, for which he hawked insurance policies to banks and finance companies. He later went on to start his own insurance firm, but all the time Harry dreamed of a career in the First Division, even though the odds were stacked against a life in professional football.

Of course he wasn't really called Harry. It wasn't even a middle name, just a convenient tag given to him by friends of the family. According to his autobiography, Bassett Junior's real name was David, but given that his old man was called Harry he was labelled 'Harry's Boy', or maybe 'Young Harry', to differentiate him from the other Davids in the street. Later, in his teenage years, the name became permanent.

Honeypot Lane Nursing Home in Kingsbury, London, was the rather incongruous birthplace in 1944 for the Bassett family's only son. Within a year he'd been handed his first football as a birthday present. By his fifth, he was kicking it around the playground of Willesden's Brent Road School. Naturally, education took a back seat, and when Harry wasn't playing in the park he was daydreaming in lessons about future footballing achievements. At weekends his granddad would take him to watch First Division football at Stamford Bridge or Craven Cottage, while Sundays were spent watching his dad slugging it out for a distinctly less glamorous side from the local transport depot. He was hopelessly addicted to football, and his passion began to pay off. At school he was selected for the U-11 side despite weighing in at a tender nine years of age. But the success came at a price, and school tests were flunked with alarming regularity. Eleven- and thirteen-plus exams came and went with disappointing marks attached; even a private tutor, paid for by his mother Joyce, couldn't drag him through education with anything approaching respectability.

But a change was just around the corner. At thirteen he managed to earn a place at Roxeth Manor School, having passed an aptitude test and secured a spot on a commercial course. Here, Harry told tutors that a career in journalism seemed like an exciting vocation. Four years later, and to his own amazement, he finished school with five O Levels and walked into a job as a trainee for the Scottish Life Assurance company in nearby Harrow. Within another four years he was decorated with a company car and the position of inspector. Clearly Harry was no slouch in the organisational department.

All the while his affection for football remained unswerving. At seventeen, he wrote desperate letters to youth-team managers at a string of professional clubs. Chelsea and Fulham, the teams he'd watched with granddad as a kid, were his preferred destinations, but initially his enquiries were greeted with muted enthusiasm. A flicker of opportunity briefly appeared when Fulham offered him a trial at Craven Cottage, where coaches were impressed and handed him a contract, but his head was quickly turned by an offer from Chelsea manager Ted Drake. Sadly, his excitement was short-lived. Once he'd signed with Drake, Chelsea didn't view him as an integral part of their youth team, often leaving him on the sidelines during matches. And when Drake left Chelsea and was replaced by Tommy Docherty, Harry was told to forget a career at Stamford Bridge.

As always, his enthusiasm remained undiminished. During

this disappointing spell, he supplemented the time spent warming the youth-team bench with games for Hayes, a side competing in the amateur Athenian League. Despite his teenage frame, he quickly muscled into the first team with his keen running and work rate while attracting the attention of professional clubs, most notably the Swiss First Division side Basle, which offered him a contract after an impressive performance in a pre-season friendly. However, by his own admission, Chelsea's rejection had pounded the ego, and Harry was desperate to prove himself at home. Basle's offer was rejected, and in 1963 he joined Wycombe Wanderers, a tidy outfit in the Isthmian League – a more competitive and talented amateur league. After half a year he returned to Hayes having failed to settle at Wycombe, but the change proved a vital turning point.

During the 1964/65 season a string of impressive performances attracted scouts to Hayes. Watford proved the most eager, offering Harry a professional contract a season later, but bizarrely, after a spell playing in their reserve team in the Combination League (a competition for the reserve teams at most professional clubs), he chose to slap it away. Watford, he felt, were not a club big enough to match his ambitions. They were playing in the Third Division after all, though more importantly he was loath to lose the company car afforded to him by Scottish Life Assurance. His friends and family figured Harry had lost his marbles. This would mark the beginning of a trend. Long after the Wimbledon years, during his managerial spell at Crystal Palace, Harry showed the same unflinching aspiration, claiming that he would leave Selhurst Park only if AC Milan offered him employment. 'I'm not mucking about with these intermediate clubs,' he said. 'I want the top stuff!'

For now, though, he would have to contend with second best. He signed for Hendon in 1966 in what would prove to be a disappointing journey, despite an enjoyable appearance for the England amateur side against Enfield. When the club was drawn against Harry's former club Wycombe Wanderers in the Amateur Cup, he missed the game through flu. Later, when Hendon progressed to the final at Wembley, Harry was sidelined with a broken leg sustained during a game for his Sunday side, Thames FC. 'Really intelligent,' he sniffed later, recalling the injury.

An eighteen-month absence from the game followed. The time was used to pick up girls and party in his Ruislip flat. But once the leg had healed he was back in business, first during a miserable three-month stint at St Albans City ('A mistake,' he later admitted). Then came another return to Hayes, before joining Walton & Hersham in 1970. By then he had long dismissed the dream of a career in professional football (he was 26), and occasionally his frustration manifested itself on the pitch. Two sendings-off during his final spell at Hayes resulted in lengthy bans and £10 fines, though Harry would show his true battling spirit by taking the FA head on and writing a particularly angry letter outlining the injustice of his punishment. He lost, but this would be the first of many showdowns with authority during his managerial life, most of them with the FA.

At Walton & Hersham, then under the control of manager Allen Batsford, Harry began to settle, and took an interest in coaching. 'Batsford got hold of me when I was a bit of a rebel at 24 – a loony you know – got me interested in coaching. He influenced my thinking.' He influenced his playing style too, and Harry was soon invited to play for the Surrey FA and FA Amateur XI sides before pulling on the England amateur shirt in a string of friendlies in 1971. He notched up a total of ten caps, and later captained the Walton & Hersham side to victory in the FA Amateur Cup in 1973, which climaxed in a Wembley final against Slough in front of 46,000. It wasn't quite the World Cup Final success he had dreamed of as a kid, but for Harry it marked an amazing triumph. Later that year, when Walton & Hersham defeated Brian Clough's Brighton side 4–0 in the first round of the FA Cup, Harry began to concede that perhaps this was to be the pinnacle of his football career.

Until Wimbledon came calling, that is.

The Wimbledon Harry Bassett joined in 1974 bore a personality as battle-hardened and passionate as his own. To Wimbledon fans their club's romantic back story was as popular as the myths that followed the likes of Sanch, Fash and Harry during the late eighties. In 1889 a group of players previously affiliated to Old Central School in Wimbledon's Camp Road decided to form a football team. They chose the imaginative moniker of Wimbledon Old Centrals and began practising and playing on a makeshift pitch by Robin Hood Road on Wimbledon Common. At this time, Wimbledon wasn't the lush South London suburb of today. In fact, it was nothing more than a village, and fixtures with opponents willing to travel to the common were initially hard to come by. Nevertheless, the team decided on a blue and white strip and began using a local pub, the Fox and Grapes Inn, to change at weekends.

Eventually the friendlies gathered pace. Matches against Peckham Adults and Rabbit & Sons were organised. Old Centrals won their first game, a 1–0 victory over Westminster on 2 November 1889. But as the games mounted up, so did local complaints. As this early incarnation of Sam and Harry's mob scrapped their way to wins in the mud and grass, long, wayward passes and shots were skipping off the turf and clattering into passing dog walkers and carriages hurtling along the Robin Hood Road. Local conservators went crazy, so the players decided to up goalposts and play half a mile deeper into the common. Symbolically at least, Wimbledon had ruffled the purists with their long-ball game for the first time – a complaint Harry would have to suffer on more than one occasion during his time in charge.

A long and difficult existence had begun that involved ground hops and financial difficulties punctuated by cup success. They jumped from pitch to pitch during the late 1890s and early 1900s, simultaneously swapping kit colours from light blue and chocolate to blue and white, and finally to blue and yellow. They looked a pretty dapper mob too: one grainy black and white photo of the team, featuring the unfamiliar names Milledge, Jenkins, Bates and Edgcumbe, depicted a bunch of stiff-lipped gentlemen complete with curling moustaches, long shorts and shirt sleeves rolled up to the elbow. This team finally settled on Plough Lane – an expanse of bog land with a football pitch marked out on the turf that would develop into a stadium for superstars in under a century – and on the name Wimbledon FC in 1913.

In between the identity changes, Wimbledon were proving habitual in victory. They rattled up 100 goals in just over 30 games in 1901/02, claimed the South London Charity Cup in 1905 and appeared in the FA Cup proper in 1906, though they were kicked out by Norwood in a 2–1 defeat. By then, the club had built up a reputation as one of the best amateur teams in the country, which was understandable given their track record. The 1920s was a barren spell – Wimbledon won only a handful of local cup competitions – but it was only a minor blip. In the 1930s they qualified for the first round of the FA Cup, progressed to and claimed (in 1931, 1932, 1935 and 1936) the Isthmian League, one of the most respected amateur leagues in the country, and also made the semi-finals of the FA Amateur Cup while gobbling up five local trophies in the process.

Fame came calling. The players were immortalised in cigarette cards, and in 1935 they attracted a crowd of 18,000 fans to a third-round FA Amateur Cup game against HMS Victory. Later, some 32,000 fans arrived for the final's replay at Stamford Bridge, though Wimbledon were hit by a 2–1 defeat at the hands of Bishop Auckland. In 1947 they returned after the wartime interruption with an FA Amateur Cup Final appearance against Leytonstone before 47,000 spectators at Highbury, though they suffered another 2–1 defeat. Despite these losses, this team clearly represented much more than the group of former school-mates who had once kicked a ball around Wimbledon Common. They were one of the biggest amateur clubs in the country.

But Wimbledon had sugar daddies. Their Plough Lane ground had taken shape during World War One as the then club chairman, Mr Headicar, used the time to build a 500-capacity stand. Over the coming decades it would develop into a full stadium complete with club house and terracing, thanks to the generosity of chairman Sydney Black, a local benefactor who arrived during the 1950s. Black was determined to drag the club into modern times and believed his players should be treated like superstars. He even flew the squad to Switzerland in 1956 for a friendly against the Division Five team FC Lengnau. Tickets for the Swiss Cup Final were thrown in too. Black was a hugely influential figure in Wimbledon's history. The west wing of the stadium, previously a grass mound, was covered, and the club house was given a facelift. Training sessions, focusing on cardiovascular work and strength training, as well as competitive fixtures could take place on week nights thanks to Black's investment in floodlights. A gym was installed too, and the players spoke proudly of the technologically advanced kit that was being introduced to their daily routine – football boots with screw-in studs and plastic balls. Legend has it that a Wimbledon physio even devised a blueprint for the shin pad.

Many of the changes on the park were the responsibility of Les Henley, the former Arsenal and Reading player who had taken charge of the team in 1955. Henley introduced a new strip of blue shirts and white shorts and took Wimbledon into the future. The club played with the M formation introduced by England manager Don Revie, and in 1958/59 they claimed their first Isthmian League title since 1936. They secured another in 1962, and even took their first League scalp when they defeated Division Three Colchester 2–1 in the FA Cup first round. The team had won with ten men too: one player had smacked his head against an opponent and was stretchered off. In an era before the introduction of substitutes, Wimbledon secured victory a player short.

By the 1960s they were amateur giants. They even picked up a goal-scoring legend, striker Eddie Reynolds, a bruiser who scored more goals with his head – 50 in one season, if myth is to be believed – than his feet, although he wasn't bad on the deck either. Many team-mates observed that his quick feet left opponents, particularly goalkeepers, bemused. He came from Ulster and was a whopping six feet three inches tall. He was a mean-looking so-and-so too, his creased features and Stan Laurel haircut often planting the ball powerfully past a goalkeeper into the back of the net. After he'd signed from local rivals Tooting and Mitcham in 1958, he helped Wimbledon to those two Isthmian League titles and secured the FA Amateur Cup in 1963. All four of the Wimbledon goals that humbled Sutton United were thumped home by Eddie Reynolds's head. Fash would have been proud.

Typically, there was also financial controversy in the early days, and for much of their shelf-life in the amateur divisions they had to resist the temptation to turn overtly corrupt. A number of Wimbledon's peers in the Southern and Isthmian Leagues actually paid their players a weekly wage rather than employ footballers who would compete for the love of the club. During the 1940s the likes of Leytonstone and Walthamstow in London were paying their players as much as £5 or £10 a game – a small fortune in those days. But Wimbledon prided themselves on being an honest team and refused to corrupt their accounts. Even if they had considered shamateurism, as it was called, it's unlikely their players would have stood for the incentives on offer at that time. Traditionally, many footballers at amateur clubs preferred the relaxed atmosphere in the non-leagues and would have refused cash handouts. A number of Wimbledon players even rejected lucrative offers from other non-league clubs in order to retain their amateur status. It felt purer. To the club and the players, it was the height of honesty.

Shamateurism was a cute turn of phrase, but a number of clubs without the financial clout of their rivals, including Wimbledon, were soon left floundering in the chase for the best players in the division. Wimbledon were still loath to go down that road, but by 1956 the club had reached a crossroads. By abstaining from shamateurism Wimbledon had handicapped themselves. The successes of previous decades looked difficult to emulate given the problems the club were having attracting quality players to Plough Lane. Wimbledon would have to stoop to the same underhand methods as their peers if they were to retain their impressive standing in the Isthmian League. In 1956 Sydney Black introduced a controversial payment scheme among his staff, but for many players this represented a modernisation too far. Several members of the squad were proud of their amateur status and the club's unswerving commitment to amateur football. At the end of the season they opted to leave Plough Lane to play elsewhere. For those who stayed, brown envelopes stuffed with bank notes were dropped off in the dressing room after every game.

It was the end of Wimbledon's innocence, but it was born of necessity. The club applied for semi-professional status in 1963, but only because the FA had sniffed rumours of illegal payments being made within the amateur leagues and had opened up an investigation. On television, Cyril Black, brother of Sydney and a Tory MP, was asked if Wimbledon had made player payments. 'No,' he'd answered defiantly. But he had lied. Wimbledon were as guilty as all the others.

Once Wimbledon attained semi-professional status in 1964 and joined the Southern League, the cracks began to show. A number of fans, disillusioned at the club's new standing, abandoned the team. Gates of nearly 10,000 dwindled overnight. Just over 3,000 attended the first semi-professional game, against Poole Town at Plough Lane – a far cry from the 18,000 that had crammed themselves in for the 1935 FA Cup tie with HMS Victory. To fans of the amateur game semi-professional football just wasn't as much fun. The new league presented geographical challenges too: fans found that they had to travel all over the country to watch Wimbledon – Merthyr

Tydfil was just one of the venues on the fixture list – whereas before, as the Isthmian League was based in London, supporters had only needed a bus ticket. The team didn't care, however: they quickly bagged promotion to the Southern League Premier (one league below the old Fourth Division) and were thus banging on the door for full professional status.

But off-the-field tragedy was about to strike. Sydney Black, an habitual smoker, was slipping into illness. Tobacco had plugged the arteries wired to his brain, and he was struggling to maintain focus. He would fall asleep at random times. Some days he wouldn't even get out of bed at all. More worryingly, his visits to the ground became increasingly scarce, and when he did muster the strength to visit Plough Lane on matchdays he required a chaperone. He died on 4 April 1968. Wimbledon's next game, against Cambridge United, was marked with a minute's silence, and both teams played in black armbands.

The knock-on effect was immediate. Without Black's cash the club was financially adrift, especially as low gates had already affected Wimbledon's bank balance. The number of semi-professionals at the club was slashed to just sixteen, the reserve team was abandoned, and the number of supporters attending matches dropped below 2,000. By the time former Walton & Hersham boss Allen Batsford was signed up to manage the club in 1974 the team was in dire straits. They had no money, next to no players and looked unlikely to escape from non-league football. The club was going nowhere, and Batsford had to improve matters quickly.

Which was where Harry came in. Almost as soon as Batsford said yes to the managerial job, he convinced Harry to join him as a player. Batsford figured he could use his enthusiasm and tireless running at Wimbledon, and Harry jumped at the chance. This was unsurprising: under Batsford at Walton & Hersham Harry had enjoyed some of the best football of his playing career, and he wanted to prolong the buzz. Under the grim circumstances, Wimbledon needed a character like Harry. The previous year he had married his long-term girlfriend and Miss Great Britain finalist, Christine. At the wedding the Walton & Hersham team had formed a human tunnel with their matchday boots in an unusually skewed show of respect. Off the pitch he enjoyed ballet and the theatre. He was a lover of fine wines and nice restaurants, and he listened to classical music by way of unwinding. He played tennis and golf to ease the strains of football. He even read books – big ones with long words – which seemed to provide a rewarding lifestyle. If verve, humour, quirkiness and desire were what was needed, Harry had the lot. So, at the age of 30, Batsford picked him as the man who could help Wimbledon out of a rut.

In 1996, when *FourFourTwo* profiled Harry's career, a journalist chose to portray the 38-year-old manager of Crystal Palace as a 'Chirpy Cockney, diamond geezer, long-ball loudmouth, top bloke, nutty boy'. Harry preferred to describe himself a little differently: 'I don't need the medals or the trophies. They're nice, but as long as I'm happy with myself ... Sometimes I don't like Dave Bassett. Sometimes I think, yeah, you're all right. Sometimes I think I'm not as nice or as decent as I could be. Or that I could be more intelligent or more talented. But generally I can live with myself. I've never tried to model myself on anybody. I'm Dave Bassett. I'm an individual. I'm me own person.' To everyone who crossed Harry's path during his Wimbledon career, both descriptions profiled him perfectly. Thanks to Batsford, in 1974 he was about to carve a cosy little niche for himself at Plough Lane.

CHAPTER TWO

When Allen Batsford and Harry Bassett arrived at Plough Lane they hadn't figured on walking into a financial war zone. Filled with bravado and swagger, Batsford had applied for the manager's job after noticing an advertisement in a local paper. It had needed only one phone call to the Wimbledon chairman Jack Bevan before an interview was arranged. This pleased Batsford, because on paper the move appeared a logical progression from his spell at Walton & Hersham while also representing a leg-up in the football hierarchy. Recently, he'd become very aware that his time at Walton & Hersham was reaching a natural conclusion. A number of his playing staff had won England amateur caps with his help and, having claimed that FA Amateur Cup trophy in 1973 and the notable FA Cup scalp of Brian Clough's Brighton & Hove Albion, Batsford believed he'd fulfilled his potential. Furthermore, he'd been at the club for nine years. Wimbledon, he knew, were a strong team in the Southern League Premier with ambitions of promotion to the Football League. With the right blend of players it would probably provide a suitably rewarding environment for him to flex his managerial muscles.

But Wimbledon were in serious trouble. Such was their financial predicament that they had only just escaped closure. A £2,500 donation from the supporters organisation was required to keep them afloat, and because of the lack of money available for wages Batsford began his tenure without huge chunks of the playing staff. The surprise was his own fault. Having met with Jack Bevan for an initial interview in June 1974, quickly followed by a second, he'd accepted the job offer and agreed to a pay cut without enquiring about the club's financial standing. He was told the bad news only when he arrived that summer: funds for new additions hovered around the zero mark. Dramatically, he was even asked for assistance in cutting the club's wages bill. Had he known these facts before accepting the position, it's debatable whether he would have gone ahead. Now he had to claw his way out of a nasty mess.

There was political despair too as Wimbledon's application for professional football status that spring had been rejected. This, though, was a common occurrence. Wimbledon had been applying for full professional status since 1965, though their attempts were occasionally delusional: they'd originally applied when they were only in the Southern League Division One. In those days such applications, based on a voting system involving 48 members – one representative from all the teams in the First and Second Divisions, and another eight representing Divisions Three and Four – were used to decide whether the professional teams at the bottom of Division Four were worthy of relegation into the amateur leagues. If that was the case, then the vote would go on to decide which non-league team should receive professional status. At the close of the 1964/65 season Wimbledon had received just one vote. A decade later the vote was still providing a similarly unwelcome kick in the teeth:

despite the fact that by this time Wimbledon were champions, they received only four votes, whereas fashionable Kettering, which had finished the Southern Premier League campaign in fourth place, were awarded twenty. Class war was already a conversational topic around Plough Lane.

Batsford set about making the most of the limited resources at his disposal. Five players were hauled in: from Walton & Hersham, alongside Harry, came Billy Edwards and Dave Donaldson, plus his former strikers Roger Connell and Kieron Somers, who had already moved to Hendon a year earlier. Connell and Somers had been involved in an argument over pay when they'd played for Batsford at Walton & Hersham, but that dispute had been with the board so they needed little persuasion to rejoin him at Wimbledon. The only snag was convincing the new additions to sign professional forms and accept the meagre wages of £14 a week. Dave Donaldson, for example, had a well-paid job with British Airways and was loath to give up his post, but with some forceful persuasion from Batsford and the help of several sympathetic work colleagues, a suitable roster was tabled so that Donaldson could hold down his job and make Batsford's training sessions without fear of the sack from either position.

The manager's next task was to mould the two disparate groups of old and new players into a cohesive playing unit. This was done with the help of Harry and senior Wimbledon player Ian Cooke. According to Batsford, both were leaders, and the pair soon set about ensuring that the two sides of the club mixed effectively. With Harry in place, a raucous atmosphere simmered behind the scenes, and practical jokes became the norm. However, before a ball was kicked Batsford had picked up his critics, and many fans remained unimpressed with his additions to the squad. But a bolshie pre-season run of friendlies, including a 1–0 win over Crystal Palace, soon silenced the complaints. And the opening-day 2–0 defeat at the hands of Nuneaton Borough? Well, that was only a hiccup and wouldn't deflate his team's confidence. Even Kettering manager David Pleat had noted what a tough team they'd been to play against. He was right too. The slump was short lived, and between 20 August (against Yeovil) and 3 December (Cambridge City) Batsford's Wimbledon side climbed the table in a match-winning stampede totalling 22 games.

It was a taste of things to come. In Batsford's first season Wimbledon snatched the 1974/75 Southern Premier League title for the first time in their history from second-place Nuneaton by three points. They also racked up a London Senior Cup in the process, though according to Harry in his autobiography the journey to success was tiring, totalling 73 games of which 49 were victories and ten were draws. In attack, the team claimed an impressive 128 goals. Wimbledon had got off to a flyer, and the new manager had something to build on.

Incredibly, sandwiched between the muddy fixtures and a timetable that included up to four games a week, Wimbledon had also managed to cram in an impressive FA Cup run, which culminated in a tie against First Division heavyweights Leeds United. Of course, the early ties in that campaign provided nothing in the way of drama, throwing Bracknell, Maidenhead, Wokingham and Guildford & Dorking into their path, though as anyone following Wimbledon's career curve could tell you, all of these teams represented potential banana skins. When they drew Bath in the first round proper, a 1–0 win took them to Kettering for another victory in the second stage. Suddenly they were joining the top teams in the hat for the third round.

Burnley were drawn, away at Turf Moor. At the time they

were a First Division club lying in seventh place, and Batsford knew the tie would be fraught with problems. For a start, while still a big side, Burnley didn't enjoy the superstar status afforded to some of their contemporaries and therefore would attract very little TV attention. The revenue from travelling supporters would also be minimal given the lengthy journey from South London to Lancashire, and Wimbledon needed the cash. Batsford also suspected that Burnley were too experienced to slip up against Wimbledon and that his team would be kicked out of the cup without too much of a fuss.

For once he was wrong. The club, with the help of British Rail, set about organising a special supporters' train that ran from Euston to Burnley. Wimbledon had to pay for the tickets up front, to the tune of £1,500, which was a stumbling block, but at least the fans would be there. In front of 20,000 supporters and the TV cameras, Wimbledon then pulled off one of the biggest upsets in FA Cup history, winning by a single goal – a strike from winger Mick Mahon, which came just after the half-time break. Unbelievably, they'd hauled a First Division side across the coals. They were looking to do something similar in the next round, and Batsford and Harry were not to be disappointed. When lot number seven was drawn from the hat on national television, Wimbledon were on their way to Elland Road.

If Burnley were considered a glamour tie, then Leeds resembled a trip to a Las Vegas casino, with the Rat Pack of Gordon McQueen, Peter Lorimer, Eddie Gray, Johnny Giles and Billy Bremner providing the gaudy entertainment. It was to be a swinging, riotous party, and Wimbledon were an important guest: Leeds may have been League champions and European Cup finalists the previous year, but having claimed one top-flight team, Batsford was determined not to be seen as a bit part. This time two trains were organised by British Rail to escort the Wimbledon fans to the game. Rather than laying on a spread of sandwiches, as they'd done on the previous journey, 2,000 fans were served with sausages, mash and baked beans. Later, as the players left the tunnel and ran on to the turf, two fans dressed as Wombles handed out the match balls. Who said Wimbledon couldn't provide the glamour?

On the pitch they held their own too, restraining Leeds for nearly 90 minutes before 46,230 fans – Elland Road's largest gate of the season at that point – until Harry upended Leeds winger Eddie Gray in the penalty area.

'You prat, Harry,' hissed Wimbledon goalkeeper Dickie Guy at his team-mate.

Harry was devastated. He'd already secured a reputation as a hothead at Wimbledon. At the start of his career there he'd increased the red-card tally that had dogged him at St Albans City and Walton & Hersham with a series of ugly challenges. The occasional wild tackle seemed a less reckless gamble in the Southern Premier League, but now he had gone and done it in a fourth-round FA Cup tie. *Against bloody Leeds United.*

Guy shook his head as Peter Lorimer stepped up to take the spot-kick. The promised wad of cash that would accompany a money-spinning replay at Plough Lane seemed more distant now than ever. On paper, a goal was a formality. *A bloody formality.* Lorimer was a feared dead-ball specialist. He was also reputed to possess the hardest shot in the English game. But on this occasion he somehow contrived to scuff his strike, leaving Guy to scoop the ball easily into his arms. Leeds now had to contemplate the horrors of a tricky visit to Plough Lane while Wimbledon had achieved the seemingly impossible.

That night, Guy became a mini-superstar. Immediately after

the game he gave interviews to BBC journalists with the aplomb of an England captain. The following morning he was driven to ITV's studios in London for an interview with Brian Moore for *The Big Match*. For a while Guy was the nearest thing to a bona fide celebrity Wimbledon had ever possessed.

But while the fuss and media buzz surrounded him, Batsford and officials at the club prepared for the replay at Plough Lane – the biggest game in Wimbledon's history so far. The match had been scheduled for the following Tuesday, but it soon became apparent that the venue would have to be switched from Plough Lane to a bigger ground. Now that Wimbledon were entertaining top-class First Division opposition, they had to cope with the demand that success had created. Match tickets were sold out within 90 minutes of going on sale and ticket touts operated at a premium. In the event, Plough Lane's turf was reduced to a boggy mess in a deluge of winter rain, but it was on police advice that the game was switched to Crystal Palace's Selhurst Park a fortnight later.

As matchday dawned, Batsford and his players set about devising a crude plan that would unsettle their superior opponents and create another upset for the media to frenzy over – equal parts siege mentality, ball-chasing manoeuvres and 'rope-a-dope' tactics as adopted by Muhammad Ali when he allowed George Foreman to pummel his torso on the ropes during the 1975 heavyweight championship bout. Having absorbed the blows, Ali later dropped Foreman, exhausted from the physical exertion, to his knees. Batsford was hoping for a similar outcome and encouraged his players to defend in numbers, encroaching into the Leeds penalty area only when necessary. The players were confident the tactics would work. 'We were tough buggers,' said Harry afterwards. Wimbledon held their opponents for the best part of 50 minutes, until a lucky break ricocheted a goal into the back of their net. Again it was Harry who was at fault, a tame shot from Johnny Giles clipping his leg and rolling past Dickie Guy in goal. Wimbledon were on their way out.

Despite the lucrative cup run, the club remained in dire straits off the pitch. Their annual application for professional status drew only three votes. Wimbledon had also managed to haemorrhage £20,000 that year and had to rely on supporter donations to transport them to a semi-professional Anglo-Italian cup competition at the end of the season. Something had to give. Then the press got wind of a story: George Best had apparently made an enquiry about buying the club, but the rumours never came to anything. Someone was interested in acquiring the team, though, and in 1976 up stepped local entrepreneur Ron Noades with a suitcase full of cash.

Noades was an impressive businessman. He'd started work as an estate agent before several lucrative deals upped his financial clout and he was able to set up his own company. He had previously been chairman at Southall, a team from the Isthmian Premier League, but felt disillusioned by their lack of ambition. Now he was looking to buy Wimbledon, and with the help of Harry – a schoolmate of Noades's brother from Roxeth Manor – he hoped to lure the club away from then chairman, Bernie Coleman. 'I used to see Dave Bassett a lot at the time,' explained Noades. 'We were old friends. He used to play for a youth team I was involved in. He was also working in insurance as his main job, but he was leaving his firm to start his own business. I gave him an office in my building in Stanmore [North London]. Bassett would come into the office on a Monday morning and talk about how Wimbledon had done and I would tell him how Southall had done. Of course, this was just after their great cup run. They'd managed to get out of financial trouble briefly with the Leeds game, but within twelve months they were in as much trouble as ever. Bassett kept asking me to come in and take over Wimbledon. Eventually he introduced me to the owner, Bernie Coleman. He didn't have any involvement in the club, he'd just inherited the shares from Sydney Black. So I went to see him.'

Within months he was in charge. 'He sold me the club for £2,768,' Noades continued. 'At that time he was offered £15,000 by QPR's Jim Gregory, but Gregory wanted to use Wimbledon as a nursery for QPR. So Bernie sold it to me on the basis that he wanted to see Wimbledon survive and continue. He owned the Sportsman's [the pub next to the ground, by the entrance] lease at that time and I said the club was only viable if he sold me the Sportsman as well. He agreed and gave me the pub for nothing, and there I was, owner of Wimbledon in 1976. But the club was in a bit of a financial mess. When I arrived the first match we played was away to Romford and we only had eleven players. We didn't have anyone on the bench because we couldn't afford it. I think we drew and got a replay. They had the bailiffs knocking on the door in July and they would have gone bust had I not taken over then. The root of their problem was that they had a board of directors who had very little nous and spent more than they were earning. When Sydney Black was in charge, he would write a cheque out at the end of each year for however much they had lost, so the board never really had to manage.'

In an attempt to balance the books, Noades trimmed the playing staff for the 1976/77 season and drew up plans for entry into the Football League. Still, he knew that a miracle was needed if Wimbledon were to join the big boys. Luckily, he possessed the self-belief and entrepreneurial skills to make people listen; whether they took him seriously or not was another matter entirely. Noades began to press palms with Football League chairmen, asking for advice and drawing opinion. By 1977, with yet another Southern League Premier title challenge under way, Wimbledon were embarking on the Dons 4 Div 4 campaign, an idea dreamed up by Wimbledon club committee member Lord Faulkner while dozing in the bath tub. Suddenly, the Southern League felt like a small pond, and Noades began calling on the supporters for help to secure promotion to the Football League, organising a thirteen-man team of volunteers and going into overdrive, paying for car stickers and lavishing the slogan across the bumpers of vehicles up and down the capital. He canvassed his fellow chairmen for votes in the run-up to the 1977 Football League election and bombarded the media with publicity stunts and photo-calls. Noades may have been an estate agent at heart, but he was no amateur when it came to romancing the press pack. He even convinced England cricket captain Tony Greig to join the campaign, though this coup soon backfired when Greig stepped down from his position.

'We had to work hard to get into the Football League,' he recalled. 'When everyone was fiddling the gates in the League, saying they were getting much less than they were, we were fiddling them by saying we were getting more. We did it the other way round. That way we would look more attractive to the Football League because the gates were influencing the votes for Football League election. Our floodlights were also crap. When we produced a brochure to assist our promotion campaign I put a picture of an evening game in there with the floodlights on. Underneath it I wrote a caption with the words "An evening game at Plough Lane showing the quality of the floodlights".

Everybody read it as meaning they were fantastic when in reality they were awful. There was a lot of kidology involved.'

Meanwhile, his team continued to do the business on the pitch. Having kicked aside Woking and Leatherhead in the first two rounds of the 1976/77 FA Cup, Wimbledon were rewarded with a tie against Jack Charlton's Middlesbrough at Plough Lane. Almost as quickly as the two names were pulled from the hat, a blaze of accusations and bickering rattled across the telephones. Ticket sales had slumped but Wimbledon were blaming Boro: their style of football was boring, not good enough to tempt the Wimbledon faithful to the ground. Boro spat back that Wimbledon had priced their tickets too high and that nobody could afford to travel south. Neither side was backing down. On matchday tensions rose even higher. In the winter cold Plough Lane's boggy surface had frozen rock solid. It was ankle-breaking stuff, and as it thawed Big Jack Charlton began his hissy fit. The pitch had been hosed down to make it easier for Wimbledon to play their scrappy style of football on. The dressing rooms were disgusting. The floodlights weren't bright enough. Nothing was up to scratch. Which was exactly how Wimbledon liked it. Amid all the foot stamping, Wimbledon managed a draw, though in reality it could have been so much more when a perfectly good goal from Dons striker Roger Connell was disallowed. By the time of the replay, Wimbledon's spirits were up. Big Jack and his international stars, including Graeme Souness, were due for a kicking. But it wasn't to be, and Boro scraped a 1–0 win. *Another penalty* (though this time it hadn't been Harry's fault). Wimbledon were sick.

From the stands, Ron Noades didn't care too much. His club's run-in with the big guns, the controversy at Plough Lane, Big Jack's tantrums ... it was putting Wimbledon on the map. His public-relations masterplan had suddenly been cranked up a notch or two without any effort from him or his backroom staff. And as Wimbledon cruised to their third Southern Premier League title on the bounce, their chances of election to the Fourth Division proper stood on a firm footing, though Noades attributed their success to another one of his financial masterstrokes. 'We lost in the FA Trophy at Chorley,' he explained, 'so in the car home myself and Bassett set up a new bonus scheme to gee the players along. They were on £3 a win in those days, so we decided that if they won three games on the trot they were given £9 extra, as well as their normal bonuses. So if we were at home for two matches and the next one was away, they wouldn't get anything for the first two matches, they had to win the third as well. So they could be away in the third match and they'd be playing for an £18 bonus for three wins, which was quite a lot of money in those days. It became quite an incentive.'

In an amazing run of form, the Dons lost one game from 25, and Noades pushed harder for promotion into professional football. The Football League AGM was scheduled to take place at the Café Royal Hotel in London on 17 June 1977. For Noades it marked the end of a tumultuous, giddy season of wheeler-dealing and charm offensives. He wasn't going to slip up now, not after the newspaper interviews and TV appearances and public campaigns. When Noades and Batsford travelled to the Café Royal, they were determined to make an impression. Despite the sweltering summer heat, the pair wore their sharpest suits and worked the room like skilled politicians.

The voting process was complex, however. Workington had been dumped to the bottom of the Fourth Division yet again; this meant that they were joining Halifax, Hartlepool and Southport in the vote for relegation. Wimbledon and Northern Premier

League side Altrincham were waiting in the wings to take one unfortunate team's place. The tension in the Café Royal was unbearable. But despite the importance of the afternoon's decision, Wimbledon were forced to face up to their lowly stature yet again. At that time they hadn't even secured membership of the Football League, and as non-members they wouldn't be privy to the final voting procedure. Batsford and Noades, after all the tongue-wagging and handshaking, would have to wait outside in a corridor.

They paced and chatted until practically the last minute. *Anything to kill the tension.* Inside, the 48 members' votes were being tabled in alphabetical order and read out slowly by the president of the Football League, Lord Westwood.

'Altrincham, 12 votes. Halifax, 44. Hartlepool, 43. Southport, 37. Workington, 21. Wimbledon, 27.'

In the corridors of the Café Royal the news slowly dawned on the Wimbledon pair. Halifax, Hartlepool and Southport had retained their League status, but Workington were on their way out; having polled more votes than Altrincham, Wimbledon would be taking their place. At last, their lowly club of scruffs and mickey-takers had made it into the Fourth Division. 'It was the best day of my football career,' said Noades. 'I can't really remember much of the afternoon. I can only remember celebrating afterwards. I was whisked away in a taxi and taken away from one studio to the next for TV interviews. It was wonderful.'

His phone rang off the hook for days.

CHAPTER THREE

If the truth be told, nobody fancied Wimbledon's chances in the Fourth Division at the beginning of the 1977/78 season, least of all Allen Batsford. He'd gone along with Ron's dream of professional competition but hadn't believed the fantasy would actually become reality. Now that it finally had, he wasn't sure whether his team could cope with the pressures and rigours of league football. They were glorified amateurs playing against the big boys.

Batsford was also feeling distinctly underwhelmed by his position at Wimbledon. On arriving from Walton & Hersham, he'd been placed on a part-time contract for financial reasons, and despite their move into the professional leagues, this hadn't been upgraded. Wimbledon, as always, were desperately short of cash, and despite Noades's wheeler-dealing and campaigning, his team still occupied a financially precarious position – a hangover from the falling attendances that had continually dogged the club since their amateur days. They might have claimed Football League status and attempted to present a professional image to the authorities, but Noades seemed unable to upgrade Wimbledon's ambitions behind the scenes. Batsford suffered as a result. His situation led him to believe that Noades was hopelessly inept when it came to running a football club. According to Batsford, the chairman was interfering with his scouting plans. He even stopped training sessions, having become fretful that the club was unable to afford the travel expenses incurred by his playing staff. And when Noades finally upgraded Batsford's managerial contract, he added insult to injury by bringing in former Chelsea and Derby County coach Dario Gradi as his assistant. Initially this appeared to be a major coup: Gradi was in demand. Crystal Palace had previously tried to secure his services, but Gradi had been unimpressed by their offer. When Noades asked him to help with the Wimbledon youth team he jumped at the opportunity. Gradi was also required to assist with coaching matters, but according to Batsford he seemed reluctant to do so. His argument was that his scouting responsibilities were too time-consuming. Batsford's resentment grew, but what really grated was that Gradi had received a superior contract to his own.

To the outside world Wimbledon's managerial set-up seemed strange at best. Batsford enhanced this oddball image by making Harry his team captain and part-time coach, which seemed a suicidal choice. Most fans viewed Harry as a hothead who lost his cool during vital games. In fact, such was his unpopularity that during his first shift as captain, in the 1976/77 season, local papers were bombarded with letters of complaint. However, the coaching role appealed to Harry: his legs weren't as sharp as they'd once been, and this new responsibility gave him an opportunity to further his football career. Enthusiastically, he began studying for an FA coaching badge.

Initially, nothing was gained through Harry's captaincy. When the 1977/78 season opened for business, Wimbledon failed to win in their first seven games, and lost four of them, to Brentford (1–4), Hartlepool (0–2), Aldershot Town (1–2) and Scunthorpe (0–3). Clearly, the gulf in fitness and technique between Wimbledon's part-time players and their professional peers was problematic. They often struggled to match the majority of their opponents and looked yards behind the pace.

Meanwhile, political chaos had taken hold. Batsford felt as if Noades was obstructing him at every turn. There was no money for new players, and the squad worked on a strictly unprofessional basis: the team travelled to away games in individual cars rather than on a coach, and several players still had full-time jobs and were unable to train during the day. When on 2 January 1978 defender Dave Galvin was accidentally left behind in Bristol after a lunch stop en route to an away match against Swansea, Batsford decided enough was enough. A 3–0 defeat that afternoon only cemented his decision. 'He resigned in a fit of pique,' said Noades. 'I accepted his resignation, although he didn't really think I would. But Allen was a good bloke. We originally tried to see if he could do the job part time, which I think was a mistake, but financially we didn't have a lot of choice.'

The players believed that Batsford's resignation had been Noades's aim all along. Harry in particular believed the manager had been cruelly undermined, but the conspiracy theorists failed to prompt a reinstatement. More controversially, Harry had already been offered Batsford's position. He turned it down, however, instead taking the option of assistant coach, a £90-a-week salary and a lower profile role in his full-time role in insurance. Gradi was placed in charge on a caretaker basis; he only discovered the approach to Harry years later.

Gradi was under pressure from the off. Wimbledon's playing

staff continued to assume that Batsford had walked from the club with a knife in his back. Elsewhere, the fans, upset by Gradi's arrival and Batsford's almost immediate departure, sniffed a stitch-up. Gradi, meanwhile, grappled with the squad's fitness levels in an attempt to drag them out of the relegation zone. Given their poor form at the beginning of the season, a tough battle lay ahead.

Surprisingly, the improved fitness techniques immediately proved fruitful. After a win against Halifax and a draw against Brentford that January, Noades felt he'd witnessed an encouraging improvement and made the caretaker manager a permanent employee. Gradi promptly signed striker and crowd favourite-in-waiting Alan Cork, then an eighteen-year-old flop from Derby County. The bank was later busted with the signing of Les Brierly (who would become a team-mate of Fash's at Millwall) for a club record £16,000 from Hereford. Money, previously unavailable to Batsford, had suddenly appeared after another Noades business deal. 'I sold a minibus we'd just bought so we could buy Les,' Noades explained. 'I sold it for £16,000 and then purchased the minibus back on HP. But we always did things a little differently at Wimbledon. I signed [midfielder] Wally Downes on an apprenticeship for £5 a week. He was seventeen and the first part-time apprentice the Football League had ever had. We had to break ground in that way because we didn't have that much money at Wimbledon.'

Still, another £20,000 appeared, and Gradi snapped up a handful of players from the Chelsea youth team for £5,000 apiece, including Glyn Hodges, Paul Fishenden and Steve Perkins on free transfers. Their fresh legs made an immediate impact and performances improved in the league. Somehow, Wimbledon pulled clear of the relegation zone and maintained their position in the Fourth Division for another season. By the end of the season nearly every player was on a full-time contract – except, of course, Dave Donaldson, who still enjoyed his role with British Airways. He was 36 and a dedicated professional. If it ever looked as if he was about miss his seven p.m. meeting for an away match in some cold corner of the north of England, he'd hop on a plane to get there. Unbelievably, he wasn't late once.

Behind the scenes, a new investor was making hay. Sam Hammam was a Lebanese business entrepreneur who travelled to England as his wife Nada prepared to give birth to their third child, fearful of the impact Lebanon's raging civil war could have on their family. They relocated to London where Nada's sister had fled several years earlier and settled comfortably with her husband and kids. Nada's sister recommended the now closed St Theresa's hospital in Wimbledon as an excellent place to give birth. Sam nested down at his sister-in-law's and travelled to St Theresa's every day to visit his wife.

At this point, myth muddies the tale. According to popular legend, Sam regularly travelled to St Theresa's by the same taxi. During his journey the driver, a Chelsea fan, would regale him with tales of his favourite team. Until now, Sam had never really talked about football – he'd always been a tennis nut (another popular myth perpetuated by more than one source is that Sam bought Wimbledon because of his love for lawn tennis, not football) – but suddenly he became enthused. One day the driver informed him of another club closer to home. Wimbledon, he said, were a newly promoted team in Division Four and had travelled through the amateur divisions. They were also skint and in desperate need of some serious financial investment – the sort only a man of Sam's calibre could provide.

According to Sam, he didn't believe it was possible to buy a football club; he'd naively assumed that teams such as Wimbledon were owned by a community or a group of people. Furthermore, the financial problems and on-the-pitch woes dogging this team, this humble club of scruffs and down-and-outs, sounded like a fantastic Shakespearean struggle against adversity. Excited by the possibilities, he contacted Ron Noades and enquired about the likelihood of an investment. This part we know to be true, given Sam's subsequent cash transaction, but according to Noades, Sam had previously tried to buy into Chelsea. Executives at Stamford Bridge, accustomed to flimsy business enquiries, had explained that a serious offer should be put in writing. Sam had apparently become impatient with Chelsea's reluctance and instructed his driver to contact Wimbledon. Noades promptly invited him to the club. 'Come on over,' he said, delighted to have found a willing investor to line the club's rapidly emptying pockets. And when Sam arrived at Plough Lane, he took little persuading to spend his money.

The truth, however, lies somewhere between these two tales. According to Noades, the apocryphal cabbie was actually a chauffeur who contacted Noades shortly after Sam had ordered a lift to Stamford Bridge and walked away empty-handed. And when he walked into Plough Lane, Sam fell in love. 'It got a hold on him,' Noades explained later. 'Like it does on all of us. His driver contacted me one day, late 1977. He wanted to invest. We had an afternoon meeting and I took his money. My first impression was that he was just another investor. When I was at Palace we had a Nigerian gun-runner and a Nigerian senator, and I always ran an open house with a maximum loan. But if you put it in, you never got it back. It was virtually an interest-free loan to the club with twelve months' notice to withdraw. He was one of the first [at Wimbledon], and I sold him 30 per cent equity for £30,000, which was quite a lot in those days.' Sam was naive, and desperate to invest. 'Apparently he was only in the country for 24 hours, which was why he didn't bother with Chelsea,' explained Noades. 'He didn't have the time, but he was keen to do it and I didn't care who wanted to invest money in Wimbledon. Thirty grand was a good deal as far as I was concerned. But it was clear he didn't know that much about football. When he sat down to talk about the club, I explained to him that we could break even without opening the turnstiles and he just nodded. It turned out later that he didn't actually know what turnstiles were.

'But he was a lovely man. He still is. He was the best man at my wedding and he did a similar thing there. At the reception I told him to read the telegrams. Twenty minutes passed and he still hadn't read them, so I said, "Sam, you have to read the telegrams." Anyway, another twenty minutes passed, so I said, "Sam! Why haven't you read the telegrams?" He looked at me and told me that he had. He didn't understand that he had to read them *out*.'

That Sam should buy £30,000 worth of ramshackle Wimbledon FC on a whim after a few encouraging words from his temporary chauffeur (or cabbie, depending on who you believe) seemed like the build-up to some ghastly punchline. But Sam wasn't laughing. The club he had bought into represented an interesting hobby, far more exciting than real estate or the Stock Exchange. It was a more romantic notion, too, than investing in a faceless business enterprise in some far-flung corner of the globe. And he'd done plenty of that.

As his infamy grew over the seasons, it became clear he was a wildcard unlike any other club owner. His gunslinging verbosity was born of a self-proclaimed peasant lifestyle. The favourite description of his back story was that he had been a man of the mountains – 'a man from the rocks' – though the self-deprecating evaluation didn't ring completely true. He came from good stock, for sure, born as Samir in July 1947 in Dhour Shweir, a small Lebanese village in the Chouf mountains near Beirut. His dad was a doctor, but Sam had limited ambitions as far as following in his footsteps was concerned. A doctorate didn't really appeal to him, but at his father's encouragement he studied English at school and quickly engrossed himself in British culture. During this education, Sam would later claim he had absorbed as much of Shakespeare's works as any Eton scholar. Modesty wasn't a word that featured on his CV.

But Sam had every reason to be a little cocky. A degree in civil engineering was his next step to fame, and he enrolled in Beirut's American University. This was his first move towards a big business break, and two years later Sam was working in construction, helping to develop Abu Dhabi's airport. By 1972 he was immersed in the Saudi Arabian construction boom that was rolling in opulence following the first financial spoils from the oil boom. Later he financed businesses in the Middle East and America where he employed upwards of 4,000 workers. Clearly there was much more to the 'man from the rocks' mythology than this flippant description implied.

As his career blossomed, Sam's friends became aware of a golden touch, and many observed his business acumen with awe. In 2002 an *Observer* newspaper journalist tracked down Bassem Afifi, one of Sam's former associates, who explained his early financial expertise and successes. 'He had a contracting company in Dubai with two Lebanese chaps. We were family friends. He moved to Abu Dhabi about 1976, and I lost contact with him for a while. He went to an oil rig, and this is where he made his money. He used to forecast events, predict the future … he was always a very happy, very nice man.'

The description painted a shamanic image, and for the most part Sam's background remained shrouded in mystery. But as Afifi mentioned, the smile never seemed to leave his face during his formative business years, and why should it? He enjoyed a happy family life and in 1971 married a Christian Lebanese girl called Nada from Beirut. Sam was also a Christian, and their first daughter, Dina, arrived in 1973; a son, Zayd, was born three years later. When his third child arrived in the world, Sam visited Wimbledon. On 15 September 1977 he became a part-owner of the club.

At the time he believed there was nothing in the way of money-making opportunities at Plough Lane. Almost immediately after the deal with Noades had been struck and Nada was fully recovered, Sam flew out to New Jersey in the United States where a wing of his construction business was making waves. He often relied on the BBC's World Service to pick up Wimbledon's results, though it was months before he realised they were even featured on the news. Little did he know that this was the beginning of a beautiful friendship.

Behind Dario Gradi's back, Harry thrived in chaos. The manager was a disciplinarian who liked his club to be run in an orderly fashion, but his assistant had other ideas. Practical jokes and mucking about became the order of the day, and if ever Gradi caught wind of the stunts, Harry would shrewdly blame the players. These high jinks officially marked the birth of the Crazy Gang. 'If Dario knew about what was going on he would have had a baby,' said Noades. 'There was even a Radio Five news report when somebody had seen one of our naked players on the top of the minibus. Dario doesn't know to this day. He would have had a fit.'

As Harry settled into his assistant manager's role during the 1978/79 season, training sessions and coach journeys were punctuated with outbreaks of violence. Pre-match warm-ups would often culminate in a mass bundle, but when Gradi pressed Harry on various incidents – black eyes, injuries – he'd claim the situation was under control. The culprits, said Harry, had been reprimanded. But the mayhem didn't stop there. One coach driver had a cardboard box placed over his head as his vehicle hurtled down the motorway at 80 mph. His bald pate was later covered in piping-hot batter scraped from the team's fish and chips. He resigned shortly afterwards. Much later, in Finland, club physio Derek French was dangled by his ankles from a fishing boat. He was then thrown into a lake by Wally Downes and held under water to see how long he could hold his breath.

Harry's insane team-bonding tactics worked. Wimbledon were promoted to the Third Division in May 1979, thanks mainly to a thirteen-game unbeaten streak at the start of the season; the only low point was the 8–0 humiliation in the League Cup second round at the hands of Everton. Meanwhile, Alan Cork was proving a shrewd buy: he scored 25 goals during the season to become the club's top scorer.

But, as had happened during the transition to the Fourth Division, life in the Third Division was a shock to the system. Wimbledon, who were now blooding a youthful team – a string of buys and sales had whittled the average age down to just 23 – lacked the experience and strength to make a fist of things at this higher level, and they were relegated in the early summer of 1980. They had, however, managed to snap up goalkeeper Dave

Beasant, an influential figure in the Crazy Gang lineage. Harry had been scouting for the club and had spotted Beasant guarding the sticks at Edgware Town. After one fixture, Beasant was informed that Harry was outside waiting to speak to him. He left the pitch and walked straight towards him without showering. Harry wanted Beasant, he explained, and in a trial and some reserve games at Wimbledon he did enough to impress Gradi too. The club offered him £25 a week for a full-time contract, which meant he'd have to drop his vocation as a printer, but Beasant wasn't bothered. It was his first step on the ladder to professional success. Wimbledon paid Edgware just £100 for him.

Gradi probably rued his decision a few months later in January 1980 when, on Beasant's debut, the keeper, who had already affectionately been nicknamed Lurch by his team-mates, let a loose shot slip from his grasp and through his legs during a 1–2 defeat at home to Blackpool. In his defence, Beasant hadn't been expecting to appear the night before, having played second fiddle in the reserves to first-team resident Ray Goddard. Back pains had cut short Goddard's hopes of making the Blackpool game, and on the evening prior to matchday Beasant was informed of his inclusion. He'd just returned from an evening out with a girlfriend, which had culminated in a pub session. After the Blackpool howler, Beasant was devastated and feared his career at Wimbledon was over before it had started. He slipped back into the reserves and stayed there for much of the season as Wimbledon dropped to the bottom of the table.

With the club back in the bottom division, however, a dramatic change was in the offing. Sam's love for the club had blossomed. The Hammams were still in New Jersey, but Sam just couldn't stay away any longer. Financial difficulties were still hounding the club and Sam found he was being called to help. Eventually he relented and flew from the States for fleeting visits. He began to watch the team rather than listening out for their results on the BBC's World Service, and soon the brief trips to SW17 became lengthier stays, taking in training sessions and even away games. He was hooked. 'He was a great person to have in your club,' remarked Noades. '[He was] very close to the players and the manager. He always wanted to be one of them. Sam would rather have been a player than a chairman. He'd always help them out. I'd cut the players a fiver as a bonus after winning a game, but he'd give them six on the side when I wasn't looking. So they'd get a bonus from me and one from Sam, but he would do it subtly. He'd lose it in a card school on the coach to an away game. He had his own ways of giving them money.' Often Hammam could be spotted on matchdays in the manager's dugout or on the touchline. He'd be as animated as any of the fans in the stands. With Dario Gradi he developed a transfer policy that would stand Wimbledon in good stead for much of their life in the top flight: spend money only on players you can afford; sell only when you have a natural replacement at the ready; and invest in the youth team. Gradi also taught Sam the finer details of the game.

As Sam's football addiction grew, so Noades's ambitions for a burgeoning empire gathered pace. By 1981 he'd drawn up plans to buy Crystal Palace, then a Second Division club. Wimbledon fans feared the worst. Rumours percolated through the club that a merger with the two teams was imminent, and obviously it was Wimbledon who would suffer most as there was very little a club of Palace's stature could glean from their playing reserves. Other whispers suggested a ground-share offer was to be tabled by Palace in order to lessen Wimbledon's crippling debts. Either way it amounted to an unpleasant end for Wimbledon FC. The fans were in uproar. 'There were loads of rumours about clubs merging,' said Noades. 'In fact, Wimbledon, Palace and Charlton talked about merging, but nothing ever came of it. Merging was never going to work. The fans didn't want to, they were set against it. We did a survey and they voted against it. Everybody felt they had a say in the process.'

Unfazed by the emotional burden, Noades took over at Palace in February 1981. But the Football Association then deemed it illegal for one person to hold stakes in two professional clubs, so he passed his Wimbledon shares to local businessman Joe McElligot. In secret, Noades hoped McElligot would fancy the ground-share offer devised by Palace, but Wimbledon's board had other ideas. Noades's plan was scuppered when a veto was enforced, leaving McElligot to follow him away from the boardroom. Sam was initially tempted to join Noades at Palace too, but the thought of owning a football club outright was too big a deal to pass up. He gobbled up Noades's offer of £40,000 and bought the remainder of the club. By 1985 he was permanently based in the capital, with his family having bought a fancy house just a block or so away from Regent's Park. His kids enrolled in American schools in London and, later, American universities. As Wimbledon's top dog, he became a fully fledged Londoner.

Noades also dragged Dario Gradi to Selhurst Park, but not before he'd installed Harry as Wimbledon manager during his final days as club owner. This could have been considered a risk: Harry had no managerial background despite his recent schooling with Gradi, but Noades was convinced that his seven years at the club as a player and coach made him the perfect choice. Meanwhile, behind the scenes, the players were laughing. They'd secured themselves a chairman and a manager in the Crazy Gang mould. And now Noades would never know that they used to break into his office to have sex with their girlfriends after games.

But Harry had walked into a tough job. At the end of January 1981 the club was lying in thirteenth place in the Fourth Division and were out of both cup competitions. Worse, he had nothing to spend on new players. Still, with his motivational patter he worked his team to a 3–2 victory over Port Vale and followed that up with an impressive run of seven games unbeaten. They only lost to Wigan, Bury and Darlington for the remainder of the season. Harry had sneaked Wimbledon into a fourth-place promotion spot and he was building an impressive team through the youth ranks and a bargain-basement scouting network; home-developed players Kevin Gage and Mark Morris in particular would prove mainstays for years to come. Meanwhile, Dave Beasant had cemented his position in goal, the blunder against Blackpool long forgotten.

Early Third Division results for the 1981/82 season were again disastrous. Wimbledon lost their first five home games and drew sub-2,000 crowds to Plough Lane. They were battered by suspension and injury too: Alan Cork broke his leg in September and was missing for long parts of the season as Wimbledon finished in 21st place. But this second relegation was to prove the last. Wimbledon secured the Division Four Championship in 1983 and picked up a £25,000 award from London's Capital Radio for being the first city side to score 80 goals. There was still no money to spend on players, but somehow Sam persuaded Harry to use his house as a guarantee against a whopping £100,000 bank loan. Naively he agreed, then spent the next two years nervously watching Sam going about his transactions. He needn't have fretted, however. Their first major signing was the £15,000 purchase of Oxford full-back Nigel Winterburn, who would later go on to represent Arsenal and England, and Wimbledon secured promotion yet again in the early summer of 1984, even beating Brian Clough's Nottingham Forest 2–0 in the home leg of the Milk Cup.

But by that stage Harry's tactics, which drew success from long balls pumped with aggressive vigour into the opponent's penalty area, had drawn disapproving comments from the Football Association. The previous year Wimbledon had been warned for their excessive numbers of bookings and suspensions. As they charged towards promotion to the Second Division that season, they seemed equally reckless. Alan Cork wasn't bothered however: he'd picked up another 29 goals in the process. Harry wasn't bothered either, though at the end of that 1983/84 season he'd decided that enough was enough at Wimbledon. Ron Noades had asked him to take over the managerial post vacated by Dario Gradi and later Alan Mullery at Second Division Crystal Palace, and he'd accepted, informing the players after the final game of the season.

It was easy to see why such an offer would appeal to Harry. At Palace the crowds were huge when measured against Wimbledon's following. The club was also bigger and had substantially better facilities, including an impressive training ground and a vast stadium that represented a tempting stage on which Harry could sharpen his managerial skills. It was certainly a step up from the public park used by the Crazy Gang and Plough Lane's limited terraces. But within days of switching clubs, Harry knew he'd made a mistake. Despite Palace's superior facilities and finances, they were a team lacking in potential. The Crazy Gang, Harry reckoned, the team he had built up during his first tenureship as a full-time football manager, was a far more talented bunch of players. So four days later he returned to Plough Lane, after asking club chairman Stanley Reed (who had taken over from Bernie Coleman in that year) and owner Sam whether the position was still vacant. To Harry's relief they allowed him back, but Sam in particular never forgave him for what he considered a bitter betrayal. Ron Noades, too, was unhappy: after two attempts to lure Harry to Selhurst Park, he'd remained a Wimbledon man through and through after all.

By the summer of 1984, then, the Crazy Gang spirit was in the ascendancy. It had even been given its official title, though again, as with Sam's procurement of Wimbledon, debate rages on the finer details. *Daily Mirror* journalist Tony Stenson was certainly the first to use *the Crazy Gang* name in print, though Sam claimed to have devised the title. He'd seen a TV show in America called *The Crazy Gang* where a character called Crazy Eddie would use the catchphrase 'It's not crazy, it's insane!' Sam loved it. Other officials at the club had debated whether to use the Wombles as an official mascot. Sam dismissed that moniker. He rejected 'The Dons' too and stuck with his own phrase – especially as he had his very own Crazy Eddie in Harry Bassett. Harry was amassing a like-minded team too: he signed striker Lawrie Sanchez for £29,000 and spent £25,000 on Arsenal defender John Kay, and Wimbledon established themselves through the 1984/85 season as a solid mid-table unit in the Second Division.

Initially, Harry hadn't really fancied his chances of promotion to the First Division. He knew his side was strong, but it seemed to him that they'd only just acclimatised to the Second Division. He figured that pushing them all the way to the top flight was still a jump too far. Wimbledon were to prove him wrong in 1985/86, however, for their physical style of play, while paying dividends in attack, was also reaping rewards defensively. With a string of 1–0 victories and miserly displays, the Crazy Gang pushed into the top three by November. But Harry needed a striker to boost his forward line and offered Milllwall £125,000 for the services of John Fashanu. To his surprise, Millwall agreed to the deal, and the striker was enlisted in March to help their final push. It worked wonders. The Crazy Gang went unbeaten for the remainder of the season, clinching promotion to Division One with a 1–0 win over Huddersfield, the winning goal coming from a Lawrie Sanchez strike after a short free kick. They'd done it with three games left to play.

The club was in fantasy land, though many figured the dream would be short lived. Harry's team had been assembled on a shoestring budget. In bringing together his team, he'd spent less than £275,000, and much of that had been blown on the Fashanu deal. But on paper it was an impressive side. Dave Beasant and Nigel Winterburn were now being eyed by bigger clubs in the top flight, while Mark Morris, Kevin Gage, Glyn Hodges, Andy Sayer, Andy Thorn and Brian Gayle were all impressive products of the youth team. Then, of course, there were the attacking qualities of Fash, Sanch and Corky. Sam was delighted. How he must have thanked his lucky stars that a London driver had given him such a rollercoaster ride.

CHAPTER FOUR

Fash was a bulldozer on the pitch, and at £125,000 Sam knew he'd secured a bargain. On paper it certainly looked that way. Prior to signing for Harry, the striker had built up a fearless reputation at a string of league clubs, most notably Millwall, where he had ingratiated himself with their notoriously racist support with his physical prowess. They had booed him when he was playing for former team Lincoln, but by his own admission John had 'bashed hell' out of the Millwall defence with a few choice challenges. The fury was unprecedented, and he later required a police escort back to the team bus. 'The Millwall fans were shouting, "Nigger, black bastard, we'll kill you!" and throwing cups of urine at me,' said Fash afterwards. 'I remember seeing the hate and the venom in their faces as we drove off. Then I signed for them shortly afterwards and the fans loved me.'

Clearly Fash didn't give a shit. This made him all right in Sam's book, but his fearless attitude wasn't that much of a surprise. Grow up in the midst of poverty, endure the knowledge that you were rejected by your parents as a child, then play out your teenage years in the shadow of your older brother – suffer all this before your eighteenth birthday and you'd fight and snarl like a cornered rat too. His journey to Wimbledon was peppered with confrontations and battles with adversity. Consequently, he was one of the Crazy Gang's most interesting characters.

Almost from the moment he was conceived, Fash was battling the odds. He was born on 18 September 1962 in Kensington, London, a year and a half after the birth of his brother Justin (who would later became the first million-pound black player and open homosexual in English football), but times were hard for the family. The home was soon torn apart by John's father Patrick, a trainee barrister from the Nigerian Ijeun Township in the Abeokuta south local council. Patrick was studying law in London, but because of his meagre lifestyle and his wife Pearl's limited income, the Fashanus often went without. Nevertheless, financial hardship wasn't to blame for the marital break-up that followed and Patrick's return home. In subsequent meetings, Patrick would assure his sons that his move to Nigeria had been at the behest of their grandfather, who had ordered him to return home on the completion of the bar exams Patrick had been close to completing when Fash was born. He'd hoped to take his family with him to start afresh, but Pearl had other ideas and decided to stay in London where she already enjoyed a large family and a circle of close friends.

Now Pearl was a single mother with a newborn son and four other children – Justin, Dawn, Phillip and Nicholas – to feed, and while she initially comforted herself with the support from her friends and family in London, the outlook seemed bleak. She was a nurse who was recalled as a caring woman by everyone who knew her, but her resources were now too stretched. Pearl would have to hand some of her children over to the social services. John was only eighteen months old.

'Obviously it was very difficult for me,' she said afterwards. 'I would have preferred to have had them with me all the time. If I had the means I would not have let them go at all, but I had no choice. The parting really grieved me.'

John and Justin were promptly rehoused in the Barkingside orphanage in Wood Green, North London. Even for a care home it was an oppressive place, and its clock tower and church spires created a gothic, nightmarish atmosphere. Inside, the uncomfortable environment toughened the brothers' personalities. Although they quickly acclimatised to their unpleasant surroundings, Barkingside affected the brothers badly. Pearl would visit them at weekends, but John was obviously missing the love and attention of a family home. He developed a speech impediment. 'I remember I was very insecure,' Fash said in the 1998 BBC documentary *Fallen Hero*, which charted the life of his brother. 'I had [the speech impediment] for three or four years and I found it very difficult to communicate. But Justin always knew what I was saying and people would say to Justin, "Justin, what's John saying?" And Justin would say, "John wants some more sweets" or "John's tired" or "John doesn't like that". So I would cling to that.'

Then in 1967, for the first time in their lives, the Fashanu brothers experienced stability and security. Justin was five and approaching the age when, according to Barnado's regulations, he would have to be fostered and separated from John – unless, of course, somebody decided to adopt them both. Alf and Betty Jackson were an elderly couple living in a small country village called Shropham, which nestled near Attleborough in Norfolk, and were looking to take in a foster child. The Jacksons, it was reckoned, would make ideal parents for the Fashanu brothers. The eldest child in the family, Susan, had already left home and although their son Edward was approaching his twenties and still lived in their care, the house seemed empty without the buzz of young children. And a picturesque home it was too. The Jacksons' two-storey flint cottage was set back behind a large holly bush and situated along a country road overgrown with hawthorn and cow parsley. More importantly, Shropham was a quiet place, criss-crossed by tree-lined lanes and hedgerows, and would provide a far more idyllic lifestyle than the one the boys were experiencing at the care home. It was perfect for the Fashanus.

In the village the Jacksons were well respected. Betty was a classical piano teacher who played the organ in Shropham's thirteenth-century church; Alf supplied the family income as an engineer. A plot of land at the back of the cottage had been used to build a modest workshop. There he worked daily on his lathes, but family friends remarked that Alf was prone to a drink or several and would sometimes suffer from 'mood swings'. Nevertheless, the couple began to indulge the boys, and the land that backed on to the house was put to good use. A set of goalposts and a football were bought to keep them occupied, and as they grew older the makeshift pitch was the scene of countless kickabouts. The Jacksons also bought the pair a dinghy to play in and toy guns to shoot in the garden. One year they were even given bikes. The Jacksons also instilled a disciplined work ethic into the brothers. As soon as John and Justin were big enough, they were taught how to hold axes and chop trees. As part of their daily chores in the winter they were often sent out to cut and gather wood to stoke the living-room fire. 'Those two lads were brought up like two young English gentlemen,' remarked one family friend.

At Attleborough High, the local mixed secondary school, a

small, rural establishment that housed around 500 pupils, the boys thrived. They were the only black faces in the playground and in the surrounding towns, but racism was something the boys never experienced. 'We didn't have any problems,' John told the BBC. 'We weren't a threat. I think it's difficult if you are a black child and brought up by a white family. I remember explaining to the other children at the time why our hair was different and why our skin was different. There are two ways you can go in that situation: you can either swim or you can sink. We took the positive route and we chose to swim.' Like most facilities of its kind, Attleborough High was made up of a number of mobile classrooms, but the boys enthused about the sports fields. There were several football pitches to play on, they told Betty excitedly, as well as an athletics track and a number of tennis courts. In the evenings the PE department ran various sports clubs, including badminton. On the pitches, the brothers really made their mark. John was obviously a handy player, but Justin made bigger waves, attracting scouts from Norwich City who soon signed him on schoolboy forms. John followed a year later, though many noted that he lacked the technical ability of his brother. Not that he cared. If Justin was going to dribble the ball past players, John would power the ball into the net. 'He didn't take any prisoners,' noted Norwich scout Ronnie Brooks. 'Even as a kid, you'd rather have him on your side than in the opposition.'

But John soon began to struggle at Norwich, which was down to the fact that his brother was a superstar in the making. As Justin began to force his way into the first team, John took to capitalising on his older brother's blossoming fame. One evening, as John watched Justin play in a reserve-team game, a number of girls fluttered to his side. When one asked for an autograph after the game, Fash was wowed by the attention and scribbled his name enthusiastically. This, of course, was understandable: at fifteen, a taste of fame, however small, is usually an unknown experience. But as John handed the pen back to his 'fan' he heard a shout. Unexpectedly, an arm then snaked around his throat in a choke hold. 'It was so powerful that I nearly passed out. It put me on my knees. It was Justin, and very embarrassingly, for me anyway, he dragged me to the corner of the stand and started asking me what I was doing. When I told him I was signing autographs he couldn't believe it. He said, "What have you done and what have you achieved to sign autographs?" At first I took it badly and I sulked for a couple of days. I thought he was really horrible and a beast. But then I thought about it and realised it was me who was an idiot. I wasn't even a professional footballer at that time and I thought I had made it because of my brother. I was signing autographs because of his hard work, because his name was Fashanu and my name happened to be Fashanu too. And on the basis of that I was signing autographs, trying to get in the limelight myself, and I hadn't even achieved anything. It took me two days to come out of my sulk. After a while, I knocked on his bedroom door and said, "You know what, Justin, mate, you were right." I had done nothing; what was I signing autographs for? I was only on the first rung of a very big footballing ladder.'

John continued to endure the swelling hero worship of his brother at school, and at times it must have been tough living in Justin's shadow. Everywhere he turned, John was constantly reminded of his brother's status. 'He was in the papers every day,' Fash continued. 'He was being hailed as a major superstar. Everybody was singing his praises. I'd go into school and everybody would have another story about Justin scoring three goals, beating eleven men on his own and putting the ball in the back of the net.' One thing John certainly struggled to understand was Justin's frivolous attitude to money. When he began to receive First Division pay cheques, they were cashed and wasted. John would ask for cash to help him through the week, but Justin would always refuse, telling him he had to learn to pay his own way. Occasionally he would resort to rummaging through his brother's pockets while he was at training. He was often shocked to find coins and notes there. John just couldn't understand how his brother could be so uncaring with his cash when he felt so poor. 'I realised it was becoming unhealthy and I was becoming envious,' he said. 'From there we were having a rift.'

John tried to boost his income by charging fellow trainees 50p for a lift in his car into the Norwich training ground. He used to cram six friends in on a daily basis. But on the pitch he was finding it difficult to make any progress in the Norwich youth teams, and still he was falling short of Justin's ability. It was noticeable that he didn't possess the flashing feet that were making Justin famous, and he worried his career was being hindered by his brother's reputation. His frustration soon manifested itself in a series of violent outbursts during competitive matches. 'At that stage he was having disciplinary problems every other week,' said the then Norwich captain Joe Royle. 'These mainly happened in the youth team, and he certainly seemed to be having problems in getting the balance right between playing football and getting involved with other players on the field.' Clearly, John had to get away.

The first separation came in August 1981 when Justin moved to European champions Nottingham Forest, smashing transfer records and making more headlines. John was now alone with

Alf and Betty Jackson in their Attleborough cottage, for the first time leading a separate existence to Justin. All of which must have seemed strange. He had often relied on his older brother to play the role of a father figure, despite their financial feuding. But when it came to football, John's career began to move at a quickening pace. After leaving school at seventeen and working as a steel erector in Norwich, he had signed professional forms at Carrow Road in October 1979. He had made his debut that same year and had quickly carved a reputation for himself in Norwich's reserve side as a promising young striker, but he'd been unable to emulate his brother and break into the first team on a regular basis. In fact, in nearly four years he made only seven first-team appearances and scored just the one goal, in a 4–1 win over Cambridge.

It was obvious to everyone that John would have to move elsewhere if he was to play regular first-team football. In August 1983 a loan deal was arranged with Crystal Palace. Only a month later John was signed by Lincoln City for £15,000. He was 21 years old, and the transfer suited him. Lincoln were a mid-table side in the old Third Division, and although they were playing a distinctly lower standard of football than Norwich, John was happy to drop down a division or two if it meant his development could gallop forward. Meanwhile, the Lincoln coaching staff were keen to encourage his enthusiasm and eagerness to learn. Their style of football was aggressive and direct, exactly the sort of environment in which a player as physical as John could thrive and score goals. The coaching staff at Lincoln also came with a good reputation. Manager Colin Murphy and his assistant, the late John Pickering, were viewed as excellent developers of youth talent. Midfielder Glenn Cockerill recalled how both trainers believed that they could succeed where Norwich had failed and fulfil John's potential. 'I think coming to Lincoln got him on the right track, because Colin Murphy brought the best out of him,' he said. 'Every young player should have been under Colin Murphy at that time, because you could learn so much from him. I think Fash really benefited from joining Lincoln. Colin was a brilliant coach. He was good on the pitch and he knew how to handle the players. He upset a few along the way too, but give me a manager that doesn't.'

On the pitch, Fash certainly seemed happier. According to his new colleagues, first impressions suggested that he was focused and ambitious, if a little raw on the training ground. Many noted that he was a physical handful who seemed determined to battle his way to success on the pitch. Off it, he was considered a gentleman, if a slightly flamboyant one who attracted attention from the moment he arrived in the club car park. 'He turned up in this silly little sports car,' recalled Cockerill. 'I think he'd made it out of Lego. It looked ridiculous. It was a strange little thing. I remember it was called a Mantra or something, and so he got the mickey taken out of him straight away for that. He took it in his stride though. He always took the jokes well, but then he always gave as good as he got.'

In his first year at Lincoln Fash scored eleven goals in 31 games. Behind the scenes, Colin Murphy was delighted with his new acquisition. Fash had forced his way into the starting line-up almost immediately and had quickly become ever present in the side; according to Cockerill, he only missed games when hampered by suspension or injury. He was popular with the fans too, although the attendances were a lot smaller than Fash had been used to at Norwich. Lincoln were only attracting crowds of around 3,000; 4,000 on a good day. He was viewed as a leader too.

Colin Murphy and the Lincoln players soon began to look to him for inspiration. His peers noted that he was a real 'driving force' in the dressing room.

'He was a massive player for the team because of his character,' remembered team-mate Neil Redfearn. 'He arrived shortly before me, but he helped me to settle in and I was there over a year with him. But John was a massive character even then, he was larger than life, and he was looked upon as a leader at the club. In some ways he was almost viewed as a senior pro, even though he was hardly out of his teens. It was very impressive. He was somebody the manager could lean on because he was a physical presence and he was confident, so the players respected him. The manager relied on Fash for that confidence, and he gave us strength.'

The flamboyant weaknesses indulged in by his brother at Norwich and Nottingham – the flashy parties, the late nights, the frivolous attitude to cash – weren't evident in Fash, though it quickly became clear to the Lincoln team that he did follow his brother's infamous sense of fashion. Friends noted that John was a 'little bit different' when it came to clothes shopping. 'His gear was pretty dramatic,' said Cockerill. 'I think he was trying to keep up with Justin's fashion sense, and he really thought he was a top dresser. He used to get a bit of stick for it because, basically, whatever Michael Jackson was wearing at the time, John was also wearing it.' Fash's tailoring exuded a healthy aura of arrogance, said team-mates. He would often arrive at the training ground immaculately dressed, sometimes even wearing a suit, while his peers arrived in tracksuits. Nobody came close to John's sartorial tastes. 'I remember he once arrived at training with a cane,' Redfearn recalled. 'But the thing was, when he pulled it apart it had a sword in it. We couldn't believe it when he showed it to us. He was definitely a little bit different in his sense of style, that's for sure. He dressed like a Premier League star even then, and he always had the latest car. But everybody accepted that flashy attitude in him. It was a little bit of arrogance in a way, but it was a healthy arrogance. There wasn't anything nasty about it.'

Fash was also beginning to show the same levels of business acumen that had inspired his brother to pick up sponsored Toyotas and free sports equipment during his time at Norwich City. In Lincoln Fash was soon securing himself similar endorsement deals, although they would come from unlikely and less glamorous sources. 'He had a business head even at an early age,' said Redfearn. 'He got sponsored by a health food store in the centre of town, but he had to have their stickers plastered on the side of his car, which he got a bit of stick for.'

Much of his work was taking place on the pitch, however. The scrappy nature of Third Division football allowed Fash to thrive during games. He could cope quite easily with the physical battering that was a trademark of the lower divisions where many more skilled players would struggle. His robust performances and his goal-scoring record meant that he was one of the league's rising stars. Scouts and managers from higher divisions were beginning to take note of his muscular potential and technical ability, which until now hadn't surfaced. Fash had made his reputation by scrapping for loose balls and using his size at set-pieces, but he was also beginning to display excellent ability with his feet, even though a number of fans didn't credit him with having any skill; they only saw the typhoon of elbows and knees that marked his arrival in the penalty area. He was, as Ronnie Brooks had previously noted at Norwich City, 'a little bit lethal'. 'It was strange,' remarked Redfearn, 'because his character off the field didn't match his character on it. Once you got him on the pitch, he turned wild. He was definitely an animal when he was playing football and he caused a lot of defences a lot of problems. Looking after himself came naturally to Fash, and he would look after one or two of his team-mates too, if it came down to it. He was a physical player, but I don't think he ever went around looking for trouble at that age. I think it used to follow him around because of the nature of his game, but he was tough. There's a saying in football: if a player was tough, you'd "want him in the trenches with you". John definitely came into that category.'

Millwall manager George Graham was one who earmarked Fash, and in November 1984 he paid Lincoln £55,000 for him. Graham knew it made for pretty good business. Fash was young and talented and therefore a sensible investment. He would also fit neatly into Millwall's style of play. As was the way with most George Graham teams, the South London club, which were chasing promotion in the old Third Division, played a defensive style of football that often required the midfield to pass the ball out to the wings. High crosses would then be fizzed into the opposition's penalty area where a target man, in this case Fash, was used to knock the ball down to his supporting strikers. Unsurprisingly, the style of play suited Fash, and his team-mates were impressed with him from the moment he arrived at the club. It was clear that George Graham had done his homework.

And all the while Fash was developing his technical ability. Neil Redfearn, for one, had already begun to appreciate that there was much more to Fash than a barrage of elbows and boots as he charged into the penalty area. He was proving to be pretty good on the deck at Millwall too, while showing a keen desire to learn from those around him. And there were few better young managers in English football than George Graham, who would later go on to win trophies with Arsenal. 'He grew leaps and bounds with the help of George Graham,' recalled former Millwall captain Les Brierly. 'George was a fantastic coach and manager and John really worked hard at his game. He was always looking to improve himself and he made that very clear to everybody at the club. He wanted better things and he always strived to achieve good things, both for the club and himself.'

The fans loved him. Throughout the early 1980s, Millwall's following had built a reputation as an aggressive and intimidating mob. On occasions, their more unhinged members instigated battles with rival fans in the streets surrounding the ground. On matchdays Fash reflected the same bloodthirsty mentality in his tackling and goal-scoring, and quickly became a crowd favourite. They even nicknamed him 'Fash the Bash'. But there were minor problems with his attitude to match preparation. One downside to Fash's development was his almost petulant resentment of training. Unlike most professionals, he seemed to dislike this day-to-day work, especially if it was cold or raining. He would resort to devious means to avoid any hard work. For instance, during shooting practice at Dartford College he would often hoof a wild strike over the crossbar and into the woods that framed the football pitch; he would then spend the next half an hour hunting for the ball in the undergrowth, much to the amusement of his team-mates, although George Graham and his assistant Theo Foley were less enthusiastic. 'There were a number of occasions when Theo Foley would take him for a bit of extra running after training because he hadn't done enough work,' noted Millwall striker Steve Lovell. Despite this adverse reaction to football practice, Fash, like his brother, was a fit lad. His reluctance to train didn't pose too much of a problem therefore, and Millwall reaped the rewards of acquiring his ability almost immediately. During his first season at the club, Fash helped push the team into a promotion spot; overall, he picked up a decent tally of twelve goals in 50 matches.

He proved his worth off the pitch too, and Brierly later recalled how Fash would involve himself in the club's work in the community. As team captain, Brierly was required to attend various functions and sponsored events. Fash would often lighten his workload. He was also beginning to appear in the media with increasing regularity, something that would become commonplace in the years to come. In later years with Wimbledon, Fash loved seeing his name in the papers. His easy-going nature, articulate speech and humorous turns of phrase made him a favourite with local and national journalists. It amused the Millwall players too: his propensity for appearing across the back pages of South London's weekly newspapers earned him the nickname 'Johnny Quick Quote'. 'I think his time at Millwall was really the start of him as a player,' said Brierly. 'He had done very well for us and he was beginning to get recognised more and more. I think Millwall was the first step on the ladder to recognition.' Steve Lovell agreed. 'We could see pretty quickly that he was a star in the making.'

At Wimbledon Sam Hammam and Harry Bassett were convinced of it too. Harry had taken note of Fash's debt-collector-like abilities in January 1986 when Wimbledon had been given an away tie at Second Division promotion rivals Millwall in the third round of the FA Cup. At The Den Fash made an impressive return after an untypical five-game suspension. Feeling rejuvenated after the short break, he scored one goal and sprang the offside trap twice to set up two more in a crushing victory. On the touchline, Harry made notes furiously. Here was a player with enough muscle and speed to complement his wily strike force of Alan Cork and Lawrie Sanchez. At over six foot three, he was also big and aggressive enough to terrify the toughest of defences. Harry enthusiastically enquired about his availability. Millwall, it became apparent, were open to offers, and in March Fash joined the Crazy Gang. Sam declared that it was his present to the club.

'We got him just before the transfer deadline in March,' said Harry. 'I'd seen him playing for Lincoln a few seasons previously and thought he was strong and good in the air, but his control needed to improve. He was very athletic though, and by the time I'd seen him play for Millwall he had taken another step forward. He'd stepped up, and his understanding of the game was better and his touch had sharpened. It wasn't difficult to convince Millwall to part with him because they were in a bit of trouble financially. I know George Graham wanted to hold on to him, but they needed to make some money, so they sold him to us. It worked out nicely for everyone concerned.' Millwall were indeed sad to see him go. 'We had a new board of directors coming in and with our money troubles we couldn't hold on to John,' Brierly recalled. 'It was a nice bit of money for us, but John had a real rapport with the fans and probably would have liked to stay, but unfortunately we couldn't refuse the money.' Fash's arrival at Wimbledon was certainly uplifting. 'We thought we needed a boost just before the transfer deadline,' said Harry, 'and we felt he'd be the sort of player who could give us a bit more firepower up front and push us through to promotion. And what he did do was to give the players a psychological boost, a belief that when we splashed £125,000 on him we were taking promotion very seriously indeed. It gave us all a little lift.'

The deal was Harry's then record expenditure for a player, and the move was impeccably timed, for both the club and Fash. Wimbledon were halfway through a sixteen-match unbeaten streak that would take them into the First Division, and in eight appearances Fash contributed four goals, although he didn't always make the starting line-up at the end of that 1985/86 season. Wimbledon, the 'alley cats' of professional football, had snatched a place with the game's elite. Sam and Harry were chuffed. Fash's rags-to-riches war against adversity had given him the schooling to take Wimbledon to superstardom. Now he was going to be the time bomb that blew the First Division to smithereens.

CHAPTER FIVE

By the time the promotion celebrations had finished, relegation was the talking point of the day. Wimbledon might have escaped Second Division life with their mob of park players, but most fans were predicting a quick return to the scrap heap. Not even Sam's quickfire verbosity could dissuade the doubters.

It was easy to see why. Harry's bolshie tactics were never going to put the squeeze on the likes of Kenny Dalglish, Glenn Hoddle and Bryan Robson in the First Division. These were experienced international footballers who regularly graced magazine covers and TV studio sofas. They had too much know-how and guile to be fazed by the Crazy Gang's primitive tactics. Meanwhile, any supporters of First Division clubs wishing to learn a little more about lowly Wimbledon would probably need an encyclopaedia of the English game to figure out who played where. The Crazy Gang were a cute little novelty, a one-season wonder which would probably drop down the divisions they'd ascended so unexpectedly in a few seasons. Most experts figured that everybody would be bored with their quaint little tale after a game or two anyway.

Nobody at Plough Lane cared. The club was in football

dreamland, though they were unprepared for the fantasy of the top flight. Compared to the top stadia in the country, Plough Lane was a ramshackle dump with rubble-strewn terraces and a rusting, corrugated-iron roof. Inside the ground the dark, dingy dressing rooms were a shock to the system, regardless of which division you played in. Unbelievably, the international superstars of Liverpool, Arsenal and Manchester United would soon be undressing there. 'It was a horrible place,' said defender Paul Parker, who faced Wimbledon while playing for Fulham in the Second Division. He would later come up against them for Queens Park Rangers in Division One during the 1986/87 campaign. 'The moment you tried to park your car anywhere near the ground you were in trouble because there wasn't anywhere to park. Certainly, when teams realised they had to go to Plough Lane they were unhappy because the facilities were so bad.'

But the snobbery didn't bother the club or its staff one bit. In fact, during the pre-season they seemed happy with the situation. Wimbledon had little money to spend on improving the stadium and its infrastructure anyway, and their poverty would give them a psychological advantage. *Anything to upset the snobs*. There was next to no cash to invest in the squad either, as Fash's transfer fee – Sam's 'present' – had drained the bank account in the spring. Only Dennis Wise, who had signed two seasons earlier as a then unknown midfielder at Southampton, was drafted into the first team during the summer of 1986/87.

Wise was perfect for Wimbledon – he was trouble, like everyone else, a self-confessed 'spoilt brat'. The cocky son of a West London publican, he played the game with a wild-eyed, reckless streak that grated with everyone he competed against, though when recalling his back story this attitude was understandable. As a kid he had grown up on war-zone housing estates in Shepherd's Bush and Notting Hill, where he often kicked a ball around with his dad's friend Stan Bowles, the legendary football maverick. A relentless ferocity soon developed on park pitches during his teens – his dad once whacked him because he refused to shake a victorious opponent's hand – and his youth was peppered with run-ins against authority. He even scuppered his chances of playing for England schoolboys after he'd got into a scrape on the train to the trials. Apparently, one of his team-mates told a fellow passenger to fuck off and all hell had broken loose. Wise also used to dodge traffic on his bike. The only time he was ever hit by the oncoming vehicles was when he flew across the bonnet of a car driven by his parents. He then set fire to their bed during an attempt to retrieve a ball that had rolled underneath. For some unknown reason he'd decided to pierce the gloom with a lighter and set the duvet ablaze. It was this schooling that moulded him perfectly to Harry's team. At five feet seven inches, he was a short-arsed powerhouse. In later years he expressed a fondness for Robert De Niro movies, which seemed apt, because he possessed the same destructive streak on the park as Travis Bickle in *Taxi Driver*, but, strangely, he also claimed his favourite singer was the androgynous Terence Trent D'Arby, revealed that he'd kept a tiny horseshoe at his house for good luck and said that his favourite cartoon characters were the Smurfs. All of which suggested he was a softie at heart. His opponents would probably disagree.

Despite the baggage, Southampton had taken him on as a kid, given him a football education and offered him a £100-per-week apprenticeship. He turned his back on the offer, and first-team manager Lawrie McMenemy, shocked at the petulance, pushed him away from The Dell. But McMenemy had tired of him long before this arrogant rejection. During one training session Wise had roughed up a team-mate, and even though 'Little' Dennis's victim was over six feet tall, McMenemy fought back for him, later pinning Wise against his office wall. 'Come on then, bully *me*! Bully me!' screamed McMenemy as he pinned Wise's throat to the wallpaper. 'Yeah, he had a little bit of a go at me,' said Wise afterwards. 'It was something that happened. I had an argument with a player: he was six foot one and I was five foot seven and I was the bully. I couldn't work that one out.' There was also an incident in which he'd involved himself in a fight with Southampton team-mate Reuben Agboola. That it took place outside a nightclub wasn't strange to Wise. He figured everybody did it, even if he was Southampton's head boot boy. Clearly McMenemy thought he was better off without him, but Wise's attitude had rattled him, and he was eager for revenge. The diminutive midfielder offered his talents to a variety of clubs in the capital, but McMenemy refused to release his registration. Wise soon saw the error of his ways and apologised for his behaviour. He even asked for a return to the south coast. McMenemy agreed and recalled him, which on paper looked like an admission of defeat. Secretly, however, the Southampton manager held a trump card, and when Wise returned to the club, McMenemy handed back the registration he'd been so reluctant to release. He told Wise to beat it.

The Dons took him on for £25 a week less than the offered wage at Southampton, and he settled in quickly. The rough-and-ready feel of Wimbledon didn't bother him, and he was immediately nicknamed 'Rat' (which later became amended to 'Ratski'). It didn't bother new boy Fash either, and they both adjusted into a new way of life at Plough Lane. The reassuring family atmosphere within the club and the boisterous team-bonding tactics of the players and its staff suited them. Fash believed he was standing shoulder to shoulder with like-minded individuals. 'We were all poor guys,' he said, 'and most of us came from difficult backgrounds – broken homes, Barnardo's, prison, you name it. Wise wouldn't turn up for training some days because he'd got into some punch-up or another, and with Jonesey [midfielder turned Hollywood actor Vinnie Jones, who signed during the 1986/87 season from non-league Wealdstone] it was an everyday occurrence. Jonesey would come in with a baseball bat still hanging through his car window. His earrings would be ripped out and he had scratches all over his face. I'd say, "Jonesey, what the hell's happened to you?" and he'd say, "Nothing, Fash, just the family." I remember when Jonesey came in late every day because he'd been having a running fight with some gypsies near his house.' Of course, Harry loved the lawless atmosphere. He later described the team as 'the Borstal of football'. Their peers weren't so enthusiastic however, and from the moment Wimbledon secured their place in the First Division they were viewed as a curiosity, a ragtag team of part-timers and pub players that had struck lucky, won the Lottery and pinched a place in English football's big league.

For much of the coming season the club would rely on most of the players who had secured promotion from the Second Division: Beasant in goal; a defence of Kevin Gage, Nigel Winterburn (who was impressing at every turn), Andy Thorn, Mark Morris and Brian Gayle; Steve Galliers, Dennis Wise, Sanch, Wally Downes and Carlton Fairweather were available for midfield duty; and Fash and Corky filled the roles up front. Outside Plough Lane nobody seemed impressed. During the pre-season campaign of predictions and 'expert' punditry within the media, most commentators spoke only of two relegation places rather than the usual three. Wimbledon, they predicted, were a dead cert for the drop even before a long ball had been kicked in anger. All of which suited Harry and his Crazy Gang just fine. Football's fancy Dans might show a galling lack of respect for Wimbledon's up-and-at-'em tactics and fearless attitude before the season started, but they would soon feel a twitching sense of unease when the close-season talking made way for competitive fixtures. Wimbledon were determined to stick to their guns tactically and play the same sort of football that had secured their top-flight status. There would be no attempt to add finesse and guile to their play in order to match the superstars of the division. They were sure their underdog image would play to their advantage. 'We'd been underestimated,' said Harry. 'And all the pundits thought we weren't a good team, but we were a good team. I knew we had better players than most people reckoned.'

On the training ground Harry's team, led by an intimidating war cry, had discovered the perfect tactic with which to ruffle the feathers of the Division One peacocks. Following Fash's shout of 'Put it in the mixer!', the ball would be pumped into the opposition half as long and as high as possible. When the ball was played on the deck the tactics were based on pub-football simplicity too. Harry hated it when players passed the ball across midfield. He became even more irate if his defenders tried anything more complicated than a long clearance upfield. He wanted the ball played to Fash and Corky as quickly as possible, and if it dropped short in midfield it was his players' job to flick it on. When the ball finally popped into the penalty area, chaos ruled in a blur of boots, hair and teeth. According to football analyst Andy Gray, central defenders would head the ball on more occasions against Wimbledon than in five or six matches against other sides.

It was ugly, but, incredibly, these aggressive tactics proved remarkably effective. In the first half of the season Wimbledon managed to hold their own. Despite a shaky 1–3 home defeat against newly promoted Manchester City on the first day of the campaign, they topped the table after consecutive wins against Aston Villa, Leicester, Charlton and Watford. On television that September Manchester United captain Bryan Robson spoke about the First Division's league leaders with an air of glazed bemusement. But Harry wasn't getting excited. When asked about the club's title ambitions he snorted with laughter. 'Win the league? That would be like Dobbin winning the Derby.'

They began to pick up defeats after that, and their peers sighed sympathetically, claiming that Wimbledon's little bubble had burst. The schadenfreude would never last for long, though: Wimbledon would inevitably bounce back after defeat with impressive victories, as evidenced by their wins over Norwich (then a top-six side) and Spurs at the end of October. Such wins, however, were always credited to top-flight complacency rather than Wimbledon's dogged spirit. Even the tabloid press, previously an ally, adopted a snobbish attitude to their style of play. At first Harry took it personally. By his own admission he'd get 'arseholey' and ring journalists after he'd read yet another scathing piece. It was easy to understand why it upset him so much. When Wimbledon knocked the big teams from their perches it seemed the elite's deficiencies were highlighted rather than the Crazy Gang's strengths. Nobody wanted to credit their performances. Harry quickly compared the media to the Mafia, but later the negative press was taken quietly. He accepted that the abuse was part of the game. Harry probably wasn't that bothered in all honesty. The only major blip in the first half of the season was a Littlewoods Cup defeat at the hands of Cambridge. His Wimbledon, it was apparent, were determined to make an immediate impression, and the big boys were taking a kicking. If they didn't like it, if the media didn't like it, if the fans didn't like it … *then fuck them*.

His tactics, it was then announced, followed a scientifically proven methodology. Former FA Director of Football Charles Hughes had conducted a study that revealed that 85 per cent of goals were scored from build-ups using five passes or fewer. He even wrote a book on the subject entitled *The Winning Formula*. Wimbledon's peers winced at the news, as did the FA. Wimbledon's direct style was being played out to the accompaniment of a flourish of cards and injuries. 'They were clearly a strong physical side and you soon realised you were in for a battering when you played them,' recalled Aston Villa winger Tony Daley. 'I'll never forget the game at Plough Lane [on 26 August, which Villa lost 3–2]. Every time I got the ball I thought I was going to get a whack and end up in the stands. I wasn't complaining about it, but they would kick and pull you around until you were black and blue.'

As the season developed pace, Fash became the heart of Wimbledon's bully tactics. Despite receiving harsh criticism from football's more puritanical experts, Harry was delighted with him. 'He was a big threat to good defences,' he said. 'He was a real handful, and he was quick and tough. Defenders knew they were in for a real battle when he played, because he was a physical centre-forward. Opponents knew they were going to get involved in a confrontation with him at some stage during a game, whether that was an aerial battle or a chase for a ball, and he used his strength to the best of his ability. He'd win all of his battles.' As Wimbledon's notoriety spread among the league's bigger teams, so did their unpopularity, particularly that of Fash. After one game an opponent was moved to grumble, 'His ideal pitch would have a rope around it, like a boxing ring.' A disgruntled David Pleat, the Spurs manager, sneered, 'If I wanted a player like him, I would go out and buy a heavyweight boxer.'

Fellow professionals, defenders in particular, described playing against Fash as 'a bloody nightmare'. 'John hustled and bustled you all the time with elbows or anything he could use to get an advantage,' recalled Paul Parker. 'I remember a game for QPR when he ripped my neck to ribbons with his nails. As a ball went up he dug his nails into the side of my throat. I had to convince my missus that something suspicious hadn't happened because she was going to beat me, but I had four gouges in my neck from what he'd done to me. He then put me into the hoardings at Plough Lane with a tackle. But you accepted that's what came with marking John. He'd never get away with it today, but at the time football was a man's game, and John was definitely one of the toughest playing it.'

Fash felt his over-exuberant aggression was all part of the sport. If a defender was pole-axed by a flailing elbow or a full-blooded volley to the head, he would take time to apologise, *sincerely*. 'What was annoying was that if he clattered you he wouldn't apologise begrudgingly and say, "You all right, mate?"' Parker continued. 'He'd apologise in a very well-spoken and polite way. And of course that would wind you up even more because you'd be waiting to have an argument with him, but he wouldn't give you the opportunity because he was so polite. Not that you'd want to row with him, that is. You just wouldn't do it because he was so big.'

It was this muscular but intelligent behaviour that would often give his team-mates the confidence to play. Many Wimbledon players would look to 'Bashanu' (as he had been nicknamed by the press) to unnerve the opposition. 'He used his brains too,' said Harry. 'He was into psychology and psyching people out. He knew when he could wind up an opponent.' Parker agreed. 'His chatting on the pitch was always intimidating, but it was never aimed at anyone in particular. It was always what he said to his team-mates that was unsettling. The big shout from him was always, "Get it in the mixer!" But the other one was when he would go up for a corner or a free-kick. Fashanu would say to one of the other players, "This is going to hurt me," and it would make you wonder what he was on about. You'd end up worrying about what was going to happen and what he had in mind rather than your own game.'

But it was the matchday atmosphere rather than Wimbledon's players that really unsettled travelling opposition. Plough Lane, while only attracting a measly 6,000 supporters to most games, quickly gained a reputation as an intimidating and uncomfortable place for teams to compete in. The bigger clubs, used to luxurious changing rooms, treatment tables and generous catering, were disgusted by Plough Lane's worn – a polite term, by anyone's standards – facilities. Plough Lane fell woefully short of the usual standard of hospitality, and the complaints came in thick and fast, but Sam really couldn't give a shit. Wimbledon's downtrodden stadium gave them the upper hand. 'It really upset teams,' Parker confirmed. 'Once you'd got to the ground, you had to walk down a little alley to get to the changing rooms, which used to really wind you up. And when you got to the dressing rooms they were horrible. You had to come out of the changing rooms to go to the toilet which meant you had to be near *them* [Wimbledon], and you couldn't even think about the game because their boys had the stereo on so loud you couldn't settle. They were one of the first teams to bring loud music to their warm-up.'

The stereo had been brought in by Fash during the pre-season break, and the music, a mix of dance and house, was provided by Paul Clark, a DJ and friend of the team. And that wasn't the only act of gamesmanship. West Ham striker Tony Cottee recalled how the heating would often be set at an uncomfortably high level in the away team's dressing room, all of which was designed to add to the unpleasant Plough Lane experience. 'It was bloody horrible to be honest,' he moaned. 'You felt drained by the time it came to warm-up.' If that wasn't enough, Sam would often fill the sugar bowls with salt, and somebody was always on hand to ensure the loo-paper holders were empty. This accompanied the specially laid 'present' in the toilet bowl. Naturally, the lights in the cubicles had no bulbs.

Later, when the players exited their dressing rooms, a territorial battle of wills would begin. 'When you got out into the tunnel you had them growling and pulling faces at you,' recalled Cottee. 'There was always a lot of shouting and hollering from that lot, but I always used to get my head down and let [West Ham captain] Billy Bonds and the bigger players do the eyeballing stuff.' The Crazy Gang loved the intimidation. 'The players' tunnel was one of our secret weapons,' said Fash. 'It was like the Tunnel of Doom. It might not be Anfield, but I tell you what, a lot of our opponents were scared to death. When they walked back in at half-time or after a game and it got dark, things happened. They got closer and closer and realised there was no light in the tunnel, and they weren't sure whether they were going to come out on the other side. We used to go out screaming and come in screaming. And when the echoes rang around, you could see the fear in their eyes.'

When Wimbledon played away games, however, the boos accompanying their arrival on the pitch rang louder. And it wasn't just Fash who endured the public's ire. Fans were disgusted at what Harry often referred to as 'the Wimbledon Way'. Wise, Corky, Sanch, even Dave Beasant took the flak, but nobody cared. Not even when their fellows pros complained. Managers, pundits and the media, meanwhile, continued to describe their style of play as 'hideous', all of which simply served to inspire Fash and his team-mates. 'We started showing off,' he said. 'We started trying things that Glenn Hoddle would do ... trying to take on a few people. It was ridiculous.'

Another indignity thrust in the faces of opposition fans centred on goal celebrations. Unlike Justin, who was renowned for scoring goals with his boots, Fash was more adept in the air. At set-pieces he would often lead the charge of blue and gold shirts steaming goalwards. And when he scored, which he did on fourteen occasions that season to become Wimbledon's leading scorer, he would anger fans with a dance that involved a touchline sprint, arms outstretched like an aeroplane, as his team-mates followed suit behind him. It was just one more infuriating thing for opposing supporters to suffer as Wimbledon body-slammed their way to another victory.

Wimbledon were laughing loudly. The rest of the First Division would have preferred them just to disappear for good, but things were about to get worse – much worse. In November 1986 Harry signed a non-league terroriser called Vinnie Jones, whose reputation as a stud-happy midfielder with a manic streak had reached the press boys long before his arrival on the pitch.

Compared to some of his new professional peers, Vinnie couldn't have been cut from a more different cloth. If Glenn Hoddle was tailored in satin, Vinnie was made of sandpaper. He was a 22-year-old midfielder and former hod carrier (which the newshounds loved), but having watched him play football Harry figured his robust style suited the Crazy Gang's tactics to a tee. After a summer spent playing in Sweden for Holmsund, Vinnie was taken to Plough Lane for trials. There was baggage, however. Vinnie was a wildcard who liked to use his fists as much as his feet. His tackles also came with Parental Guidance tags attached. During one FA Cup game for his non-league side Wealdstone against Reading he came on as a sub and started a punch-up within minutes. Seconds earlier he'd launched a violent tackle at an opponent. Later he would claim it was a great challenge, though today he often expresses shock at how he remained on the pitch after landing a right-hander on his opponent as he lay on the floor. He reckoned it would have been one of the quickest sendings-off of all time. But Vinnie impressed in a series of practice games for Wimbledon. He knew it too, and when he was called into Harry's office after a training session a smile spread across his face. In the changing rooms, the players began to shout, 'Contract! Go on, son, get a contract!' Once inside, Harry told Vinnie he was going to pay Wealdstone £15,000 and handed him a two-year deal: £150 a week, £50 a goal, £50 per first-team appearance. Vinnie was chuffed. And could he have a signing-on fee? Harry's face creased into a scowl. 'Fuck off.'

Vinnie was drafted into the team on 22 November for the game against Nottingham Forest. Harry had to lend him the £150 for a matchday suit. Before the game London Weekend Television tracked Vinnie down for an interview, and he ballsed it up, stuttering his way through the answers. On the day of the game he spent his £2.50 food allowance from Harry on a fry-up and involved himself in a water fight in the team hotel. He'd settled in quite nicely, even if he did give away a penalty for a handball in a 3–2 defeat. A goal a week later helped to settle his nerves. He scored it against Manchester United at Plough Lane, and Wimbledon won the game. Vinnie was delighted, but of course these football aristocrats sneered yet again at the Crazy Gang's style of football. 'I remember when we beat United,' said Sanch. 'It was during the time when you could kick the ball back to the goalkeeper and he could use his hands. We got it straight back to Dave Beasant from the kick-off and he kicked the ball upfield and it bounced on the edge of the United box. I'll never forget Bryan Robson's face. He looked around as if to say, "Fuck me, here we go. We've got 90 minutes of this." We loved it.'

Within weeks Vinnie was crowd favourite and public enemy number one in equal measure, endearing himself to Wimbledon's fans with a series of horror-show tackles and body charges. On 6 December he threw himself into a punch-up with Chelsea, scored his second goal in three games, and Wimbledon ran off the victors by four goals to nil. 'When you're building a team,' explained Harry when asked about his new signing, 'you're looking for good players, not blokes to marry your daughters.' Vinnie also had a spectacularly long throw-in technique, which was used to hurl the ball into the penalty area at any given opportunity. Every fan in the country outside Plough Lane hated him. Secretly, the Crazy Gang were proud as anything.

Officialdom began to quake. Alex Ferguson admitted that he'd been terrified of Vinnie, even though he had been safely ensconced in the dugout rather than sharing the midfield –

Vinnie's midfield. But the violent streak caused problems. Come April 1987, when Arsenal's Graham Rix claimed Wimbledon weren't even fit to walk the pitch, Vinnie brained him and was sent off, driving Harry into fits of apoplexy. 'He wound me up, I elbowed him,' explained Vinnie. In another game he picked up a booking after five seconds. Off the pitch, Sam had told reporters, 'We take nothing from no one and give it out to everybody, always. Football is war.' On the pitch, Vinnie was the literal embodiment of his boss's gunslinging gob. He scared the hell out of everyone. And Sam stuck by his side through the negative headlines and the wars with the authorities. 'He took all the blows,' said Vinnie. 'There is not another chairman who would have backed me for the aggravation I caused. Either the bell would ring on my phone at seven in the morning or the bell would ring on my front door, but I knew straight away who it would be – Sam. "Hey, baby," he'd say. "We have to sort this out now." He wanted to fight every corner for you. That's how he got his buzz, by standing up and defending his team to the hilt.'

Sam had his work cut out then. Alongside Fash, Vinnie intimidated teams with verbal insults and mind games. Both Vinnie and Fash daubed their faces with whitewash before a January FA Cup tie against Portsmouth, a game they won 4–0. And when Wimbledon travelled to Liverpool a couple of months later, Vinnie plastered a scrap of paper over the legendary 'This is Anfield' sign; on it he'd scribbled the word BOTHERED in marker pen. The club's groundstaff were rumoured to have gone 'apeshit' and Vinnie to have responded with a simple 'Fuck off'.

The Wimbledon players were already household names – especially after they beat Everton 3–1 in the fifth round of the FA Cup in February, which was their first televised game – and none more so than Vinnie. 'It put us on the map,' he said afterwards.

'Take a team like Coventry. Who do you know from Coventry? Even a grannie has heard of Fash, Beas, Wise and Vinnie Jones.' And, of course, the entire First Division had heard of them too. Wimbledon had ruffled feathers and upset football's giants. They were in the quarter-finals of the FA Cup against Tottenham. Clearly, the quaint fairytale drawn up by the media wasn't going to have a logical ending. The little club from South London that had travelled from non-league football were not about to plummet like a stone. The Crazy Gang, unbelievably, were still punching their weight. Everybody else felt physically sick.

The aggression and bravery didn't always come easily, though. For the most part Vinnie's yelling and hollering proved an inspirational form of leadership, but his new pal Fash sometimes struggled to draw it from himself. And when he was feeling off colour, the rest of the team would suffer. At times, with an out-of-form Fash in the line-up, Wimbledon seemed drained of strength. 'When I played with Fash,' said Vinnie, 'if he was on his game, flying and winning all the headers, roaring about, he would give the rest of us such a big lift. But if he wasn't at it, all the other boys used to say to me, "Hey, Vinnie, set your mate going. Get him livened up," because we were looking for him to spark it all off for us. I used to shout at him, but sometimes Fash wasn't at it. He'd have five good games and one bad one. Sometimes you'd know before the game that Fash wasn't at it. On the coach going to the game he'd say, "Who have we got today? Who plays at the back for them?" The manager didn't know it, but I did. If I'd been picking the team I'd have said, "Leave him out today."'

But whenever the opposition smelt blood and roughed up Wimbledon with the same tactics employed by Fash, Wise and Vinnie, they usually took a volley back, harder and wilder than they could have imagined. Sunderland's Eric Gates once had the cheek to goad Glyn Hodges after scoring against Wimbledon. As the players headed down the tunnel for half-time, Gates decided it was time to tell the Wimbledon player that his team 'were shit'. Harry didn't have to give a team talk after that. When Wimbledon hit back with two goals to win the game, the team rounded on Gates and gave it back harder and louder.

The bad games were actually few and far between that season. Much to everyone's surprise, Wimbledon maintained their position in Division One. They had beaten Manchester United and Chelsea home and away, and Liverpool at Anfield. More miraculously, they finished the campaign in sixth place, behind champions Everton and the big guns of Liverpool, Tottenham and Arsenal, and the slightly smaller but impressive gun of Norwich City, which had also been promoted the previous season. They were knocked out of the quarter-finals of the FA Cup 2–0 by Spurs, but the goals had come only in the last ten minutes of the match. Midfielder Andy Sayer even picked up the FIAT Young Player of the Month award for February. Wimbledon had made their mark. 'They weren't a stylish team, but they were effective and it helped to keep them in the division,' said Tony Cottee. 'It wasn't an entertaining style of football and I didn't particularly like it because I was brought up as a football man, but playing against that Wimbledon team was one of the great challenges in English football at the time. Nobody could believe it when they got to sixth place, and once they'd stayed up they built on the success.'

Opposition fans, of course, didn't want to acknowledge the club's achievements. Harry put the finger of blame on the sneering press pack, which had mocked his tactics and delivered a volley of criticism with every game. The press even claimed they were the worst team to have played in the First Division. But Sam, Harry, Fash, Vinnie, Wise, Sanch, Beas, Corky … none of them cared. 'Everybody looked down on us,' said Sanch. 'At first, everybody thought it was a great story, especially the press, and they expected us to enjoy our year and then go away. But we didn't see it that way. We hung on, and the longer we stayed there, the nastier it got for us, especially from the press side. Their new attitude was, You've had your fun, now go away. But that bonded us. The bunker mentality kicked in.'

If the press were right and Wimbledon were the worst team ever to have played in the First Division, then the joke was on everybody else. The Crazy Gang had taken the piss.

It was no great secret that season that Fash and Sanch were the best of enemies. In fact, the words commonly used by club insiders to describe their fraught relationship was 'confrontational at best'. The simmering tension between the two festered from the moment of Fash's arrival, but friends of the pair struggle to pinpoint the exact moment when the atmosphere between the two really began to bristle.

To those insiders at the club it was obvious why Fash and Wimbledon's dour striker disliked each other so intensely. Fash naturally irritated Sanch, who was angered by the truth that, deep down, Fash didn't share his passion or enthusiasm for the game. The fact that Fash really couldn't give a toss about the sport disgusted him, and he found his lethargic attitude to training a real pinch on the nerve endings. Fash would complain about injuries and spend a week on the treatment table. Miraculously, he would be fit again by the time Friday's five-a-side sessions kicked in, and he would be razor sharp by Saturday afternoon. Sanch, who worked throughout the week, and worked hard, used to twitch with rage. Fash did much to antagonise away from football too. During a pre-season trip to Spain he charged the team's drinks bill to the rooms of Sanch and Dave Beasant. The spat became public. 'I don't like Sanch and he doesn't like me,' said Fash later when explaining their feud. 'Hate is a strong word, but we agree to disagree.' For Sanch, though, emotions ran at an extreme. 'You could say we hated each other,' he said.

All of which made for a confusing situation. The Wimbledon team Fash had joined in 1986 was one that prided itself on its sense of camaraderie and team spirit. But if Wimbledon's football achievements during their first season in Division One were newsworthy, their off-pitch antics were a headline writer's dream. The feud between Fash and Sanch added a little spice to the newspaper writers' questions. And there was plenty more to report alongside that. As that 1986/87 league campaign progressed, tales of practical jokes and ritual beatings at the Wimbledon training ground – a handful of public pitches in Roehampton – had filtered through to the national press. Even trashing hotels and matchday high jinks weren't unusual occurrences. The ringleader of this unruly mob, of course, was Fash, a man who had built a reputation as a practical joker from the moment he'd started at Attleborough High School. 'I think Fash was in a league of his own,' said Wimbledon defender John Scales, who joined the club at the beginning of the 1987/88 season. 'He was one of the most eccentric characters. You had to laugh when Fash did some of the antics he got up to, whether it was on the pitch winding players up or coming into training with his briefcase and his suit on with a chauffeur dropping him off. He was unique, eccentric and just perfect for Wimbledon in those days.'

But while some of the Wimbledon team took the joking to its extreme conclusion – smashed property, broken ribs – Fash made it clear to team-mates that there was a line and it wasn't to be crossed. 'He was crazy like some of them were,' said Harry, 'but he wasn't into cutting people's clothes up, or letting people's tyres down. He didn't like that. He said at the start, "I'm not going to interfere with anybody else's stuff, so nobody interfere with mine. I don't care what anybody else does but I don't want anybody slashing my gear to ribbons or my tyres." He wasn't anti-jokes, but he laid the law down that he was slightly different and he wasn't going to take liberties. So he expected people to treat him the same way.'

In that respect, Fash was unique. Certainly the other members of the Crazy Gang were eager to promote their aggressive public image – Dennis Wise, for instance. 'Everyone took it in good stead,' he said of the practical joking. 'Basically, they knew that it was an enjoyable thing. If you got your shirt ripped, you got your shirt ripped. You could always get another one.' But Wise was and always had been a tearaway. Players spoke of having their hotel rooms rearranged by him in the corridors while they were at dinner. Even Harry was a reasonable target. The protagonist was often caught out though. 'As we were putting [Harry's] bed down at the last minute,' said Wise of one incident, 'the manager of the hotel came up, so me and Vinnie came a bit unstuck and we didn't actually know what to say. We had to put it all back in the end and Harry was standing there just laughing at us. So we'd mugged ourselves off, really.'

When it came to training and matchdays, Harry ratcheted up the anarchy. He would often order his players to run around the training ground with their arms in the air, shouting 'Power!' until they were hoarse. The method behind this madness was simple:

to the outside world, Wimbledon resembled a bunch of lunatics released from a nearby asylum. Unsurprisingly, it unnerved their opponents. The players became terrified of one another too. Training sessions would often end with a ten-minute game of 'Harry Ball'. Based on the rules of rugby and the aggression of the ultra-violent 1975 James Caan movie *Rollerball*, the game was played on a rugby pitch at their Roehampton training ground and would often culminate in a mass brawl. During one bundle, a player suffered two broken ribs. But injuries were of no concern to the Crazy Gang, and on Friday mornings Harry Ball became a regular part of the team-bonding process.

Away from the club environment, Harry would occasionally encourage his players to socialise, often in the pub. Most of the team, Vinnie in particular, took to it enthusiastically, but Fash remained sober. Harry insisted that the fact that he didn't drink wasn't a problem ('You didn't have to drink to be part of the Crazy Gang'), but Fash's teetotalism did give him a unique role in the Wimbledon squad, and he installed himself as unofficial spokesman for the team. 'I feel honoured to be associated with such a great bunch,' he said in one interview. 'They were awesome, mad. And what people don't realise is that although I acted like the statesman, calming everybody down, breaking up the fights – I was really egging them on.' It was often his duty to act as a representative for the players or to ensure that everyone was in a fit shape mentally and physically before games and practice sessions. 'It was like counting sheep in,' he said. 'To get everybody in training would be wonderful.'

Away from Plough Lane, a strange subplot was unfolding in Fash's life. During the PFA dinner at the close of the 1986/87 season he was confronted for the first time by rumours regarding his brother's sexuality. Justin had been leading a closeted life: he was gay, though he hadn't yet found the courage to announce this publicly. His friends had their suspicions though, particularly his colleagues in the game. Since his spell at Forest, Justin had been dogged by vicious comments criticising his private life. His increasing bravery when it came to visiting gay clubs in London and Nottingham had heightened the rumours surrounding his lifestyle. Subsequently, his footballing peers began to point fingers, not only at Justin but at his brother too.

As the evening progressed, Fash was beginning to feel slighted at the veiled comments and sly jokes from club outsiders, and when one member of the Crazy Gang was attacked, the others fell in line behind him, as Paul Parker recalled. 'If you gave one of their players a dig,' he said, 'they would stand up for each other and they wanted to have a go back. They wanted to go eyeball to eyeball with you, that's for sure.' As the whispers regarding Justin became increasingly audible from one player in particular, Fash took offence. Sure enough, the Crazy Gang quickly fell in line behind him. Fash recalled the ugly incident: 'We were running the joint that night – me, Wise, Jonesy, a few of the boys. We were rogues, and I remember a QPR player, someone who I always thought was a bit flash, shooting his mouth off. Someone came up to me and said, "He's putting it around that your brother's gay," and I remember thinking that was such an insult. I remember watching him go up to the toilets and thinking, "No, no, no. Goodnight, mate." I was so mad that he could insult Justin and my family that I took it really personally. So I followed him in and I wanted to have it out with him, one on one. Jonesy and a few of the boys cleared the toilets and stood outside. And lo and behold, as I was about to settle it, Justin came in. He had seen what was going on and flashed me that look as if to say, "Don't be stupid, John. Don't even think about it." Today, even though we're without Justin [who later killed himself], without Justin we'd be without that [QPR] player too. So if he's reading this, he'd better say his prayers and thank my brother, because without him he wouldn't be around, mate. And those in the football world know I would have done something about it.

A forceful point had been made: Wimbledon were a fearsome club with a grim resolve to stick together, both on the pitch and off it. 'That team would have been all right against Frazier and Tyson,' Harry commented with a knowing smirk.

CHAPTER SIX

Everything was different in 1987/88. Wimbledon, whose sixth-place finish had confounded the experts and shocked their peers, were experiencing a crisis. For the first time since the club started its dizzying climb from the Fourth Division to the First they would be without the leadership of Harry Bassett.

Sam had fallen out with Harry, and Harry with Sam. The chairman figured his manager was stealing the limelight, that his hard work and investment behind the scenes at Plough Lane had gone largely uncredited, which was down to Harry's resounding success on the pitch and the rapport with his players off it. Harry, meanwhile, believed Sam was holding a grudge against him as a kickback from those brief days he'd spent with Ron Noades at Crystal Palace. During the previous season Sam had done the gentlemanly thing and offered Harry a new contract, though its terms were greatly devalued. They'd discussed an improved deal, but this new offer failed to reflect their negotiations. It also stated that Sam had a choice in player selection on matchdays. Clearly Harry was being nudged into an awkward situation and would have to leave.

Fortunately, he was in a strong position. Other clubs had

taken note of his impressive achievements at Wimbledon. Several agents had even approached him during the spring of 1987 when the rumours of his discontent first began to filter out of the club, though he was often unsure of their validity. On one occasion he agreed to meet an employee of Spanish team Athlético Bilbao at the Post House Hotel near Heathrow, believing it was a prank worked up by the Crazy Gang. When a Spanish representative who bore a passing resemblance to Sanch strolled into the foyer, Harry grabbed him in a headlock and ruffled his hair. Big mistake. A business card was produced and the man was identified as an official of the Spanish club. Harry cringed. The job was then offered to Everton's Howard Kendall, and it was forever marked as another lost opportunity.

But aside from the contractual bickering, Harry had also been experiencing doubts regarding his managerial ambitions at Plough Lane. Having dragged Wimbledon kicking and hollering through the English divisions, he worried about whether he could improve on those achievements with the resources available. His work, under normal circumstances, would have made the club eligible for European football, but the behaviour of English supporters abroad and the Heysel Stadium disaster – a shocking clash between Liverpool and Juventus fans during the 1985 European Cup Final that resulted in 40 deaths – had forced FIFA to ban English clubs from overseas competition. Despite their now lofty status, the Crazy Gang would not be using their passports that season – professionally at least. 'I think he thought he'd taken the club as far as he could to a certain extent,' Lawrie Sanchez observed. 'He thought he'd added to a great story and it was time to move on.'

The Bilbao approach was a confidence boost. Harry knew he was coveted on the continent as well as at home where a raft of

First Division chairmen respected his results-on-a-shoestring-budget approach. When clubs wanted a manager who could spend, spend, spend, they plumped for a flamboyant figure like Ron Atkinson, argued Harry; when they wanted something done on the cheap, they went for a manager cut in his image. He grew confident that resignation wouldn't leave him strung out on the dole. *And quite frankly, sod Sam.* The tabled Wimbledon deal was rejected, and Harry walked away from the club on 9 May 1987, just after the last game of the season, an away win against Sheffield Wednesday.

Typically, the news had leaked from the boardroom long before then. A week earlier, Wimbledon fans had invaded the Plough Lane pitch during the match against Chelsea and sung the words 'Don't go, Harry'. Despite the board's subsequent public announcement of his resignation, a number of supporters rallied under the same chant at Hillsborough. Harry left the ground in tears. Wimbledon were his club, his boys, a team he had guided from non-league football to the First Division over thirteen years. Despite the political scrapping with Sam, he felt sick rather than relieved.

Nevertheless, his suitors came in thick and fast, and Harry was keen to court them. As the season closed, a roundabout of player transfers and big-money transactions cranked into action. One of the most prominent switches that summer involved the Watford manager Graham Taylor. Attracted by their bulging bank account and swelling ambition, Taylor, who would later go on to manage England, accepted the manager's post at Aston Villa. His employers at Watford reluctantly accepted the decision and quickly drew up a shortlist of targets for the vacated position. After much discussion and speculation it became apparent that only one name was considered suitable by the board: they wanted Harry Bassett. After much consideration, Harry accepted the generous offer of Watford's chairman Elton John and headed up the M25 to Vicarage Road. He could hardly have refused: the flamboyant singer had even popped round to Harry's house for tea to sway his decision. Harry later convinced his backroom staff to join him, leaving a bitter aftertaste in Sam's mouth.

These changes, twinned with the sales of full-back Nigel Winterburn to Arsenal for £400,000 and Glyn Hodges to Newcastle for £200,000, prompted another summer of gloomy predictions for the Dons' forthcoming season. Without the aggressive managerial tactics of Harry and two top players, could the Crazy Gang maintain their impressive standing in the top flight? Many fans and experts felt the answer was no.

Sam believed the solution to Wimbledon's problems was to screw the doubters and employ Bobby Gould. The former Bristol Rovers and Coventry City manager was well respected within the game. He also pre-empted Sam's move by informing the club that he would love to take on the job. After some discussion, Bobby was contacted by Wimbledon chairman Stanley Reed during his holiday in Corfu. The conversation went something like this:

'Hello, Bobby, it's Stanley Reed from Wimbledon. Would you be interested in the managerial job?'

'Yes, Stanley, I would.'

'Then it's yours.'

It was as simple as that. Bobby was in charge, and he soon began to face up to the mess left by Harry's departure. He called in a rather prominent assistant to work the team in pre-season – Don Howe, the former Arsenal manager who held a part-time position with Bobby Robson on the England coaching team.

According to Bobby Gould, Howe was 'the best coach in the world'. He would also bring some much-needed tactical knowledge to the club. 'I wasn't working at the time,' said Howe, 'and all of a sudden I get a phone call from Bobby saying, "What are you doing these days?" And I said, "Nothing," so he asked me to come to Wimbledon.' Bobby Gould remarked of Howe's appointment, 'It was like finding out Miss World was free in a ballroom and asking her to dance.' But Howe wasn't convinced he could cope with the Crazy Gang mentality and initially committed himself to a month of pre-season work only.

Bobby, meanwhile, was given a glimpse of Wimbledon's non-league infrastructure after taking his team away for a string of friendlies in Sweden. The trip had been inherited from Harry's reign, and both the accommodation and facilities provided for his club were typically down at heel. 'When we got there,' Bobby recalled, 'it wasn't a hotel it was a motel. Don had been at Arsenal and England for most of his life so to find himself in a motel, well, it was a bit of a comedown, wasn't it? So I looked at him and he looked at me and I said, "It's not our standard this, is it, Don? We're four-star merchants, aren't we? Tell the lads not to unpack their cases. We're going somewhere else." So I called the Swedish tour agency and said, "This was arranged with Dave Bassett and with all due respect my management style is a little bit different. I prefer things a little more plush. You've got half an hour to get us into a four-star hotel or we go home." So we moved into a four-star hotel. When we arrived and got out of the coach, the players could not believe it. I said, "Lads, this is the standard now."'

Despite their plush facilities and improved day-to-day surroundings, the squad were initially unconvinced by Bobby's appointment. As the trip progressed, many worried that this new manager would have great difficulty filling Harry's shoes and most reckoned Bobby lacked the charisma to carry the club through another season in the First Division. And in his office at Plough Lane, Bobby was just as aware of the challenge ahead. 'When I went in, it was like going into a bomb crater,' he said. 'Dave Bassett had left and he'd taken everybody with him apart from the kitman, Sid. Other than that it was a war zone. Every time you put your foot somewhere it usually landed on some of the shrapnel that had been left behind. The lads were disappointed too, because they'd had a fantastic run with Harry in the First Division.'

Bobby soon became aware of training-ground mutterings and decided to stamp his authority on the club. Granted, he was not as outgoing as Harry, but his character cut a domineering streak. The players were told that now they would be doing things his way. If anyone felt uncomfortable with the new arrangements they were more than welcome to follow Harry out of the club. In training he even scrapped Harry Ball and implemented a new sense of discipline. For a short while a buzz of resentment crept in among the senior professionals, but the players soon adjusted. The new manager fell in line with them too, allowing the team to continue with their robust playing style, though admittedly he had little say in the matter. 'When I first got there we had a big meeting,' said Bobby. 'Myself and Don started talking and all of a sudden Sanch, Corky, Beasant and some of the others stood up and said, "Look, before you two start, this is the flip chart and we'd like you to sit down. We'll tell you how we've been successful and how we've earned a lot of bonuses over the last couple of years." Two hours later they'd explained everything in detail and how and why they played in their style. Then they said, "We're not changing because the rest of the First Division don't like the way we play, and they certainly don't like playing against us." You've got to remember that Don had coached England and I'd played a lot of football in the First Division. So I looked at Don and he looked at me, and he said, "I'm staying. This has never happened in my professional career before. Those lads want to be successful." I thought, "Right, I'm not changing anything here."

'And their style of play worked,' he continued. 'With all due respect, the media can talk about Jose Mourinho or Arsène Wenger, but the way these teams have scored goals recently has been developed from the Wimbledon way. I saw Chelsea score from a long throw-in once. Sure, it might have been scored by a £24 million striker, but that was a technique used by Vinnie. Whipping corners in on the near post? Wimbledon started that.'

Howe had, of course, been aware of Wimbledon's reputation; he'd heard about the Crazy Gang's mentality and their skewed attitude to life as professional footballers. He feared chaos during his first day at the training ground, but his worries were unfounded. The rowdy bunch who greeted Howe as the season got underway were a far different proposition to the ones so often criticised by the national media and football fans. 'It wasn't difficult to step into that club,' said Howe. 'In fact I was very impressed. What happened with Wimbledon was that, because people looked upon them as being a little bit different, they didn't think they were professional, but in reality they were dedicated players. The first thing I noticed was that there was always a demand to understand the playing side of things. They were very keen on asking tactical questions like, "How are we going to play against this team?" or, "How are we going to deal with this problem player?" They were good pros, good technical pros. They wanted to get their game right.' The affection was soon reciprocated. 'I've never seen players have so much respect for a coach or manager as they do for Don Howe,' said Vinnie. 'He really knows what he's doing.'

Fash was impressing too. Few players came packaged with as much dedication, and Howe noted his hunger for success. Fash had relished battering defenders in his first season in Division One. The fact that Wimbledon had finished in sixth place and he'd notched up fourteen goals had convinced him that success, either in the league or in one of the cup competitions, was well within Wimbledon's reach, managerial change or no managerial change. But he was looking even further than domestic success. He harboured international ambitions too. 'On the training ground [Fash] was a great person to have around,' said Howe. 'He was one of the lads, and he would be getting about and having a laugh and a joke with the rest of them. But he was also very ambitious at that time. Very, very ambitious. He wanted to get on and win things, and he was determined to make a name for himself and the club. He was always thinking about whether he could play for England. That was one of his major goals.' Like so many others, Howe and Gould were impressed with his leadership qualities too. 'He was a spokesman for the lads,' Howe continued. 'He was the type of bloke who would take it upon himself to sort out any problems in the dressing room. If there was a problem he would head into Bobby's office and say, "Look, boss, this is wrong and the lads are unhappy about this thing or that thing," and he'd get it sorted out. I think the players appreciated that. It was something that came naturally to him. That leadership wasn't something he had to manufacture or force. He never had to say "I'm the union" or anything like that, he just wanted to make sure everything was running smoothly at the club.'

So Bobby began working with the same football philosophies

that had worked successfully under Harry Bassett. On the pitch he pursued Wimbledon's aggressive and basic approach, and off it he continued to upgrade the club's demands: hotels for away games went from two stars to four. 'The players loved it,' said Howe. 'They enjoyed the Wimbledon way and their style of football, especially that whole "Put it in the mixer" attitude. That was right up their street. They would steam into the box during games because they were strong. They were powerful, they had good pace. They could hold people off and they were very good in the air, so you could see why they loved that style of play because it brought the best out in their game. Up front, Fash had Corky by the side of him and they loved crosses; in fact, they lived off crosses. They loved the ball coming up early from the back. They certainly didn't want to be playing in a team that thrived on keeping possession or playing the ball around on the deck. They wanted the ball played up to them in the air as early and as quickly as possible, and that style of play worked really well for us.'

Bobby brought in full-back Terry Phelan and defenders Eric Young, John Scales and Clive Goodyear to strengthen the team (later, he would also sign striker Terry Gibson from Manchester United). Goodyear made an immediate impact on his new manager. The defender had been playing with Plymouth for three years, but the club appeared to be going nowhere. Bobby noted his combative style and arranged to meet him to discuss a transfer. He was unprepared for Goodyear's appearance, however. As part of their training, Plymouth's squad had been working with the armed forces. On the shooting range a rifle kick to the face had left Goodyear with a rugged, military-style black eye to match his sergeant-major facial hair. 'You'll do,' said Bobby approvingly and handed him a contract.

But some of Bobby's additions found it difficult to adjust, most notably Phelan, who struggled to fit into the Crazy Gang's day-to-day routine and aggressive dressing-room mentality. 'It was very difficult for the new lads to come into a club like that and play with players of that reputation,' said Bobby. 'It was tough. There were so many strong characters and you had to prove yourself. When Terry Phelan started, he was in tears. He said to me, "I can't handle this lot." I said, "Why, Terry? What's up?" He started crying and said he had to leave. Basically it was taking a while for the lads to accept him. Later that day I said to Don, "In today's training you've got to make sure Terry Phelan wins everything." He ran them 50 yards, 100 yards, 400 yards and cross-country. And what happens? Terry Phelan was such a great athlete he won the lot. All of a sudden the lads started to say, "What a great athlete, what a great player." Their psychology meant that he was accepted.'

As Bobby tinkered with the line-up, the fixture computer was delivering typically unkind news, pitching Wimbledon against Harry Bassett's Watford at Vicarage Road on the opening day of the season. More surprising, however, was Wimbledon's uncharacteristically generous mood that August afternoon: they gave way in a slack 1–0 defeat. A further two draws followed against Everton and Oxford before the Dons grabbed their first win at Derby County. It was not a good start by anyone's standards.

Still, the new boys were settling in well. Eric Young in particular had made his mark on the club, though not in the way his team-mates would have liked. Most mornings he'd swagger into training carrying his old Brighton kit bag. The swagger didn't last for long, and the bag, along with its contents, were soon smouldering in the training-ground changing rooms, setting off the building's smoke alarms. When the fire brigade responded to a 999 call, they arrived to see the entire Wimbledon squad cavorting around the charred hold-all doing an Indian war dance. But the bag was just the start. 'Wimbledon upset people and gave them no respect,' said Beasant. 'Eric was involved in the Brighton side that made the cup final against Manchester United [in 1983], but that carried no credibility with us at all. He used to wear his cup final suit all the time, so one day we emptied all his kit on the floor and set fire to it. We burned the suit. That's what we were like.'

Bobby soon discovered that his team played fast and loose with authority both on and off the pitch. When Sam leased the training-ground car park to a local motor dealership, the company began to leave their vehicles there overnight. When the players realised that the keys were often hidden under the windscreen wipers, they would borrow them for a day or two. The lease was later cancelled when the brother of one unnamed Wimbledon player drove away several cars – and failed to return them. Bobby even became involved in the brawls that regularly accompanied the daily training sessions, usually with little Dennis Wise. 'Me and Gouldy, we were in this circle,' the midfielder recalled, 'and he said, "Come on then, we'll have a fight." He'd have a fight with so many people, just jokingly, so I had a little mess-about fight with him and I caught him wrong. I didn't find out until a couple of weeks later that I'd actually cracked one of his ribs, so I think I won that one.' Despite the bruises, Bobby felt he was at home. He even took to bringing a pair of boxing gloves to training, just in case. 'Wimbledon was my club,' he said, beaming. 'I loved the players, every single one of them, though sometimes it was a handful. It was like going into a senior school where all the kids are out-of-control teenagers. But with my levels of professionalism and Don's levels of professionalism, we were going to get there.'

The first half of the season developed a consistent pace, but only because a Wimbledon win would kickstart a short run of losses and draws. Fash was equally erratic in front of goal, scoring only six times in the first twenty fixtures. Meanwhile, his team-mates were winning new enemies and critics with every passing game, as boots, elbows, fists and foreheads began to connect with increasing regularity. Not that it bothered the players: it was all done for the team's cause. But their robust attitude, and one challenge in particular, would come back to haunt Fash.

The incident took place against his old club Norwich City on 18 December. Former Northern Ireland international John O'Neil was left horrifically injured by a typically aggressive Fash challenge and had to be stretchered off the pitch. It was his first and last game in a Norwich shirt, and in 1994, resigned to the fact that his career was over despite various attempts at rehabilitation, O'Neil took Fash to court to seek £150,000 in damages. 'I was aware of John Fashanu coming into the picture,' he told the court. 'Everything happened so quickly. I knew from the manner of his approach I was in trouble. Then he did me. He certainly wasn't going to play the ball, and in all probability he was going to land on top of me. At the split second I played the ball I felt a severe blow to my knee and I thought I had broken my leg. When the physio came on, he told me he thought it was my ligaments. I was carried off. I have not been able to kick a football since. It is a serious thing to say about a professional footballer, but it was his intention to go for me and not the ball.' Wimbledon's insurers later paid O'Neil approximately £75,000 out of court.

Fash's reputation was beginning to precede him. The boos accompanying Wimbledon's arrival on the football pitch were reaching a hysterical volume. And it wasn't just Fash who was causing an upset on the park. Pretty much all of the Crazy Gang had one run-in or another during the course of the season, particularly Vinnie Jones. During one match against Liverpool Kenny Dalglish caught him with a weighty tackle. 'Do that once more, pal, and I'll rip your ear off and shit in the hole,' hissed Vinnie. Dalglish's team-mate John Aldridge later recalled how Vinnie had tried to claw at his ear during a corner. And anyone who tried to play him at his own game would know about it the next day, usually as they recovered on the treatment table. Nobody messed with Vinnie. 'If you're going over the top on me,' he warned his fellow pros, 'you've got to put me out of the game, because I'll be coming back for you, whether it's in the next five minutes or next season.' And nobody disbelieved him for a second, not even Sam. But then Sam had his own twisted take on most things when it came to Vinnie. 'He's a hero of the masses,' he countered as the media criticism of Vinnie's aggressive playing style increased. 'He represents the bulldog spirit of England [even though he later represented Wales]. He's never set out to maim anyone.'

Wimbledon's reputation might have been unsteady in the eyes of the public, but in the league and FA Cup they were proving prolific. They eventually finished the season in seventh place, having beaten Newcastle, Spurs (twice), Manchester United and West Ham, among others. But it was the FA Cup, figured the backroom staff and players, where Wimbledon would have their greatest chance of success. 'You could sense the hunger in the dressing room,' remarked Howe. 'I'd been there with the Arsenal and I'd been to Wembley, and I knew what it took to get there. I could smell the same sort of desire in those players. They wanted to prove themselves in one of the cup competitions.'

The team spirit at the club, so often buoyed by the moods of Vinnie, was on a high as 1988 dawned. Several players began wearing ju-ju bands, small leather straps tied around the wrist. As the team progressed through the rounds, these bracelets began to represent some strange form of lucky charm. Don Howe and Bobby Gould loved it. Wimbledon were causing far too much chaos on the pitch for anyone to handle. They swept aside West Bromwich Albion 4–1 on 9 January, in the third round. Dennis Wise, after being hit with a 'thumping great knock', hobbled across the pitch to score with a 25-yard shot. Bobby later convinced him to leave the pitch and receive medical assistance. 'But that was typical Dennis,' sighed Bobby. 'Always involved.'

Mansfield Town's boggy pitch in the fourth round gave Wimbledon the opportunity to play the ball in a manner they preferred: high and ugly. But the difficult conditions made the tie an unexpectedly tricky affair, and the 2–1 win saw them through only by a hair's breadth.

The televised draw for the fifth round pitched them against Newcastle United at St James's Park. Everything was prepared down to the finest detail. 'We'd had quite a week that week,' recalled Howe, 'because we were preparing for the game against Newcastle and we decided that Vinnie would be marking Paul Gascoigne. We worked on it in training, but Vinnie was doing it half-heartedly. Bobby was watching me with the players and all of a sudden he stopped the session and blasted Vinnie. He really tore a strip off him. Vinnie put his hands up and apologised, but it was the best thing that happened because it shocked all of the players. They watched Vinnie taking a hammering and it got them going.' The bust-up was important. Gascoigne was one of the best young players in the First Division and an England superstar in waiting. He possessed the ability to tear the Wimbledon team apart single-handedly. Bobby was adamant that Vinnie (or Vincent, as he called him) should stick to Gascoigne for the entire 90 minutes. He'd scared Vinnie enough to ensure he stuck to his task.

The two players had met a couple of weeks earlier in the league, and Vinnie had got the upper hand on the prodigy with typically underhand results. 'Before that game [on 6 February],' said Bobby, 'I said to Vincent, "You follow him wherever he goes, today and tomorrow. If it gets to a situation and you've got your back to him, you put your hand on his chest, run it down his stomach and have his bollocks. Don't let him walk away from you." Lo and behold, what happens the next day? Vincent gets hold of Gazza's testicles, and it was in all the papers.' The incident, which happened in full view of photographers, was plastered over the back pages on Sunday. During the game Vinnie had stuck to Gascoigne as instructed, hassling him, verbally intimidating him and mocking his tubby physique. When the pair went in for their first challenge, Vinnie came out on top and whispered, 'It's just you and me for 90 minutes, Fat Boy.' When the ball went out of play and Vinnie went to the sidelines for a throw-in, he told the Fat Boy to stay there; he'd be returning in a few seconds. And when Gazza managed to duck behind him, Vinnie reached around and clawed at his balls, squeezing hard. The resulting photos secured both players' iconic reputations within the English game – Vinnie as the reckless thug, Gascoigne as the talented victim. In the Newcastle dressing room after the game, Gascoigne was reportedly in floods of tears, though he still summoned the cheek to send a bouquet of flowers to Vinnie.

Vinnie responded by sending a toilet brush as a thank you, furthering his pantomime-villain status.

With the FA Cup tie looming, much was written about their imminent clash. 'I got involved in a lot of controversy over the Paul Gascoigne incident,' said Vinnie in the understatement of the season. 'After everything that was said and written about my clash with Paul, I was really worried about going to St James's Park [on 20 February] to face the Newcastle fans.' He needn't have bothered, for Bobby's tactics proved effective and Wimbledon won by three goals to one. After the final whistle, when Newcastle's midfielder Mirandinha spat at Dave Beasant, the entire team chased the Brazilian around the stadium. But who cared? The Crazy Gang were in the quarter-finals of the FA Cup. Vinnie was even named man of the match and sent home with a brand-new television.

As the team boarded the coach, he placed the box on the table and ordered the driver to park up at the nearest hospital. Howe panicked. 'We thought he was in pain,' he explained, 'so we found a hospital and Vinnie got off, walked into the reception, stuck the TV on the desk and said, "There you are, put that in the children's ward." That was one of the things people never realised about the Crazy Gang: for all their aggression on the pitch they were a thoughtful bunch of lads off it.'

Come the quarter-final draw, again Bobby seemed dogged by coincidence. In yet another bizarre twist of fate, Wimbledon were pitched against Harry's Watford. This time there would be no repeat of the generosity afforded them on the opening day of the campaign. By now Watford were relegation candidates, and Wimbledon, despite a shaky start to the season, were sitting comfortably in the upper half of the table. 'If we play our usual game I fancy us to go through,' bragged Dons defender Andy

Thorn. But Watford's Nigel Gibbs was equally confident. 'I think it will be very tight, but I think we can at least force a replay and sneak a win back at Vicarage Road.' Gibbs's claims were laced with pessimism, however. 'During our 2–1 win at Plough Lane [on 16 January] they had three players that really impressed me: John Fashanu, who is always a difficult opponent with his strength; Dennis Wise, who always seems to have a good game against us; and Andy Thorn, who is a very hard man to beat.' Nevertheless, the Dons stuttered, and after a disastrous first half Wimbledon were 1–0 down to a Malcolm Allen strike. Midfielder Brian Gayle was also sent off for thumping Watford's goalscorer in the face during an angry rush of blood to the head. Clearly there was work to be done at half-time. 'At the break we swapped the team around,' said Howe, 'and I've got to say this: that game was won by Fash. He took the match by the scruff of the neck. It was so important to him. I mean, every game was important to him at that time, but that one match seemed to be a personal crusade. He was putting himself about in the second half and we pulled it back to 2–1. John got the winning goal. He was man of the match. He ran his goolies off; he was outstanding. It was one of the best 45 minutes I'd ever seen a player play.'

Only a semi-final against Luton Town at White Hart Lane stood between Wimbledon and a cup final appearance. A measly 25,963 turned up to watch the game. You could still buy tickets on the morning of the match, but that didn't bother Wimbledon's players. They would later claim that, at times, it had sounded 'like 100,000' cheering them on. Their manager nearly didn't make it to the game when, unexpectedly, he arrived at Tottenham in a minibus. It took some persuading before the doormen at White Hart Lane allowed him to park inside. 'I'm superstitious, you see,' explained Bobby. 'If we were playing in away games in

London we never met up and travelled together. For the semi-final we didn't meet up at a hotel, we met in the White Hart Lane dressing rooms at half past one. Somebody had to take the kit, so I offered to do it in the minibus. When I got there, there were two coppers waiting for the Wimbledon team coach. When I told them I was the coach they said, "Do us a favour! Piss off, will you? We're waiting for the Wimbledon coach." They eventually let me in after some persuading. But when I got in the jobsworth in the car park wouldn't let me in either because I wasn't driving the official coach. Somehow, I convinced him too.'

Inside the stadium, chaos reigned. The Wimbledon mob had already set about intimidating their opponents, particularly Luton's harassed physio who had been involved in an accident on the M1 on his way to the match. When he arrived at White Hart Lane his nerves were in shreds. A steady commotion pouring from the Dons' dressing room only worsened his trepidation. He began to tremble. On the treatment table one of his players patiently awaited a painkilling injection. 'The physio didn't arrive until about five minutes before the game,' said Bobby. 'He got this dirty great needle out for the jab. As he's about to stick it in, all the Wimbledon boys started screaming and hollering in the tunnel. The doctor started shaking. He was terrified. Every time he tried to put the needle in, he kept missing, and he eventually stuck it in the wrong place.'

Still, the Crazy Gang were left wondering whether their intimidation tactics had been a wasted effort when, three minutes after half-time, robust centre-forward Mick Harford popped up to head Luton into the lead. But then, as he had done against Watford, Fash began to show the sort of form that more often than not inspired his team-mates to victory. His nerve was stretched to the limit too, especially when Luton conceded a penalty in the

56th minute and Fash stepped up to take the spot-kick. It was cooly dispatched. 'He hit it so slowly I remember thinking I could have run the length of the pitch to save it,' said Vinnie. The Wimbledon players raced around the pitch, screaming 'We're going to Wembley!' somewhat prematurely. *But it was as if they knew.* A scrambled goal from midfielder Dennis Wise in the 80th minute secured the win. Somehow, against the odds, Wimbledon had grabbed a place in the FA Cup Final.

The celebrations began before the team had even left the stadium. 'The big thing I remember about the semi-final,' said Don Howe, 'was that the actress June Whitfield, who's a big Wimbledon fan, came into the dressing room afterwards. She's a lovely lady, but most of the lads were naked and getting into the bath, which could have been a bit embarrassing. That didn't bother June though, and she ended up kissing all the boys and thanking them. And we didn't care, we were on our way to Wembley.'

That night, the squad travelled back to Plough Lane and then on to Nelson's nightclub in Wimbledon, which was located next door to Plough Lane. The drinking didn't stop until the early hours of the morning. Like everything Bobby Gould had implemented during his time as manager, the partying was done with four-star class too. 'I couldn't believe it,' he commented with a laugh. 'Getting Wimbledon into an FA Cup Final after walking into that war zone was amazing. Absolutely amazing.'

CHAPTER SEVEN

On the evening before the cup final Fash's anger was simmering inside. On the exterior, his eyes had glazed over and his right hand was clenched into a fist. He paced the corridors of the Cannizaro House Hotel for a moment or so, still buzzing with fury, before stopping at his bedroom. Suddenly, without warning, he drove a powerful punch into the door. Vinnie, who was standing inches away from what was a huge dent in the woodwork, dived away as his room-mate prepared to unleash another knuckle volley. But Fash backed off. His fingers were swelling and he began rubbing the buckled digits.

Vinnie fumbled with the keys, opened the door and dragged Fash inside. 'Come on, mate,' he said, 'let's get you looked at.'

Tremulously, Vinnie examined the battered hand. He guessed Fash could be patched up OK – he was a tough character after all – but even to his untrained eye the bruising looked serious. Fash's knuckles were popping back into their sockets with each gingerly flexed motion of his fingers. The experience made Vinnie nervous. Fash was a feared character, but he'd always enjoyed control. He never played the role of loose cannon; that was left to the others in the Wimbledon team.

Even the infamous run-in with Sanch was, to a certain extent, a measured response. Certainly Vinnie couldn't recall seeing Fash lose his temper like this, although the reason for the uncharacteristic outburst was understandable. Minutes earlier, the pair had been approached by a tabloid journalist in the foyer of the swish hotel in Wimbledon where the team had chosen to gather on the eve of their game at Wembley. The night had been set aside for some relaxing preparation. Instead, it was developing into a nightmare.

The *News of the World* had received information that Fash was cheating on his then girlfriend, Maria Sol. As was typical with journalists trailing a sleazy news exposé, a story had been researched and written during the week and the subject – in this case Fash – approached a couple of days before the article was due to be splashed across the weekend's pages. The paper wanted a defensive quote for an exclusive feature, and a reporter had been dispatched to the Cannizaro to collect. Audaciously, he'd approached Fash after Wimbledon's evening training session with the details. Which is when Fash stormed upstairs and pummelled the hotel woodwork.

The immediate problem wasn't the story, the journalist downstairs or the pain throbbing in Fash's knuckles, but the implications of this new injury. Fash had to be 100 per cent for the game the next day. For the first time in their career the Crazy Gang would be appearing in the FA Cup Final, against Liverpool, the best team in the country by a long shot. It was the biggest David and Goliath final in the history of the competition. It also represented the most exciting clash of recent times: Liverpool's celebrity eleven against Bobby Gould's glorified pub team.

Wimbledon's physio Steve Allen was called to the room. Bad news: at first glance Fash's hand looked broken. Nevertheless,

Allen bandaged the injury and passed him fit to play, which came as a major relief because as Fash, Vinnie and the *News of the World* were aware, Saturday, 14 May 1988 was the biggest day in Wimbledon's history. Fash was determined to play his part. It was just a shame that the tabloid press were determined to play a starring role too.

The evening had begun in the pub, though alcohol hadn't featured in the plans of the coaching staff at all. Before dinner, Bobby subjected his starting eleven to a little light training for an hour ('They didn't complain,' said Howe). They then returned to Cannizaro House, the hotel where the team were resting up before matchday. Despite Bobby's insistence that his players should relax indoors, Vinnie, Dennis Wise and Brian Gayle were going stir crazy with nerves. Discreetly, they escaped Howe's attentions and slipped away to the Fox and Grapes for a quick drink. This was nothing out of the ordinary for the players. Wimbledon occasionally approached their games with a casual attitude to drinking, and besides, Bobby wanted them to 'relax'. If one or two disappeared for a quick livener, nobody would be too fussed, even if there was a cup final the following day. In hindsight, Bobby was in agreement. 'Don said to me the night before the game, "They're a pain in the butt. You can't take them up to that lovely hotel before the FA Cup Final because there's a lot of functions going on." I figured that if we met at the hotel and trained, that would kill the afternoon. So anyway, after the practice session we went back to the hotel. During the meal, bread rolls started getting chucked about. I said to Don, "I can't have this, what are we going to do? Have you got fifty quid? I can send them to the pub down the road." The players couldn't believe their luck. When they went, there were three players missing – Wisey, Gayle and Jones. I'll never forget it. Beasant and the others went off for a couple of halves of lager and shandies to calm down. Then the others returned to the hotel. I said, "You've been down the pub, haven't you?" And they all laughed. I said, "Well, you spent your own money, you've lost out. All the other bastards are down there having a drink on Sam's cash." They turned around and sprinted as fast as they could.'

Truth be told, Bobby needed the peace and quiet. Inside the hotel, the players had been driving him crazy. As he walked the corridors, checking on his staff and chatting with them, minor chaos greeted him at every turn. In one room, striker Terry Gibson was curled up in bed asleep, still wearing a shiny pair of football boots. He'd scored a lucrative boot deal for the final, but the new leathers hadn't worn in properly; he was desperately trying to soften them for the next day. Had Bobby turned up an hour earlier, he would have seen him soaking in the bath. He was stark naked, save for the boots.

For Bobby's sanity at least, the players were heading in the right direction. And the Fox and Grapes was certainly Wimbledon's style of pub – gaudy decor, grainy photos on the wall, a jukebox. It had, of course, doubled as the Old Centrals' dressing room a century earlier. As the team drained a quiet pint and talked tactics, an elderly woman recounted her memories of the club. The players loved it.

The drinking didn't last long for Fash, of course. After a couple of Cokes – he only ever sipped at soft drinks anyway – he headed back to the hotel with Vinnie in the fresh air. As the pair entered Cannizaro House's main entrance, Fash was approached by the news hack. He seemed to appear unnaturally from the upholstery, gesturing to them in a sinister fashion. Vinnie didn't like his attitude.

'What's going on here, mate?'

The hack pointed at Fash, which meant trouble. 'I'm a reporter and I'd like to speak to you.'

Fash's heart sank. No journalist would turn up, tonight of all nights, to deliver good news. Vinnie knew too. He tried to body-swerve the reporter, bee-lining for the stairs. The journalist, presumably used to dealing with reporter-shy celebrities, lashed out with a chilling response: 'The *News of the World* have received word that you're messing around with another woman,' he shouted at Fash as the pair walked away. The paper wanted a few quotes.

Fash stopped dead. *Not now, please not now. This can't be happening.*

According to this reporter, the story was going to be splashed across the Sunday papers like a bloody car crash, whether Fash liked it or not. A mystery girl had called the editorial team that week claiming that she'd had an affair with the Wimbledon striker. It looked pretty bad, too. Now the paper wanted to run a confession or denial, in Fash's words, as a juicy feature to accompany the weekend's football. A sleazy side dish to the cup final coverage. *Trust a tabloid rat to piss on our fireworks.*

Vinnie turned nasty and warned the reporter to stay away. He wanted to kick him out of the hotel, to swing at him, but somehow he managed to calm his temper. The pair went back upstairs, and Fash forced his fist into the bedroom door like a madman. 'Bear in mind this is a real classy hotel,' said Vinnie, 'no cheap furnishings, no plywood or chipboard.'

Bobby was relaxing in his bedroom at the time. 'Suddenly I heard this shout,' he recalled. '"Boss, get down here quick. It's Fash. He's got his fist stuck in a door." So I went in there. Fash had punched the door. I couldn't believe it. I said, "Fash, you learned karate. It doesn't teach you to kick doors down, does it?" Vincent was explaining to me that the paper had set him up. He reckoned they had sent a girl round to his place. Apparently the bird picked him up, Fash had gone round to her place, had his wicked way with her, and the bird had told the papers. We just bandaged him up.'

Bobby forced the pair back to the Fox and Grapes for another drink, but even under orders Fash couldn't relax. He refused anything stronger than a Coke. Vinnie even tried to spike a lime and lemonade with two shots of vodka, but Fash caught him out after one sip. More surprising, however, was the reaction of Lawrie Sanchez, who for the first time chummed up with Fash. It made for a pretty strange atmosphere, but despite the booze being handed around like an end-of-season celebration, this was exactly the spirit Bobby had wanted to kick up before an FA Cup Final. *It was his boys against the world.*

It all got out of control pretty quickly. The drinks kept on coming. The bar staff were more than happy to pull them, startled that a team of professional footballers could booze so greedily the night before the biggest game in their careers. Clive Goodyear, who sipped Guinnesses all evening, left around eleven – way past the responsible hour. He wasn't the last back either. Most of the team were still drinking at the bar. 'It was a great way of settling our nerves,' said Dave Beasant later. 'But, typically, something I think only we could have pulled off.'

When the boys finally returned to the Cannizaro, laughing, joking and relaxed, Bobby counted them in and sent them to bed. There was no harm done. He knew his players would be up for the game tomorrow regardless of the sore heads. A few beers didn't worry him in the slightest.

By morning, however, Bobby's mood had soured. The

papers were full of the usual crap – that Wimbledon couldn't play football, that they'd somehow set the game back 50 years. Pundits cried about the long-ball tactics; one writer claimed they were killing the beautiful game. But it wasn't just the press who were having a pop. During the week Liverpool player Steve McMahon stirred up controversy in a column for *Match* magazine entitled 'I'll Make Vinnie See Red!' His rant detailed how McMahon intended to embarrass Vinnie on matchday. 'Wimbledon's Vinnie Jones will see red on Saturday – the colour of my cup final shirt as I go past him!' he wrote. 'The fiery South London midfield hard man has gained something of a strong-arm reputation this season, but it doesn't worry me in the slightest. I relish the prospect of a hard, but fair, midfield confrontation with my opposite number and I will be aware that all eyes will probably be on the pair of us as the game warms up. I saw newspaper pictures of what Vinnie did to Newcastle's rising young star Paul Gascoigne in a League game earlier this season, but Wembley will be no place for him to try those tricks on me … Vinnie Jones is just another player to me. I have come to terms with midfield hard men throughout the season and one more of that ilk won't make any difference.'

Angrily, Bobby wandered around the hotel. He goaded the players with the media's insults as they changed into their cup final suits. Each jibe wound them up a little more, turned the screw a little tighter. But deep down, Bobby knew the odds were stacked against Wimbledon. Liverpool were already confirmed as champions of the First Division; they were considered by many to be one of the greatest teams in the world at that time (*FourFourTwo* later ranked them ninth in a managers' poll of the greatest teams ever). A couple of weeks before the final, this side, which included England internationals John Barnes, Peter Beardsley and Steve McMahon as well as Scotland's Alan Hansen and prolific striker John Aldridge, had even dismantled their closest title rivals Nottingham Forest by five goals to nil. As former England legend Tom Finney watched the performance in a TV studio he gushed: '[It's] the finest exhibition I have ever seen. I haven't watched a better display in all the time I've been playing and watching the game. It was absolutely tremendous. You could not see it bettered anywhere. Not even in Brazil.' Liverpool were feared.

Back in his room, as he prepared his suit and his game plan, Bobby knew his lads were fired up. Some of them had been awake and pacing around the building for hours. Vinnie, for example, had risen before seven. He was washed, shaved and twitching with nerves. Wisey too. The pair even met in the hotel gardens for a stroll to calm the tension, though both were too wired for relaxation. Vinnie mentioned he wanted a new haircut, and the pair discussed driving into Wimbledon Village to find a barber after breakfast. Bobby pleaded with Vinnie to level off on the adrenalin – he feared a burnout before a ball had been kicked – but Vinnie and Wisey didn't care. After a sit-down meal with the rest of the team they disappeared for a trim. On their way into town they passed actress June Whitfield and stopped to chat – about the game, about Terry Scott, about the weather, *anything*. Had she enjoyed the semi-final? Where was she sitting? All three were jangling with excitement. Whitfield wished them luck, waved the Wimbledon scarf around her shoulders and walked off down the high street. It was like a surreal interlude from a movie.

Was this really happening?

Wisey blew a tenner on sweets while Vinnie had his hair

carved into a mohican. Nobody was going to forget his cup final appearance. And before heading back to the hotel they stopped at a florist's and picked up a dozen blue and yellow flowers for the team's cup final suits. The plan was to hand one to the guest of honour, Princess Diana, during the traditional meet and greet on the Wembley turf before the game.

Meanwhile, back at the Cannizaro, the other players were starting to ready themselves. Outside in the sunshine Sanch, Clive Goodyear, Eric Young, Terry Gibson and a few others prepared themselves for the coach journey to Wembley Stadium, although the glare was too much for Alan Cork. He wore sunglasses to ease his hangover. With everyone ready, they boarded the coach. Vinnie's haircut lightened the mood, as did a card game on the coach. Somehow, motor-mouthed agent Eric Hall had wangled his way on to the bus and was handing out soft drinks and promotional caps to everyone to wear as they walked in front of the cameras. There was a cash bonus being paid by the company, of course, and Hall was never one to miss out on a money-spinning opportunity.

Strangely, the journey to Wembley began to take on the routine of a typical away game, until some bright spark flicked on the TV and the BBC's FA Cup build-up kicked them all into life again. The cameras were focused on Liverpool's centre-half Alan Hansen. He was sitting on the team bus looking relaxed, bored even. Although a respected player, Hansen was a smug sort at the best of times. Worse, the cocky Scot was sneering at Wimbledon's fans from his seat. 'Can you see any Wimbledon fans out there?' He sniffed. 'It's all Liverpool.' For Andy Thorn, Corky, Sanch, anyone in earshot, this was the sort of comment to start a grudge. Anyone who hadn't caught Hansen's sour jibe was quickly filled in on the details. In the minds of every single

member of the Crazy Gang, it was game on. Not that Vinnie
cared. He'd just taken £80 in the card school.

When they arrived, the Wembley dressing rooms were bigger
than they had ever dreamed. There was a bar stocked with soft
drinks and a bartender, a medical room – even the team bath
was huge. Everywhere they looked the tiles gleamed. As they
arranged their kit, Bobby and Don talked tactics. John Barnes
was threat number one: he'd terrorised defences all season. But
there were other dangers too: England striker Peter Beardsley,
Steve McMahon in midfield and, of course, Hansen, whose
swaggering passes fuelled so many Liverpool attacks. Don and
Bobby wanted it simple – it was the only way to beat Liverpool.
No fancy stuff. Vinnie on McMahon, Wise and Goodyear on
Barnes, and Gibson on Hansen (after the TV wisecracks, Terry
was looking forward to that one). The Wimbledon line-up was
pretty predictable too: Beas in goal; a back four of Goodyear,
Young, Phelan and Thorn; across the middle Vinnie, Wisey,
Corky and Sanch; and Fash and Gibson up front.

The only debate surrounded the subs. During the run-up to
the final a number of players had been reluctant to throw
themselves into challenges with the usual venom, such was
their fear of missing Wembley. The choice was now among
three players (teams were allowed only two subs in those
days): defender Brian Gayle, a regular in the side until his
sending-off against Watford in the quarter-final, full-back
Laurie Cunningham and defender John Scales. On paper it was
a simple decision – Cunningham and Gayle. Scales was a
latecomer to the team after all, having signed for the club from
Bristol Rovers the previous year, but Bobby didn't see it that
way. He decided to drop Gayle, which sent a shockwave across
the dressing room. Vinnie and Fash seethed. Only Gayle

seemed unfussed as they made their final preparations. It was the closest Bobby had come to slipping up all day.

On the tactics board, Wimbledon were determined to keep their attack as basic and as raw as possible, relying on the aggressive tactics that had made them so unpopular in the First Division. Such was their determination to unsettle their clean-cut opposition that Fash even suggested the team should forgo basic elements of personal hygiene such as washing and shaving in the run-up to the game. By looking and smelling like a rough-and-ready football team, he believed they would play like one. Much to the relief of Bobby and Don, only a couple of players avoided the washrooms. 'We felt rough and felt unclean, but we felt mean,' said Fash. 'If you see Dennis Wise after he hasn't shaved for a week you think, "I'm not sure I want to play against that."'

Vinnie was in an equally determined mood and pulled Fash to one side before the start of the match. He knew his room-mate better than anybody at the club and was keen for him to rattle the Liverpool defence from the first whistle. He wanted Fash to match his own dogged ferocity. As Paul Parker had explained the previous season, Vinnie was aware that beneath his tough exterior, Fash was a gentleman who believed in shaking hands with an opponent lying in a crumpled heap on the turf after another ball had been pumped into the mixer. Both players were aware that such courtesies would have to be in short supply if they were to unnerve Liverpool's sophisticated players. 'We wanted to be Raggedy Arsed Rovers,' said Fash afterwards.

They were more wired now than ever. The stereo was typically noisy, on full blast. 'It was always a mad dressing room,' said Don Howe. 'They had this ghetto blaster which they took to Wembley. I didn't like it, but Bobby was happy for them to have it, so it stayed. But I have to say it had a negative effect on the other team because they didn't know what to make of the boys when they heard it. They used to think we were mad. It created a problem for the opposition, and it was intimidating, so it helped us. But if it had been left to me it would have been taken away. I was too old for that sort of thing.'

Bobby and Don were well aware that their players were in an aggressive mood. Bobby was even forced to calm down a few players as they left the team bus. The Wimbledon side that prepared itself in the Wembley dressing rooms that May afternoon didn't need any extra motivation from the coaching staff. 'You can sense in the changing room if a team are up for it,' said Howe, 'and they were up for it. They wanted it really badly.'

Fash and Vinnie were in their element. The mind games they had used to frighten the life out of opposing defenders in the First Division were put to good use again. On Fash's instructions, the team delayed their exit from the dressing room, leaving the Liverpool players to wait nervously in the tunnel for five minutes. When they finally emerged they exploded through the door, the entire team screaming the battle cry 'Yidahooo!' as they lined up alongside their opponents. Liverpool's fearsome midfielder Steve McMahon remained unconvinced. He would later claim that Wimbledon's attempts at intimidation were ineffective. 'The Crazy Gang were not a crazy gang,' he said. 'I don't buy into that whole Crazy Gang thing. You're not going to tell me that they intimidated us, because they never did.'

On the day, nobody believed him.

'Big-time Charlies!' somebody yelled in Kenny Dalglish's direction. No response.

'They don't want it, boys!'

Again, silence. If McMahon was standing steady, it wasn't showing.

Back in Wimbledon's dressing room, the flowers Vinnie and Wisey had bought for Princess Diana had been left in a corner at the behest of Don Howe. It was a nice thought, but any royal diplomacy had long been forgotten. Time for business.

Once the usual pre-match dignitaries were dispensed with and the business of football got underway, Wimbledon were determined to leave their mark in more ways than one. The physical onslaught began from the kick-off, unsettling a nervous-looking Liverpool side. The first victim on their hit list was McMahon. 'At 3.01 p.m.,' Fash recalled, 'Vinnie went in for a tackle with Steve McMahon, and that was the key moment. The tackle started at his throat and ended at his ankle. That was the game won; psychologically we had made our mark. Vinnie had hit them like an express train. We were in the FA Cup Final; how could we go too far? We were either going to win or we were going to get sent off. We were not going to hang around. We didn't want to be there at the end with sad puppy-dog eyes as Liverpool got the trophy. We were not going up those stairs as losers.' Vinnie later admitted he had been 'bricking it' as the referee, Brian Hill, reached into his pocket. Fortunately, the card was only yellow.

For the neutral, it was a blood-and-guts performance. 'It was like something out of Hackney Marshes,' said TV commentator Andy Gray later. As the game progressed, Liverpool came on strong, and on ten minutes Beasant was forced to make a great save from John Aldridge. The striker had hit a speculative shot, which clipped defender Eric Young's legs, sending the ball fizzing in an unexpected direction. Shifting his feet quickly, the keeper repositioned his body and forced the strike away with his thigh. But the ball wasn't safe, and as it looped into the air, John Barnes bore down, poised to score. Just as the Liverpool winger appeared destined to flick Liverpool into a one-goal lead, Beasant's arm appeared from nowhere to scoop it away. Vinnie then hoofed it to safety.

Clearly, as they had throughout their First Division career, the Crazy Gang were determined to play a ballsy role, and after Aldridge's effort it was Wimbledon's turn. They applied the squeeze, harassing Liverpool's strikers out of the game. Dennis Wise attached himself to John Barnes. Such was the winger's skill that he'd been awarded both the Players' Player of the Year award and a football writers' trophy. This sort of reputation meant nothing to Wise however, and he closed him down, snapping at his ankles at every opportunity. He was working elsewhere too, choking the supply lines from midfield and chasing lost causes all over the park.

But Liverpool's attacking strength wasn't totally nullified. Later in that first half Peter Beardsley wriggled away from an illegal Andy Thorn challenge to score. He'd been kicked just outside the penalty area but had decided to stay on his feet, poking the ball past Beasant, who stood stranded. Fortunately for Wimbledon, Brian Hill refused to play advantage and pulled back the play. 'It was an incredible decision,' said Steve McMahon after the game, 'and one which I thought was wrong at the time.' Even Vinnie thought the goal should have stood when he watched the replay afterwards.

The Liverpool moans were to get louder in the 36th minute, when Lawrie Sanchez looped a glancing header over Bruce Grobbelaar and into the back of the net. The goal, typically, had been fed from the feet of Wise, who had placed the ball defiantly on the turf when a free-kick was awarded to the Crazy Gang

The essence of the Crazy Gang: new boy John Hartson's clothes are ritually burnt then thrown from a window at Wimbledon's training ground. He later discovered the word "bollocks" had been scribbled on a piece of paper and stuck to his back. © Empics

Dave "Harry" Bassett. "Chirpy Cockney diamond geezer, long-ball loudmouth, top bloke, nutty boy."
© Empics

Sam Hammam. "He would have much rather been a player than a chairman,"
remarked former Wimbledon owner, Ron Noades. © Empics

Being ejected from the Old Trafford dug out in 1997.
Drama and Sam walked hand in hand. © Mirror Group Newspapers

Lawrie Sanchez glances the winning goal past Liverpool goalkeeper Bruce Grobbelaar to win the 1988 FA Cup Final. "I had a habit of scoring important goals for the club," he said. © Mirror Group Newspapers

Dave Beasant saves John Aldridge's penalty in the same game. "We practised John Aldridge's penalty style the night before the game, just in case," said Wimbledon manager Bobby Gould. © Empics

Dave Beasant lifts the FA Cup. He was the first 'keeper to lift the trophy as captain.
© Mirror Group Newspapers

Beasant, Sanchez and Alan Cork parade the trophy before Wimbledon's fans.
"Every one of us was drunk the night before the game," said Alan Cork.
"Probably that's what won us the final." © Mirror Group Newspapers

Cards showered down on Vinnie Jones like confetti. "For all his aggression on the pitch, he was a good lad off it," said Wimbledon coach Don Howe. © Empics and Mirror Group Newspapers

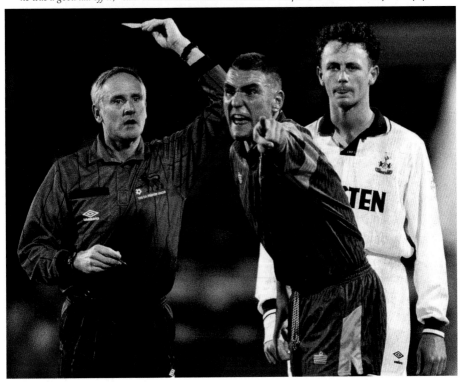

John Fashanu scores another goal. Note the socks dragged down around his shinpads.
This would later become a trademarked look. © *Mirror Group Newspapers*

Celebrating with John Scales and Dennis Wise. "We were all poor guys," said Fash. "And most of us came
from difficult backgrounds – poor families, broken homes." © *Mirror Group Newspapers*

Joe Kinnear barks orders from the Wimbledon touchline. © Mirror Group Newspapers

A typical English summer's day for Egil Olsen:
sunglasses and wellies.
© Mirror Group Newspapers

The saddest day. Wimbledon are relegated from
the Premiership in May 2000. © Empics

Mr Unpopular: fans paraded Charles Koppel "Club Killer" t-shirts. © Mirror Group Newspapers

Milton Keynes Dons' Pete Winkelman © Empics

Milton Keynes Dons at the National Hockey Centre. "Some bastard's nicked our football club," said AFC Wimbledon chairman, Kris Stewart, of the team's relocation. © Mirror Group Newspapers

deep in the Liverpool half. An argument raged around him over who should take it, but Wise didn't care. Such was Wimbledon's quality at set-pieces he knew a well-aimed lob would cause chaos in the Liverpool box, particularly if Fash or Eric Young could connect with a forehead. So Wise floated the ball into the area. The ball arced towards Sanch's head and the striker lobbed it goalwards, over Grobbelaar's head and into the net. Wimbledon were 1–0 up. 'I'd scored a goal which got us promotion from the Second Division a couple of years previously,' said Sanch. 'I had a habit of scoring important goals for the club.'

On the pitch, pandemonium broke out, though most players hadn't even seen the ball go in, such was the tangle of bodies in the box. Vinnie only knew the Crazy Gang had scored because of the look on Grobbelaar's face. He raced over to congratulate Sanch with the rest of the team, though Andy Thorn didn't have the energy. He was exhausted already.

On the sidelines, Don Howe grew concerned. He knew that his players were physically tiring in the May heat, so as Wimbledon played out the final few minutes of the first half he filled the bath in the Wembley dressing-room with ice-cold water, soaked towels and prepared water supplies. Once Bobby and the team were inside, he wrapped their heads in cooling cloths and made sure that they drank as much water as was physically possible. Meanwhile, Bobby busied himself telling his players to keep on playing in the same style. He could sense Liverpool were rattled.

Bobby was right. When play resumed, Terry Gibson was the first to come closest to scoring when he screwed a shot into the crowd after pushing the ball past Grobbelaar in the Liverpool box. Undeterred, Liverpool fought back, playing deft passes around the penalty area. In the 61st minute John Aldridge was kicked to the floor by Clive Goodyear. Referee Brian Hill pointed to the spot and awarded a penalty. The Crazy Gang surrounded Hill, shouting and screaming, adamant that the referee had screwed up, but he was unmoved. The spot-kick stood. 'All the players were convinced the ref had made the wrong decision,' said Beasant. 'But there was nothing we could do, and it was all down to me.'

Aldridge stepped up to take the kick, but Beasant had done his homework. The night before the game he'd insisted on several players imitating Aldridge's penalty-taking style by way of preparation. 'I'll never forget it,' said Bobby Gould. 'Corky, Wisey and Dave Beasant went down to the bottom end of the training ground. Beasant says, "We've got to practise Aldridge's style of penalties, just in case." Dennis Wise went up. Checked his run. Side-footed it left. Alan Cork ran up, put the ball down, side-footed it. They practised this for a quarter of an hour. After that Beasant was happy.' On the day itself, Beasant read Aldridge's jog to the ball. He dived the right way and palmed the ball to safety to become the first keeper to save an FA Cup Final penalty. 'Of course the practice the night before had paid off,' Bobby commented, 'but that's how professional the Crazy Gang were. People didn't give them the credit for it.'

They played out the remainder of the final in pain. The heat had sapped any remaining strength, and the ice-cold towels Don Howe had provided earlier were a distant memory. Alan Cork seemed delirious, and when Bobby Gould decided to bring the exhausted Terry Gibson off, he seemed delirious too. The manager decided to bring on defender John Scales and positioned him up front. On the pitch, confusion reigned. Every time the whistle blew, Andy Thorn believed it was signalling the end of the game. Players constantly harassed Brian Hill for the time on his watch. When the final whistle eventually went, Fash dropped exhausted to the floor, and Lawrie Sanchez was still the only name on the scoresheet, but only because Wimbledon had dug in so resolutely and defended with a relish for physical violence. Wimbledon had once again toppled the aristocrats of English football, in the process securing an historic FA Cup victory. Just two years earlier the result would have been unthinkable. It was a day of landmarks for Dave Beasant too. In addition to the penalty save, he'd become the first goalkeeper to lift the FA Cup as captain, which seemed apt: Lurch could see the Wembley towers every time he looked out of his bedroom window.

The achievement was made all the more impressive because of the raucous drinking session the previous evening. 'Everyone was drunk the night before,' said Alan Cork. 'Every single one of us went down the pub. Probably that's what won us the final. That and taking me off after 60 minutes because I was delirious.' Most of the players couldn't even remember the post-match chain of events, such was their heightened mood. In interviews Wise struggled to recall shaking hands with the Liverpool players or waving to the fans after the game. He just wanted to get to the pub and celebrate as soon as possible. Meanwhile, Steve McMahon was left to rue his bravado. He later described the game as the lowest point of his career.

In the dressing room the Wimbledon players were reduced to silence. Only Alan Cork shattered the disbelieving quietness, enquiring whether anyone fancied joining him for a pint. Bobby, meanwhile, was fuming. There was an axe to grind, and he was desperate for his moment with the press pack. 'They never gave us the credit we deserved,' he reiterated. 'I've been clearing out the loft recently and I've found a lot of the old articles and cuttings, and the press were disgraceful. One journalist said if Wimbledon won the FA Cup today it would set football back two decades. That really hurt. I went into the press conference after the game and I said, "Gentlemen, you had your say this morning. I've got my say now, and it's nothing." I turned around and walked out.' Even Sanch was denied his glory by the media. They described the cup final as poor, his goal as unmemorable. 'After the final I spoke to a journalist,' said Sanch. 'He said, "Well, your goal won't be remembered very much because it wasn't a particularly great one and it wasn't a good final." Today, I'm dragged out every time the FA Cup's on. They show my celebration on Sky TV all the time. I've done documentaries on that final and it's gone down as one of the greats. I see that journalist now and I've asked him whether he remembers saying that to me, but he denies it. But I remembered it because I was so gutted after he'd said it.'

The players returned to the Cannizaro and danced around the trophy. They then headed to Plough Lane, where chairman Stanley Reed had erected a marquee. By 5.30 a.m. the players were so drunk they had to hitch a lift in a police van that had been keeping a watchful eye on the proceedings. The last person went to bed at nine. Bobby had a pretty eventful evening: he later woke up with an unfamiliar bed partner. 'I was in London in my flat and the wife had gone home to the West Country,' he explained. 'I didn't know what to do with the trophy overnight, so I put it in bed beside me. I actually slept with the FA Cup. I was so proud, because we won that cup on the cheap. The money wasn't there but we cut the corners accordingly. I think the top basic wage was £300 at the time. And the players who played in that FA Cup Final were later sold for £14 million. It was an amazing achievement.'

Football's elite scratched their heads in disbelief – it was their biggest nightmare made real. Wimbledon's success had secured a place in the sport's hall of fame. Now nobody could forget their cute little fairytale.

PART TWO

DEATH OF
A PARTY

CHAPTER EIGHT

At Alan Cork's testimonial game only days after the FA Cup Final victory, the entire team, led by Vinnie, flashed their backsides at the crowd. The scene was captured by a *Daily Mirror* photographer, and it caused a scandal; the players were fined £750 each. This was a real pain, but it got worse when Bobby refused to take them on a post-season holiday. Apparently they were so uncontrollable that nobody, not even Bobby and Don, could keep them in line. The players were crestfallen, but discipline was desperately needed.

As soon as the FA Cup was safely ensconced at Plough Lane, the bubble encapsulating their little adventure popped. A number of the club's high-profile players were suddenly viewed as hot property and were coveted by the First Division's more established sides. Naturally, the Crazy Gang seemed eager to flirt with the league's elite class – at Highbury, Old Trafford and Anfield the pay cheques were fatter, after all. Certainly the cars parked there were a lot sleeker than the ones sitting in Sam's training-ground car park-cum-showroom. Naturally, Bobby was concerned. The Crazy Gang, *the hardcore*, had ensured success for the club by bludgeoning defences and terrifying opponents with their relentless enthusiasm and a fearless physical presence. Now they began to think about a future outside Plough Lane. With the romance of the FA Cup fresh in their minds, several players realised that the next dream, a First Division championship, could be fulfilled only at a richer club. 'It was summed up by Sam,' said Sanch. 'He reckoned that by winning the FA Cup, Wimbledon lost their virginity. By that he meant that the players realised we were worth an awful lot more than what we were being paid. We were FA Cup winners. People wanted winners, and we were a team of winners. Suddenly people realised we weren't being paid that much. Other clubs wanted us to play for them. We realised we weren't small players playing for a little club, we were big players, and other clubs would pay top dollar for us.'

Dennis Wise, for one, seemed desperate to leave. Spurs were trailing his career, and they allowed their interest to drizzle into the papers during pre-season preparations for the 1988/89 campaign ('Terry Venables was trying to tap him up,' said Bobby). Wise tried everything to attract an offer from White Hart Lane. He even attempted to skive Wimbledon's pre-season tour of Scandinavia. 'He told me he was ill and couldn't come on tour to Sweden,' said Bobby. 'So I sent our physio round to his house to pick him up. I was sitting in my hotel preparing notes for training the next day when suddenly these rockets came whizzing past the window. I looked out and there was Dennis letting off fireworks. He said, "You've got to send me home now, gaffer." I told him he was staying and fined him two weeks' wages instead. I enjoyed the challenge, and he knew I had a pair of boxing gloves behind the door anyway.'

West Ham, Everton and Arsenal were rumoured to be after Fash, and the striker was making no bones about his desire for success. 'Admittedly it would be very hard to leave a club that had just won the FA Cup,' he said, 'but it would be a great way to go out. I'm ambitious, and I realise that if I were currently playing for a club like Tottenham or Arsenal, then I might also be playing for England.'

Two players did make it away from Plough Lane in high-profile circumstances. Goalkeeper Dave Beasant and defender Andy Thorn were snapped up by Newcastle for £850,000 apiece. Each was a major loss, particularly Beasant, who believed his Wimbledon career had reached a natural conclusion when Harry left for Watford. At the time Bobby convinced him to stay, but at the end of October 1987, when Wimbledon beat Newcastle in a Littlewoods Cup tie, a £350,000 bid had been tabled by the Magpies. Bobby cheekily asked them to return with £750,000 – then a transfer record for a goalkeeper. After the FA Cup Final Newcastle responded with the requested amount plus an additional £100,000. Sam couldn't turn the cash down, and Beasant was allowed to leave. The keeper seemed pleased to be exiting on a natural high. He had played in an unbroken 351-game run. 'Newcastle didn't have to ask twice when [manager] Willie McFaul made an offer just a few weeks after our Wembley win,' he recalled. 'Despite all the good times I'd had, culminating in that famous FA Cup win, I realised it was time to move on and seek a fresh challenge.' Thorn wasn't so happy. 'I didn't want to leave Wimbledon,' he said.

Away from the transfer market's trials and tribulations, Wimbledon's biggest characters – the movers and the shakers, Fash, Vinnie, Wise – became advertisers' dreams. Each one was ideally suited to boot sponsorships, high-profile parties, advertising contracts and TV deals. No longer were they the scum of past seasons. Suddenly the Crazy Gang were associated with victory, though to outsiders it still seemed like a novelty that would disappear as quickly as it had arrived. Nevertheless, they'd hit the big time, only a quarter of a century after winning the FA Amateur Cup.

Bobby fretted about the new-found celebrity status sparkling around Plough Lane; he worried that it might send negative shockwaves through his team. Almost overnight, player enthusiasm had waned. According to Don Howe, some of the squad's passion had appeared to dip as soon as they had changed out of their Wimbledon kit, showered and driven away from the Wembley car park. And when pre-season training arrived in July, people were noting that the players arriving at Wimbledon's Roehampton training ground every morning seemed less passionate, less motivated.

The catalyst for this change in attitude was clear to those who understood the club's back story. In becoming FA Cup winners the team had developed into a marketable commodity. Like their League peers, Wimbledon were determined to enjoy the luxuries that accompanied success. 'It happened to a lot of players in that team,' said Don Howe. 'They became distracted with their own success and instead of giving the same attention to their playing side, the playing side became the second most important part of the day. Previously it had been their priority.' The feeling eventually trickled down into Bobby Gould too. Having secured the FA Cup – a nice little feather in Sam's cap, it had to be said – he also felt entitled to a bonus, like everybody else. Surely if his players were able to pick up the perks of an FA Cup win, he should be in line for a slice of the action too. Somehow he convinced Sam to buy him a shiny new BMW. 'He was normally mean,' said Bobby, 'but he got me one. I got the registration G88 CUP put on it.'

Such trappings only stoked public resentment. Despite their survival in the top flight, despite the scalps, the scraps and the FA Cup wins, journalists following the league's premier teams refused to accept the Crazy Gang's place within First Division history. Certainly this side had moved on in leaps and bounds since their inception to the Football League, slamming down on the superstardom pedal, but the press didn't seem to care. It drove Bobby and Sam mad that still nobody would credit their achievements. 'Where were you nine years ago?' Bobby sniped at those journalists who persistently criticised his team's playing style. 'How far have you progressed? I bet you lot haven't progressed half as far as Wimbledon.'

Behind the scenes at Plough Lane there was another bitter aftertaste to success. In winning the FA Cup the Dons would have been eligible for the European Cup Winners' Cup competition. Yet again, the post-Heysel ban enforced on English clubs put paid to that. This meant Wimbledon would have to sit out another year of continental excursions. Bobby could only wonder at how the likes of Barcelona and Juventus would have travelled to Plough Lane in order to battle the Crazy Gang. And then there was Sam's unique attitude to hospitality. How would AC Milan and Bayern Munich have coped with cold showers in the away dressing rooms? How would Real Madrid and Ajax have dealt with salt in their sugar bowls?

To temper his disappointment, Bobby simply focused on the season ahead. He sold Brian Gayle to Manchester City for £350,000 and invested in Keith Curle from Reading (for £500,000, then a club record). He would also give games to Paul Miller (a youth player turned reserve) and midfielder Detzi Kruszynski. He then settled down to begin what proved to be a difficult motivational process. 'When you've had success, you have to get back to the grindstone and start again,' he said with a sigh. But Wimbledon took a kicking even before the season was underway. The discipline problems that had dogged the club week after week, month after month, hadn't been dulled by their new-found glory. Unsurprisingly, Vinnie was in the thick of it. Following a brawl against Isle of Wight village team Shanklin – a pre-season friendly arranged by Bobby as a favour for an old friend – he was sent off for hurling his fists around in the midst of a small-scale brawl. Bobby was disgusted and reprimanded him, both privately and in front of reporters.

Rumour dominated the papers: apparently an ultimatum had been delivered to Sam in which Bobby claimed that he'd leave the club if Vinnie's temper wasn't brought to heel. Vinnie was later privately suspended for the return match against Liverpool, in the Charity Shield fixture at Wembley on 20 August, which was disappointing because Steve McMahon was making statements about revenge. How Vinnie would have loved to stand in his way, especially as he'd been making cocky noises of his own, claiming that the Charity Shield meant nothing to the Crazy Gang. They already had 'the big one' in the bag. It didn't matter if they were thrashed either. The players, claimed Vinnie, were simply happy to spend another afternoon on the Wembley turf, regardless of the result.

This was just as well: Wimbledon were beaten 2–1 by their resurgent opponents. Vinnie and Sam watched the game as telly pundits from a BBC studio. Clearly Wimbledon's fighting spirit flowed from the well of Vinnie's tackling and aggressive passion, and as the competitive matches got underway with him still in the doghouse, Wimbledon struggled. The departures of Beasant and Thorn had made minimal impact; the most problematic obstacle, it seemed, was the team's champion status. The Crazy Gang, once a squad of twenty unknowns, were now bona fide superstars. They were the team to beat. The majority of the First Division viewed them as a club with ideas above their station, and at times opponents appeared determined to bring some of their bigger personalities down a peg or two, particularly after the bruises of previous years. In the campaign's opening exchanges they were overrun by Arsenal (5–1) and beaten by West Ham, Middlesbrough and Coventry. Vinnie didn't start a game until the end of September, by which time the team had slumped to the table's basement, leaving many pundits and fans to speculate yet again on their life expectancy in Division One.

Bobby tinkered between the sticks, using two goalkeepers (Simon Tracey and Ron Green) before signing 26-year-old Dutchman Hans Segers from Nottingham Forest for £125,000. Segers had endured difficult times under Brian Clough. He'd been shipped out on loan from club to club, including stints in Scotland and Belgium. By September he'd grown weary of playing second fiddle to the rapidly improving Steve Sutton, which is when Bobby stepped in, though on paper Segers lacked the experience and charisma of Dave Beasant. 'People asked me, "Why have you bought him?"' Bobby recalled, 'and I said, "Because he kicks the ball a fucking long way."'

The transfer proved shrewd business. Segers became a hero on his debut at Plough Lane, setting up Wimbledon's first goal in a 2–1 win over Everton – their first victory of the season. The build-up was typically Crazy Gang: a long ball was launched by Segers from a free-kick deep inside Wimbledon's half; the ball dropped on to Fash, who planted it into the back of the net. Not that anyone outside the club expressed approval. It was just another example of Wimbledon's culturally bereft tactics. Segers fumed. 'If someone like Glenn Hoddle played a 40-yard pass for a striker to run on to and score it was labelled beautiful, Brazilian-style football,' he wrote in his autobiography. 'When Vinnie Jones or Keith Curle knocked the ball forward for Big Fash to get hold of and score, it would be labelled "route one" football. Double standards indeed.'

When the victories finally started to come, they were celebrated in a typically Wimbledon way: the entire team, led by Sam, would jump around singing football songs. The party wouldn't stop until the team, sometimes including Bobby Gould and Don Howe, were sinking a couple of beers on the team coach. Segers settled well in this environment. During his first week he had been treated to a special Wimbledon initiation when the team travelled north for an away game against Aston Villa. After dinner in the team hotel, he returned to his room only to find its contents rearranged around the building. His TV was in the bathroom, his clothes were strewn around the room, and the bed had been pushed through an open window and on to the street below. He laughed it off. He was enjoying himself, and on the practice ground he relished working with the 'professional' Bobby Gould. The shock and awe he'd experienced under Brian Clough at Forest was not in evidence on the Crazy Gang's training pitches, where the players rubbed shoulders with dog walkers and joggers. And though his new manager enjoyed being treated like one of the boys, he retained a tactical sharpness. Segers was surprised to discover that Bobby's team talks and briefings were more in-depth and advanced than the ones given by Clough.

Still, his introduction couldn't halt a Wimbledon slide. After a powerful surge from the beginning of December through to the beginning of April, the team capitulated, claiming only one victory in the last nine games. At the season's close the First

Division elite had got their wish: Wimbledon's defiance seemed to be crumbling, their shock tactics nullified. The club finished in a disappointing twelfth place having been kicked out of the FA Cup in the quarter-finals. The glory of their FA Cup win had, it seemed, gone to their heads. 'Success has always been a test of people's character and people's attitudes to their job,' said Don Howe. 'It affects all those things. Some people can handle it and some can't. And it really showed [in 1988/89] because we finished in the bottom half of the table.'

As if that wasn't enough, they had been masterful when it came to appalling the public at large too. Often this happened with a string of X-rated tackles. Vinnie, in particular, just couldn't behave himself. He roused tabloid ire on an almost weekly basis. One clash, which came during the 2–3 defeat against Spurs at White Hart Lane on 12 November, even ended the career of England defender Gary Stevens. Typically, the incident had started innocuously when Stevens and Fash began jostling for a ball in the middle of the park. They soon became knotted in a bundle of limbs, and as the ball came loose Vinnie drove in hard, sending the pair to the floor and shattering Stevens' knee. On the touchline, the Spurs management were apoplectic. After the game, Don Howe was forced to drive Vinnie home as a mob of 500 Spurs fans gathered for him by the team coach. 'I won the ball, so I don't know what the fuss was all about,' said Vinnie. 'Gary Stevens had bad knees anyway. I've always said that it wasn't the tackle that done it, it was the weight of Fash falling on him. Fashanu and Stevens were tussling in the corner, I came over, and bosh, I've gone in and they've both gone down. The thing is, he's always held a grudge. I went to see him in hospital the next morning. I took a load of magazines, and the next day he slaughtered me in the press saying I bought him a boxing mag. I probably did, but there were all sorts of mags, on football, motoring, sailing and probably boxing. That got the headlines though. He's always had a chip on his shoulder about that.'

Despite the casualties and headlines, Sam still loved him. Whenever the press attacked Vinnie he defended him to the hilt, even if his efforts seemed stretched to the limit. In February 1989 he was sent off for two yellow cards against Everton – the first for a tackle against England midfielder Peter Reid, the second for an apparent head butt in the face of Kevin Ratcliffe. Vinnie later claimed that Ratcliffe had feigned the attack, but few believed him. After the match a crowd of Everton fans swarmed around the Wimbledon coach and bombarded him with accusations. Fash punched the emergency exit button, flew from the back door and sent them packing, but the damage had been done. Howe vowed to leave the club. He was tired with working with 'a bunch of maniacs', and by the next morning the media were tearing the bones from another Crazy Gang car crash. 'A TV company came round to interview Vincent after the alleged head butt, when Ratcliffe had taken a dive,' Bobby recalled. 'I always got to work early. I saw a little VW in the car park and I thought, "That's a bit strange. Somebody must have left it there overnight." About an hour later Vincent came out shouting, "Boss, boss! The press are here!" This guy with the VW had doorstepped Vincent, saying, "You're the worst player in England, everybody hates you." Anyway, I got to his car, the VW, and waited for him. When he returned I told him he was outrageous and that I was calling the police because he was on private property. I said to him, "And don't think about getting away." He said, "What do you mean?" I said, "I've let your tyres down." So the police came along and took him off.'

After the Stevens incident, Vinnie was public enemy number

one yet again, even though he hadn't picked up a yellow card all season. Now Sam was struggling to justify his player's actions. Worse, he had become a major embarrassment to the club. Bobby couldn't deal with the bad PR, the pieces probing his public image, the TV interviews that made light of his harsh temper and robust attitude to the game. Vinnie couldn't stand it either. He hated it when the press splashed witty headlines across their pages or when flashy TV presenters held up imaginary red cards at the end of chat-show interviews. Vinnie was suffering from a peculiar syndrome that seemed unique to him: if he went in too hard during challenges he was labelled a psychopath, a savage; if he didn't display his tenacious spirit during a game he was often labelled 'soft' or criticised for losing his bottle. Most people seemed to have forgotten that Vinnie could actually play. Indeed, one broadsheet newspaper compared his touch to that of a Brazilian without a whiff of irony.

But it wasn't just football writers who were getting up Vinnie's nose; his team-mates angered him too. In the final game of the season he even waded into midfielder Detzi Kruszynski for his apparently lethargic attitude. The referee had to pull the pair apart before Vinnie dropped Detzi to the floor. Clearly things were no longer working out for Vinnie, and he wanted out. Not even Sam, for so long his confidant when things were going badly on and off the pitch, could dissuade him. 'Vincent's attitude became harder to deal with,' Bobby recalled. 'It was hard work. I recommended to Sam that we got as much as we could for him. But he was a good player. He was underestimated. He was technically very good, but you just couldn't control his emotions.'

Fortunately, there were offers during the summer of 1989, most notably from Howard Wilkinson's Leeds United side. For

£650,000 in transfer cash, a £1,400-a-week salary and a yearly £25,000 signing-on fee, they got his signature. At Wimbledon Vinnie had claimed a wage of only £500 a week. Suddenly things were looking up for him, though his move was tinged with sadness. 'When I left Wimbledon,' he said, 'I left behind the two men who made me a professional footballer. Bobby Gould and Don Howe turned me from a hot-headed youngster into the £650,000 footballer I am today, and I owe them everything. When he arrived at Plough Lane, (Bobby Gould) told me that while I was playing First Division football, I wasn't what he would call a pro. But he soon took hold of me, disciplined me when I got out of line, and showed me what I could, and could not, do. It took a while for me to toe the line but I soon learnt, and I'm very grateful for his advice.'

Despite the Crazy Gang's disappointing campaign in 1988/89, things were looking up for Fash too. England manager Bobby Robson had been impressed with his powerful performances in the First Division and marked him down for a spot in the England side for the fixture against Chile at Wembley on 23 May. The game was later noted for holding the record for the lowest attendance at an England international at Wembley – a disappointing 15,628 fans. Not that Fash cared – he was representing his country at last. On reflection, he performed well on his England debut, proving that he was gifted enough to compete in top-class football away from the blood-and-thunder style of the Crazy Gang. 'He played very well when he represented England,' said Don Howe. 'It was the end of the season, and you do get one or two players who get a bit tired at that stage, but John wasn't. He ran his socks off.' He played again a few days later in Glasgow against Scotland, but those two games would represent his only international recognition. Fash would later claim that race had played a greater part than his ability in terms of the caps drying up. 'At that time I was scoring fifteen to twenty goals a season,' he said, 'but getting in the national team was not about being as good as the other players – you had to be better than them. It was because I was black and playing for Wimbledon, but there was no striker who could touch me at that time. Even Gary Lineker said that the one player he wanted to play alongside was John Fashanu.'

But again, Fash seemed to view England as another marketing tool, like Wimbledon's FA Cup win. Don Howe attributed the end to Fash's international development to his increasing interests away from football. Like Sanch, he'd also noticed Fash's lethargic attitude to training. 'John was strong, powerful, and he knew where the goal was,' said Howe. 'He had a great shot on him and he was fantastic in the air. But his lack of commitment stopped him from becoming a great player. I really believe that. His ambition was to play for England, and that came to him, but he played for England and then he lost interest.'

Bobby couldn't believe it, but by the beginning of the 1989/90 campaign his mini-crisis at Plough Lane was spiralling out of control. Don Howe, his trusted ally, was leaving Wimbledon. The coach had only intended to work for a pre-season campaign two years ago. He'd stayed, but a diagnosed heart condition meant that operating with the Crazy Gang was officially a health hazard. As a replacement, Bobby drafted in former Doncaster Rovers assistant manager Joe Kinnear. He was slapped on an £18,600-a-year contract with twenty days' holiday. Not a bad deal all in all in 1989.

But with Vinnie gone, Bobby's team was sapped of strength. Certainly the players missed his enthusiasm, passion and fuck-you attitude. They also missed the practical jokes – the time, for example, when he – along with Fash – had thought of planting an old man in the front row of a game. The idea was to hurl a ball in his face when it rolled off for a throw-in or corner. Nobody would have known he'd been put there by the players and it would have caused chaos in the papers. The idea came to nothing. Sam missed him too, but carried on gooning around regardless. His new challenge was to race the players the length of the Plough Lane pitch for £100. He was given a head start at the penalty box with one of the players acting as a starter. When the green light was given, Sam would sprint as fast as he could along the touchline. For some reason, though, he could never win a single race. This was probably due to the fact that the race 'judge' wouldn't set Sam off until his challenger was two yards behind him.

This proved a minor distraction, however. On the training ground and during games at the season's start, Wimbledon were battling against familiarity. Opponents had worked out how to play against the long ball and were outsmarting them at every turn. The elbows, knees and body slams that had intimidated much of the First Division for so long were now being counteracted with guile and finesse. Bobby knew his team would have to adjust their tactics accordingly, though with only a few weeks of the 1989/90 season gone they were battered by injury and hampered by a drop in form. Age, in the likes of Alan Cork and Sanch, went against them too.

Dramatically, Bobby scrapped the long-ball game and dropped Fash from the team. Well, desperate defeats against Chelsea, Crystal Palace, Liverpool and Nottingham Forest, and only one win from the first ten League games of the season, called for desperate measures. In the stands, Wimbledon's fans were getting restless, much of the blame being heaped on

Vaughan Ryan, the young midfielder who'd been called upon to fill Vinnie's boots. Wimbledon were second from bottom by October. Bobby mixed it up a little. He ordered his players to compete in the style the critics loved – with passes on the deck. It worked too: on 2 December Wimbledon battered Chelsea at Stamford Bridge with a performance of crisp footwork that produced five goals. The club began to poach games by the odd goal, and, more impressively, with finesse too (well, by their standards anyway). The players even had a mantra for their new work ethic: 'We came, we scored, we fucked off home.' Fash earned a recall to the team and scored ten goals in the last thirteen games. In the dressing room the team stereo was being played at deafening volumes. 'The louder the music,' said Segers, 'the more we got psyched up before games.'

The Dons finished the season in eighth place – a pretty impressive placing considering their poor start. But the club's fragilities had been laid bare for everyone to see. The long-ball game had been neutralised, mostly Wimbledon seemed ineffective in front of goal, and they were failing to win games at Plough Lane, for so long their pokey, ramshackle fortress. The professionalism of the top-flight clubs ensured they were no longer ruffled by the cramped dressing rooms and poor facilities. The advantage of their poverty had been wiped away.

Meanwhile, Bobby was enduring another financial cat-and-mouse game with Sam as he haggled for a better contract. He'd improved the team on limited resources, dealt with Vinnie's battles with authority, scrapped the long-ball game and saved the club's arse time and time again, yet Sam refused to up his pay to the desired level. Bobby had been through this before: when he'd previously asked for a rise, Sam had agreed, but when Wimbledon won the FA Cup he offered him a deal that was

£10,000 less than the original asking price. Bobby didn't really want to leave Wimbledon – he loved the club – but he felt he had no choice. Sure enough, at the close of the 1989/90 season he walked out of Plough Lane. 'It was financial,' admitted Bobby. 'I'd been on £30,000 a year and I'd blackmailed Sam. I said I think I'm worth £50,000, so he gave me £50,000, so I said I think I'm worth £70,000, and he wouldn't give me the £70,000. He offered Don £70,000 but not me, and I left. I miss it. Wimbledon was my team. I always called it the Cinderella club. It was a magnificent place. I loved all the players, I've got to say that. You couldn't single out one, they were all magnificent. But the beauty of it is how successful the players were after they left football as well. I think that [proves] what a strong bunch of characters they were.'

A replacement was chosen almost immediately and Ray Harford took charge for the 1990/91 season. He was a naturally dour man – in comparison to Bobby anyway – but his pedigree was rock solid. He'd worked at Luton Town, another Division One club restricted to working on limited resources, and Sam reckoned this experience would make him perfect for Wimbledon. He drafted him in as soon as Bobby had left.

There were other exits too. Eric Young went off to join local rivals Crystal Palace for £850,000. More dramatically, Dennis Wise had finally been granted his wish, though he was sold to Chelsea rather than Spurs, for £1.6 million. It was a club record transfer fee. Once again Sam had bought small and shrewdly before selling at a very, very big mark-up price. However, the new arrivals at Plough Lane under Harford did little to motivate the fans. Warren Barton, a £300,000 signing from Maidstone, was about as exciting as it got, and his signing was fraught with complications. 'Bobby Gould signed me on the Tuesday, and by the Thursday Ray Harford had taken over,' Barton recalled. 'So it was a strange situation for me. I'd heard all about the Crazy Gang and what they got up to, and when I got there it didn't let me down. It was a really exciting time. They turned me from a boy into a man at Wimbledon. I remember in one of my first games we played against Everton. John Scales had gone in with a clash on one of the Everton players. I ran over to break it up and suddenly Fash came over, pushed my arm down and flew in to let them know not to mess with any of our players. As we were walking away, he turned round to me and said, "Don't ever do that again. We always look after our own, never try and separate it. These teams have to know that if they want to take one of us on, they'll have to take us all on." That's how it was at Plough Lane.' Barton suffered a traditionally violent Wimbledon initiation too. After practice, he was dragged across the training ground stark naked. His humiliation was completed when the Crazy Gang pushed him in front of a pack of photographers who had gathered for a club presentation. 'They were there to see the royal dress designer,' Barton explained. 'She was doing a publicity shoot, and I had to walk past her with a plastic cone covering my privates.'

A few months later it wasn't fashion the press were interested in at Plough Lane, but Fash – again. The cup final story, which had frustrated the striker so much that he'd punched a hotel door, had indeed appeared on a Sunday tabloid cover, but it had all blown over quickly. This time the attention focused on his brother's lifestyle, for Justin had finally come out in the *Sun* as football's first openly gay professional. The British media were having a field day. A deal had been struck with tabloid reporters, and Justin had detailed a string of affairs in return for sums of cash; he'd alluded to relationships with fellow players, MPs and celebrities. Fash had got wind of the news before it was splashed across the newspapers and begged his agent Eric Hall to help pull the story. But Hall had brokered the deal and saw the confession as a positive move for Justin. A reporter had obtained several photos of the striker cuddling up to a man in a gay bar in Canada, where he was living at the time, and Justin had had to come forward or run the risk of being outed against his will. This way he could procure some cash while retaining his dignity. Hall was a renowned manipulator of the media, and despite his almost comical public persona – that of a fast-talking, cigar-chewing spiv who communicated with a barrage of catchphrases, most notoriously the term 'Monster, monster' – he was considered to be the best person in the business when it came to mopping up a sleazy mess. But Fash didn't share his enthusiasm for the revelations, and on the evening before Justin's story was due to run he contacted Hall.

'Pull the story,' he pleaded again. 'It mustn't go in.'

Hall was astounded. He outlined the benefits of the deal with *Sun* editor Kelvin McKenzie and explained that Justin would be receiving peace of mind and a large sum of money. When Fash asked him for details of the fee, Hall advised him to ask Justin himself, and the call ended. Only an hour later, Fash was on the phone again. He knew the agreed sum was £100,000 and was prepared to match it if Hall agreed to pull the story. 'I explained that the money was not important,' Hall recalled. 'It was the only way to solve Justin's problem, and anyhow, the *Sun* had spent too much time and effort on it now and they wouldn't pull out even if I asked them to. I'd also signed a contract, and anyhow, suppose they did pull it? The Sunday tabloid story would put Justin in an even worse light. John refused to listen and just kept on telling me what it would do to him. He said that if the story did appear he would never work with me again. So much for brotherly love.'

On Monday, 22 October 1990, the *Sun* hit the news-stands with the headline 'I'm Gay' plastered across the front page. As Justin was tied to an exclusive deal with the *Sun*, rival papers turned to the next best source of information – his brother. Journalists became desperate for his reaction to the new revelations, and Fash was hounded, bombarded with questions. In an interview with the BBC's *Football Focus* he expressed anger at the scandal surrounding Justin's sexual orientation. Sitting in the grounds of Plough Lane on the eve of a First Division derby game with South London rivals Crystal Palace, Fash spoke of feeling embarrassed at the situation. He also appeared agitated and aggressive. 'He's come out and expressed his sexual preferences,' he said angrily. 'I mean, other footballers don't come out and say "I love women". He'll have to suffer the consequences. I certainly wouldn't like to play or get changed in the vicinity of him, and if I feel like that then I'm sure the rest of football feels like that.' Fash later expressed regret at the reaction to his brother's sexuality. 'I reacted to Justin's news in conjunction with the times,' he said sadly. 'I think I learnt a lot from Justin and his situation. And I think I grew up a lot when Justin came out. In hindsight, maybe I would have reacted differently, but life is a learning curve … The successful people are the ones who learn. The people who don't learn fall by the wayside. Had I heard the news of Justin's sexuality now, I would have reacted differently. If somebody now comes up to you and says they enjoy driving on the wrong side of the road, how you react now and how you react in ten years' time could be very different, because circumstances change.'

Professionally at least, the tabloid storm didn't affect Fash: he was banging in the goals again. On the pitch he quickly became a target for terrace abuse, as fans taunted him with wolf-whistles and homophobic chants. The most vitriolic response was experienced during that game against Crystal Palace, the first match since Justin's public revelations. Fash suffered a barrage of insults, but despite the shock 4–3 defeat he answered his critics in the best way possible, with a stylish twenty-yard chip that arced over goalkeeper Nigel Martyn's head and into the back of the net. The final whistle was a welcome sound. 'I've never been one to hide,' he said in the post-match interview, 'but that's been the longest week in my life. It was a relief to get that game out of the way. I needed that goal badly. That's the best way to shut [opposing fans] up – let your football do the talking. I was pleased as punch when my shot went in. I saw Nigel Martyn off his lines and went for it. You've got to try to take [the chants] in good humour. Life's far too short to let it get on top of you. If you're not getting any stick it means you're probably not doing your job properly. I'd have been worried if none was dished out because it would have meant I wasn't a threat. The other Wimbledon players have been as good as gold, as were the Palace team.'

Today, Fash is more revealing about the levels of abuse aimed at him during those traumatic games. 'People didn't say anything to me on the pitch about Justin once he came out,' he said, 'but they thought it. Spectators sang things at me when I played, but who cares if they're shouting "Fash, show us your bum"? Being strong and six foot three, you're expecting a lot of abuse anyway, and I loved that.' Under Ray Harford in that 1990/91 season it was a case of business as usual: he dragged Wimbledon back up to seventh place. Clearly, Sam had fallen on his feet yet again. The inference of this and of Fash's words was clear: the louder you booed, the stronger the Crazy Gang became.

CHAPTER NINE

Without warning, Sam pulled the rug from underneath his club. He moved the team away from Plough Lane and relocated Wimbledon to Selhurst Park as part of a groundshare scheme with Ron Noades's Crystal Palace.

Rumours of a move away from SW17 had hounded Wimbledon fans for years. There had, of course, been whispers of a merger with Palace when Noades first moved to Selhurst Park a decade earlier. Later, once the club had been promoted into Division One, many still believed Sam was hoping to turn Wimbledon into a South London hybrid with Palace. Ludicrous names such as South London United were even bandied around at fan meetings. 'We did a survey,' Noades said, 'but again the fans voted against it. But if there had been a merger, in my point of view, Crystal Palace's name would have been the only one that existed afterwards. The only advantage of a merger for us would have been taking some of the Wimbledon players. The team would have been called Crystal Palace & Wimbledon for a while. After that we would have been called Crystal Palace again. We would have retained the identity of the club because Crystal Palace owned the ground and Wimbledon didn't.'

As Noades said, when the merger plans were mooted in 1986/87, both sets of supporters had been against a union. Wimbledon fans rallied under the flag of a protest organisation called the Save Wimbledon Action Group; their counterparts at Selhurst Park created the Palace Action Campaign. Sam was bombarded by letters and press conferences. Leaflets were distributed outside Plough Lane as members investigated Sam's investment in the land around the ground. They also questioned the legality of Noades and Sam having an involvement in two football clubs. Clearly the Wimbledon owner hadn't banked on the determination of his own fans. They were showing the same battling spirit as his team on the pitch. Sam quickly backed down and apologised, later inveigling a handful of select supporters into a meeting to witness his new vision for the club: a luxury stadium in the nearby Wandle Valley area. Here he hoped to build a ground capable of fulfilling Wimbledon's football ambition as well as generating extra revenue for the club by hosting pop concerts and boxing matches. The new ground would also come equipped with a state-of-the-art sliding roof and an artificial pitch. But its development was accompanied by a hitch: Sam would have to rely on outside investment to realise his dream. Of course, this meant that the ground would be leased to the club and they wouldn't actually own it outright. He later told fans that if they assisted him with this vision he'd forget the proposed Palace merger.

Sam pressed ahead with investment meetings as his team gained a solid foothold in the First Division, but his dreams of a new ground failed to bear fruition. The FA's decision to scrap plastic pitches meant that plans to turn the new ground into a venue for sports events and rock shows was in tatters before the first brick had been laid. The rumours of a new ground development briefly faded away. Sam also failed to produce environmental and traffic-impact assessments for the Wandle Valley, and his planning permission lapsed. Later, Merton Council agreed to remove a covenant restricting the use of land on Plough Lane to recreation. For £800,000 Sam could now sell his plot of land to another investor and build a brand-new football stadium elsewhere, if he so wished. Plough Lane's future appeared to be limited at best.

By 1991 the football landscape had shifted dramatically. On a tragic afternoon in April 1989, 96 people had died in a crowd crush during the FA Cup semi-final between Liverpool and Nottingham Forest. Overcrowding and poor policing were blamed, as were inadequate facilities – metal fences, unattended gates – at the stadium. The upshot of this tragedy was the Taylor Report, a dossier of ground improvements which outlined the cause of poor crowd safety and solutions for it. Clearly football stadia across the country would have to undergo an extensive makeover in a concerted effort to reduce terracing. Within five years, grounds like Plough Lane would have to be all-seaters.

This sounded the death knell for Wimbledon's stadium. Converting the ground to seats would reduce its capacity to only 6,000, severely limiting the profit margins on ticket revenue. Rumours therefore circulated the terraces that another move or merger was in preparation, though nobody seemed entirely sure what Sam was planning. He dramatically revealed his ideas for the club on the final day of the 1990/91 season, outlining the details in his match notes in the programme. Wimbledon, he explained, were now tenants at Selhurst Park as part of a nine-year agreement with a get-out clause accompanied by one year's notice. They would remain there for the foreseeable future – well, until the club could afford a new ground or felt financially secure enough to refurbish Plough Lane to a suitable standard. But either way the club would be returning to Merton Borough. Fittingly, their final match at Plough Lane, on 4 May 1991, was against Palace.

Again, the fans were in uproar. After the match – to rub salt into the wounds, Palace had won 3–0 with an Ian Wright hat-trick – meetings were called in pubs around the ground to decide on a course of action. By Monday the following week an action group had been assembled (Supporters Against Merger), and it began railing against the move; that the initials spelt out SAM was intentional. But the group was shortlived: it imploded after several fractious meetings, indecision on protests and media campaigns hampering their progress. The move to Selhurst was on. Meanwhile, Sam became publicly adamant that any failure to comply with the Taylor Report would force the club out of Division One, though his claims were disingenuous. Wimbledon had five years to implement the required improvements, and Sam owned the gypsy site behind the ground and could have expanded into the land there. *Daily Mirror* reporter Tony Stenson revealed that Wimbledon were offered thirteen alternative sites to develop a new ground; they were also granted planning permission for Wandle Valley and Tamden Works, though neither of these options was exploited. Stenson also claimed there was no restriction on the height of the Wandle End of the ground and an extension could have taken place there. According to the journalist, Wimbledon were being disastrously premature. Sam countered that he had blown £500,000 of his own cash on drawing up plans for a new ground and that he'd been let down by Merton Council. He also had difficulty enticing investors: many bankrollers worried that the club would drop down into the lower divisions as quickly as they had been promoted.

Either way you looked at it, Wimbledon were in a bloody mess. But at least Ron Noades was pleased. 'We were very happy to have a groundshare deal,' he said. 'It saved us 50 per cent of the stadium costs and Wimbledon helped us pay for some executive boxes. It was a beneficial move for Crystal Palace.' Sam was smiling too. Over the coming seasons he would steadfastly refuse to contribute to any stadium improvement costs. As the rest of English football paid millions in post-Taylor Report improvements, Sam kept his hands in his pockets. Meanwhile, supporters took comfort from the fact that Sam was publicly denying the merger proposals. 'I'd rather die and have vultures eat my insides than merge with Crystal Palace,' he said.

But still the fans hated the new ground. Selhurst Park was miles away from Plough Lane and the transport links were awful; many had to drive there, and once they arrived at the stadium it was almost impossible to find a parking space. The complaints came thick and fast. The move also represented a loss of identity for the Crazy Gang. Wimbledon had been neutered; the advantages of their small ground, where the showers ran cold, the fans hugged the touchlines and visiting players were exposed to abuse from both supporters and their opponents, had disappeared. Selhurst was vast in comparison, and subsequently Wimbledon's crowd, which packed Plough Lane's stands was swallowed up within the enormous stanchions. But then the supporters had voted with their feet, and Wimbledon initially amassed gates of just 3,000. Palace, meanwhile, attracted five times that number. 'It was very disappointing for the fans,' said Warren Barton. 'The club had tried everything with Merton Council to stay in the area, but they weren't very accommodating, and neither were the residents. Then we looked to move elsewhere, because we had to. We were getting bigger crowds when we were at Plough Lane and Sam wanted to push the club on to a similar playing field to the Norwiches, Southamptons and those clubs. So we had to move on.' When the media later laughed at Wimbledon's dwindling support, Sam hit back with his trademark ferocity. 'Why do you make fun of our gates?' he said. 'You don't mock a handicapped person in their wheelchair, do you? And our gates are our handicap. We are like featherweights going in against Mike Tyson. Not just once, but every week.'

The players hated Selhurst Park too. The raw atmosphere of Plough Lane had been lost. They missed seeing the same punters in the crowd. Warren Barton's grandparents would go to games at Plough Lane and he would always look for their faces in the stands, but at Selhurst Park, with its extended touchlines, it was difficult to pick anyone out. 'It was never the same after we moved to Selhurst,' said Lawrie Sanchez. 'The attitude we had in the dressing room was that we had to play 38 away games a year. This didn't really help us. I didn't like Selhurst at all. It was a difficult place to get to and it didn't feel like home.'

The players also missed their favourite haunt – Nelson's, the small nightclub attached to Plough Lane. It was here that the team used to congregate after games, most notably after their FA Cup semi-final victory over Luton Town in 1988. Although Barton was still a newcomer at the club when the Crazy Gang relocated to Selhurst Park, he was aware of its iconic importance. 'After games we used to come out of the changing rooms at Plough Lane and go straight into the chairman's bar,' he said. 'We'd have a drink there and the next thing you knew you were in Nelson's with the supporters. You'd still be there talking to the fans and reminiscing about the game as the disco lights came on.

It was always a really good Saturday night. The Crazy Gang spirit ran through everything at that football ground.'

Behind the scenes, Wimbledon tried to establish an identity separate from Crystal Palace. They had their own offices, and brought their own stewards to the grounds. They even tried to play the odd prank on their landlords, though Palace's players were equally quick to extract revenge should any Wimbledon player interfere with their sugar or clothes. Off the park, the two clubs got along; on the pitch, when the teams clashed, the atmosphere was competitive but respectable. 'There was no animosity between the teams,' Ron Noades confirmed. 'Not even when we played each other. It certainly wasn't like Palace against Millwall or one of those games. The two clubs got along.'

Despite the upheaval, football still seemed to be a relatively simple game for the Crazy Gang. By September 1991 Ray Harford had pushed Wimbledon into seventh place in the League with impressive early-season wins against West Ham, Coventry City and Luton Town, though sadly they'd conceded their first 'home' derby against Palace 3–2 in front of 17,000 fans. Subsequently, Harford's talents were being eyed enviously by other clubs. That month, Blackburn Rovers manager Kenny Dalglish offered him the lucrative number two position at Ewood Park and Harford was tempted. Blackburn might have been a Division Two outfit at the time, but they were bankrolled by the cash of millionaire Jack Walker and looked primed for success. Harford accepted the offer, and Sam found himself managerless yet again.

It was a major loss – one to match that of Plough Lane. Harford had dragged Wimbledon into the top half of the table and kept them there. His talented eye had also brought striker

Robbie Earle to the club from Port Vale in a record £775,000 deal. Infamously, when Earle entered into transfer discussions, Sam had locked the boardroom door mid-meeting before dropping the keys into his underpants. Earle seemed reluctant to commit to Wimbledon and was given two options: the unpleasant task of retrieving freedom for himself or signing a contract with Sam, the latter ensuring a dignified escape route from the building that afternoon. According to legend, Earle duly signed. Elsewhere, Keith Curle was sold to Manchester City for £2.5 million, and Sanch and striker Carlton Fairweather were conspicuous through an injury-plagued absence for much of the season's early stages. Suddenly, Wimbledon were a team in flux. They were also without a manager. The papers began to speculate wildly, claiming that assistant manager Joe Kinnear and former Liverpool player Phil Neale were aiming for the job. Sam even called Joe into his office for a chat, though he remained unimpressed by his demeanour. According to the chairman, Joe lacked a manager's confidence and subsequently talked himself out of the running. When asked for his opinion on the managerial vacancy, Joe even listed a string of potential suitors; what Sam really wanted was for Joe to bring his own CV to the desk. The Phil Neale rumours also came to nothing.

Eventually, after much consideration and a discreet chat with Aston Villa chairman Doug Ellis, Sam employed Peter Withe. As a player, Withe came loaded with pedigree. He had scored the winning goal for Villa in the 1982 European Cup Final and earned eleven England caps in the process. As a manager, however, he was unproven. And his appointment would prove disastrous almost immediately.

On the training ground, Withe was old school. He believed in discipline and order, and unlike Wimbledon's previous taskmaster Don Howe, who seemed malleable and willing to fit into the Crazy Gang's spirit, Withe desperately tried to redesign the club's public image. He enforced a dress code: no beards, no long hair, no earrings; definitely no jeans or trainers; players had to wear suits to training as well as on matchdays. He dropped the recovered Lawrie Sanchez and Alan Cork to the reserves; he brought in Scunthorpe's Mick Buxton as his second in command and demoted Joe. Everybody at the club was alienated within weeks. The players rebelled. When Withe organised a silly-tie competition to galvanise the team, Terry Gibson wrapped a bow tie around his manhood and flashed it during practice. One morning, everybody arrived at the training ground in matching T-shirts.

Meanwhile, the team went into freefall, exiting the League Cup in October after a 2–2 second-leg draw with Peterborough. That the first tie had been a home defeat under Harford's command didn't seem to matter. Withe was made the scapegoat, and disharmony ran riot behind the scenes as Wimbledon plucked only one win from their next seventeen games. They dropped like a stone in the League, plummeting into the relegation zone from seventh place and a shot at European qualification. Worse, the team scored only eight goals. 'I think Peter tried too hard to change the club and stamp his authority,' said Warren Barton. 'If you look at a manager like Arsène Wenger, when he went into Arsenal he knew he didn't have to change the club's spirit, which was the back four at the time. Wimbledon was Peter's first big job. He was trying to make his mark. But he learnt the hard way. Trying to dictate to people wasn't going to work at Wimbledon. And to be honest, he didn't have to change it that much. He tried to fix something that wasn't broken.'

In the stands, Sam was panicking. After much media talk,

Premier League football was arriving the following season. The top flight would be radically improved and boardroom talk focused on the promised TV cash and improved revenue for upper-tier clubs. Consequently, relegation was unthinkable for any First Division team in 1991/92, especially a club like Wimbledon, which could use this lucrative competition to bolster its bank balance. By the time Wimbledon lost to Chelsea at home in January 1992, Sam knew that for the Crazy Gang to survive and profit, Withe would have to go. He'd survived just 104 days in charge.

The subsequent sacking was like something from a Mafia movie. Sam was driving up to Scotland for a couple of days of *goose* shooting (yes, goose shooting) and arranged to meet Withe at a motorway service station. There he delivered the bullet. It was the first time he had ever sacked a manager. Sam later asked Bobby Gould to come back, but, despite his love for the club, Bobby was contracted at West Bromwich Albion. 'I told him to give it to Joe,' he said. Sam knew Joe Kinnear was a man in tune with Wimbledon's personality: he understood the club's mentality and had grown in confidence since their last interview. Fortunately, he was also a good coach and an excellent man-manager. The players loved him too. If Joe could show a little more enthusiasm in his job interview this time, the spot would be his. During the drive home from Scotland, Sam called Joe and explained his plans. This time there was no hesitation. Joe put himself forward and told Sam he was ideal for the job. The chairman agreed. Suddenly, to quote Joe himself, he was 'Johnny on the spot'.

But the Crazy Gang were in real trouble. Joe, more than anyone, knew a huge improvement was required if they were to escape relegation. He told the players during his first team talk before the match against QPR on 1 February that he needed every ounce of their fighting spirit. If they were going to get out of this mess they'd have to win every single game to the end of the season, and by any means necessary. They started encouragingly against QPR, earning a 1–1 draw. Joe then promoted youth-team coach Terry Burton, previously a coach at Arsenal, to the role of assistant manager and watched proudly as his motivational patter further stirred the Crazy Gang's players. Unbelievably, Wimbledon won four of their next five League games, turning over Aston Villa, Manchester City, Oldham and Notts County. According to Sam, Joe had fitted in immediately. He referred to him as a 'genius'.

The players thought so too. Under Peter Withe, Fash had asked for a transfer; suddenly, he seemed happy to stay. Joe informed the press that he'd be scrapping his predecessor's sartorially charged regime. The suits and ties would go; the players, he said, could wear ladies underwear as far as he was concerned. As long as it didn't affect their training or matchday performances he simply wasn't bothered. He'd even endured his traditional initiation ceremony with a smile when, like Harry before him, his bedroom furniture was rearranged around a hotel the night before his first away game (against Aston Villa). Fearing the team would be kicked on to the streets, Joe avoided informing the night manager and slept on the floor. Which was all he could do: his bed had been thrown into the road outside. The team-bonding process quickly gathered pace. After games, Joe would ask his team to vote for the worst player. The offender was then forced to watch the Chekhov play *Uncle Vanya* at the National Theatre. On the training ground, Joe set about restoring the Crazy Gang's team spirit. The pranks were in full force again, and anarchy was encouraged at every turn, though typically Joe, so often the protagonist in many of the practical jokes that rattled around the club, would often leave his players to take the high jinks to their conclusion.

On the sidelines, Sam beamed as wide and as bright as he'd ever done. 'I thought, "He's my man",' he said. 'I will support Joe 100 per cent for ever – and I have done ever since.' His devotion was unsurprising: by April, Joe had ensured the Crazy Gang's involvement in the inaugural year of the Premiership, and Wimbledon would be spoilt with all the trappings and TV cash that would accompany its unveiling. In the meantime, Sam and his cohorts continued their search for a new stadium and an escape from Selhurst Park, though a number of people seemed unconvinced that the club would move back to SW17. 'In the background there were always rumours that we were going to move back to Wimbledon,' said Warren Barton. 'But I think deep down the people upstairs knew that wasn't going to happen.'

But as the 1992/93 season got underway, it was clear that Joe's work the previous year might have created a false dawn. In the summer he had picked up promising striker Dean Holdsworth from Brentford in exchange for a cool million plus the use of Detzi Kruszynski and Mickey Bennett. He also sold Terry Phelan to Manchester City for £2.5 million. Subsequently, the team drew just two points from their first six fixtures, a dismal run that included three home defeats, against Ipswich Town, Coventry City and Manchester City. In the papers, Sam promised free season tickets to every fan should the club walk away with the title, but despite his chairman's public bravado, Joe wasn't smiling. He desperately needed to instil some grit in a team that had just lost Fash in the campaign's early exchanges through a hamstring injury. Only 4,000 fans were visiting Selhurst Park and very little money was coming through the turnstiles. Things were looking bleak.

Dramatically, in September Joe encouraged Vinnie Jones to rejoin the club. Since leaving in 1989, the midfielder had left a trail of studmarks at Leeds, Sheffield United and Chelsea. His reappearance in a Wimbledon shirt for £640,000 cheered both Joe and Sam. 'People wondered why I did it,' said Joe, 'but we were losing a lot of the characters. I like characters to come and create a buzz. It's never a morbid place here, it's close, and if there are a few comedy moments it lifts the mood. I don't want everybody being tedious and boring and miserable. I allow the players to have a laugh and a giggle. As long as they do their jobs, I like to have a laugh and a giggle with them as well.' But it would be a while before the results turned around, and it would take even longer for Vinnie to settle, despite the fact that Joe had made him club captain. He hadn't wanted to leave Chelsea, but the club's managing director, Colin Hutchinson, had convinced him they were looking to sign new players and offered a lucrative signing-on fee of £160,000 (with £80,000 being paid by both clubs). He would also be able to pursue his coaching ambitions at Wimbledon, but still the move was tinged with bitterness. 'Chelsea was a great time for me,' Vinnie said. 'I wish I had never left. But the circumstances didn't allow for that. They sold me and signed Nigel Spackman. I had to go, but you feel like a pawn at Chelsea. They sell you when it suits them.'

Vinnie made his debut against Ipswich on 12 September, a 2–1 defeat. In his second game, a week later against Blackburn Rovers, he was sent off for two yellow cards. The first was flashed for a tackle from behind on Rovers' Kevin Moran; when Vinnie reacted with a blitz of profanities he was hit with another. Away from the pitch he initially felt uncomfortable too. The Wimbledon he'd rejoined was far different from the one he'd left. Sure, his old mate Fash was there, but there was a crop of unfamiliar established players Vinnie had to convince of his role as third coach (behind player-turned-trainer Lawrie Sanchez and Dave Kemp). Settling in would take a while, particularly after his typically hot-headed return. But Joe knew he had secured a good player. 'Vinnie has qualities both on and off the pitch,' he said. 'I should know because I've been a very close friend of his even when he was out of football. He was one of my first buys when I got him back from Chelsea and he's never given me a single moment to regret that. His influence on senior and young players is immense. Unfortunately he has been targeted by certain people who have given him a name which has stuck. He does a hell of a lot outside football to help people out of the goodness of his heart, but never gets the credit he deserves.'

Nobody, least of all the fans, really cared what Joe thought about Vinnie's self-destructive public image because off the pitch more stadium rumours were circulating. Apparently, Sam was taking the club back to Wimbledon, this time to the dog track located on Plough Lane. 'I remember we even had a night out there when we thought it would be our new home,' said Warren Barton. 'But it didn't work out.' Later, more press rumours suggested another merger with Palace was in the offing again. This time the team would be called the Crystal Dons, but Sam reiterated that he was dead set against the idea. Again he claimed he would rather die than amalgamate the two teams.

On the pitch, Wimbledon continued to look as though they were dying a slow, painful death at the bottom end of the table – until March, when the team got their act together, beat Middlesbrough, QPR, Norwich, Crystal Palace (4–0) and Nottingham Forest, and escaped to mid-table security (though only five points clear of the drop zone). Spurs striker Gary Lineker was so unimpressed with their performances he claimed he'd rather watch Wimbledon on Ceefax than on the telly. Vinnie called him 'an arsehole'. It had been a disappointing campaign, but it had its plus points. Their position in the League bagged them a nice little cheque for £407,605 thanks to the Premiership's bonus scheme. The boxes and private suites at Selhurst were bringing in a bit of cash too. It wasn't enough to match the players' wages or to fund the other aspects of life in the top flight, but it was a start.

When the 1993/94 season began, Vinnie was under pressure to be on his best behaviour. A couple of months after his red card against Blackburn Rovers the previous season, Vinnie had been in the shit again when the FA made it clear they were enraged about Vinnie's publicly endorsed video *Soccer's Hard Men*. The compilation film, which depicted a string of horrific tackles from 25 years of football, was garnished with a voiceover from Vinnie. He hadn't even received that much cash for his input – £2,000, less £400 for his agent's involvement. According to Vinnie, the video was sold to him on the basis that a number of other players were also contributing.

Once he'd done his bit, several months passed but the video never appeared. Its rights were passed from film company to film company, until finally it arrived on the shelves just after Vinnie's return to Wimbledon. The cover included an image of the Wimbledon player rather than other players who appeared on the video, and its contents glorified a string of unpleasant challenges, most of which were accompanied by Vinnie's comments. Some 100,000 copies were sold, and the gory details of the video's contents were plastered over the tabloids for days, particularly when Vinnie was reported to have gleefully discussed picking an opponent up by his armpit hairs. The subsequent uproar was like a media time-bomb going off. Sam called him a 'mosquito brain'. Vinnie shamefully donated his £1,600 fee to a children's charity. This didn't hold any sway with the FA however: they fined him a record £20,000 with a six-month ban suspended over three years for good measure. Tabloid journalists dogged Vinnie's every move for much of the 1993/94 season too.

Violence also seemed to be in a regular orbit around Fash. On 24 November, 1993, Wimbledon took on Spurs at White Hart Lane. Despite the fact that the game was played out as a stifling 1–1 draw, the events surrounding it were splashed across the papers the following morning. Typically, the drama centred on the striker. With only seven minutes left on the clock, a long, high ball was punted towards the Wimbledon front line. As Fash and Spurs' centre-back and captain Gary Mabbutt jumped to reach it, Fash rose higher, swinging his elbows to propel himself through the air. An arm caught Mabbutt in the face with a sickening crack and his body dropped to the turf at an unnatural angle.

Time seemed to stand still. As Mabbutt lay prostrate, it was obvious to everybody that the injury was serious. Fash the Bash had struck again. The Spurs defender's cheekbone and eye socket were shattered, and in the interviews that took place after his recovery it was revealed he'd almost lost an eye in the incident. Referee Keith Hackett took no action at the time. He later claimed he hadn't witnessed the clash clearly. On watching the replay he announced that Fash should have been booked for dangerous play. He also noted that there appeared to be a measure of intent in the challenge. In the modern game, Fash would have been sent off. In all probability he would also have been punished with a lengthy ban.

The FA quickly intervened and announced an inquiry. Fash was livid and pleaded his innocence, but the FA were not in a lenient mood. Nevertheless, after trawling through four and a half hours of video evidence, the authorities announced that no charges would be brought against Fash, much to the frustration of Tottenham Hotspur's legal experts who had busied themselves throughout the investigation. 'Spurs had two lawyers in there spouting legal jargon,' Fash told *News of the World* journalists in 1994, 'showing lots of videos from hundreds of angles and piling on the pressure. I took one look at that and thought, "If this is what football is coming to, I want no part of it." Yet all that was hanging over my head was a suspension, not even a fine.'

A number of professionals were quick to condemn publicly Fash's aggressive style of play, claiming that he was 'dangerous and reckless'. Mabbutt, a renowned diplomat, expressed regret that the matter had gone so far, but claimed that nobody was above the law on the football pitch. Today, Fash is keen to point out that the challenge was considered unintentional by the authorities. 'I think most people know it was a complete accident,' he said. 'When I jumped for the ball, I naturally moved my arms up to propel myself – I was known for that. I didn't even know who was beside me, but my sixth sense told me there was another presence there. I tried to win the ball, and when I got up I was injured myself. I wasn't aware Mabbsy's injury was so bad. Mabbsy is one of my best friends and very similar to me – a tiger on the pitch, a gentleman off it – but unfortunately the politics of football came into it. [Spurs chairman] Alan Sugar stuck his oar in, other people got involved, and it turned quite nasty. Yet the tribunal cleared me completely. Mabbsy shook my hand and we moved on. Because I was playing for Wimbledon and because I was Fash the Bash it was blown out of all proportion.' Warren Barton agreed with Fash's assessment of the incident. 'It was sad to see,' he said. 'Obviously a lot of things were being made of the use of the elbow and the arm in football at that stage, so that incident was the next thing to highlight those problems. The fact that he was a Wimbledon player didn't help him. I think if John had been at Norwich or Derby or a club of that nature, the publicity wouldn't have been as bad. Our reputation backfired on us. But that was one thing about Wimbledon: we went out to play hard and fair, but nobody was going out of their way to do anyone, or end anybody's career. That just wasn't in our nature, and it's very sad that people remember Fash for the Gary Mabbutt incident. There was so much more to him than that.'

In the early months of that campaign Sam had been causing trouble too. During the first game of the 1993/94 season, at Upton Park, he scrawled a string of 'inspirational' messages on the dressing-room wall, including 'Vinnie is shit!' West Ham's manager Billy Bonds didn't see the funny side, however, and called the police. Sam was publicly condemned and was quick to apologise. 'What I did was light-hearted and between my players and myself,' he said afterwards. 'We are a lively bunch and would never go around hurting anyone.'

Like Vinnie and Fash, Sam took a media beating. He began to devise his own form of justice for reporters who tarnished the image of the club. A list was drawn up. If any reporter in Sam's black book had the misfortune to arrive at the training ground, they were hijacked. Minor offences – critical think pieces, sneering editorials – were dealt with by dropping a bucket of ice-cold water over the offending journalist's head; for more serious crimes – exposing affairs, stitch-up stories – the water was exchanged for blackcurrant juice. Some writers were not so lucky however: those who were deemed to merit special treatment were stripped and dragged through the mud and dog shit at Wimbledon's training ground, then dropped in a puddle. Sam called it his 'baptism'.

Joe, meanwhile, was trying to live up to a bold prediction he had made before the start of that 1993/94 season: he had claimed his team were worthy of a spot in Europe. Certainly as the season developed the club were in resilient form, beating Manchester City, Norwich and Southampton in September and cruising to fifth place in the newly named FA Carling Premiership. It was their best start to a season for over half a century. Joe even picked up a Manager of the Month award. Fash was regularly hitting the back of the net again, though this may have had something to do with the fact that he was bagging £2,500 per goal.

The cash was coming in handy. Off the pitch, he had been busy and was beginning to take his business responsibilities very seriously. Fash Enterprises now encompassed a number of money-generating interests: he ran a management company called Blue Orchid, which represented the needs of African footballers competing in Europe; he looked after the Nigerian football team's account with the sports company Admiral; and later he started up a building and property maintenance company called Hanler Construction. As if that wasn't enough, he also took on the position of director at the London-based dance radio company Kiss FM. Fash seemed determined to maximise the free time afforded to him. His afternoons were soon eaten away by his spiralling business commitments, and friends and family noted that much of his life was spent working on deals, deals and more deals. Even when he was playing football Fash was forever thinking about the next financial opportunity. One day, after injuring himself during a Wimbledon training session, he was driven to the local hospital in a converted Bedford van with a makeshift siren stuck to the roof and two beds welded into the back. As he fretted about the severity of his injury, Fash also noted that maybe there was money to be made from buying these old vans in bulk, converting them into ambulances, and selling them to Africa. Suddenly the injury was of no concern. 'He was the one who got us all interested in the business side of things,' said Warren Barton. 'I remember we were all chatting one day and John turned round to us and said, "Don't be one of those lads who just goes home and puts on the telly with the *Sporting Life* in front of them. Try and do something with yourself after training."'

Clearly, Fash's desire for financial wealth was driven by his terror of poverty as experienced in the Banardo's home. A fear of hardship had already driven him to succeed on the pitch, and with that secured he was determined to match those accolades in his business deals. During media interviews he spoke of being unable to relax unless he'd achieved something notable that day. He was a workaholic, he said, while speaking warily of the days before his success, the days when he would often tuck himself tightly into bed to create a feeling of security. And Fash had succeeded. His penthouse apartment, which was located between London's Regent's Park and Lord's cricket ground, was lavish. He was rumoured to be earning in the region of £200,000 a year, before goal bonuses. Author Dave Thomas noted: 'Gossip about his riches became so pervasive at the club that their chairman, Sam Hammam, was forced to reveal that three other Wimbledon players earned even more. Alan Cork, the team's longest-serving member, was not convinced, and told John, "I've pledged £100 to Children in Need if you show me your wage packet."'

Later, Joe changed Fash's contract. He paid him £90 a week, with a £10,000-a-goal bonus. Elsewhere, players were picking up around a £1,000 a week, while Joe by his own admission was one of the best-paid managers in the country, earning a whopping £100,000 a year after bonuses. Clearly Premiership status was boosting the Crazy Gang's pay packets, though it was also draining the club bank account. A desire to survive in the top flight had guided Wimbledon's forward thinking too, and Joe picked up midfielder Marcus Gayle from Brentford for £250,000. 'It was a snip,' said Gayle. 'A big snip, by the way.' This attitude probably made his initiation ceremony typically aggressive. 'They hid my clothes,' he moaned. 'Then, when I went back to my room, they'd ransacked it, turned everything upside down – it looked like a bomb had hit it. Still to this day I don't know who was involved. I think Sam the Man may have been behind it. He's absolutely crazy. If there's any craziness, it comes from Sam.'

The craziness and the Premiership cash certainly solidified the team. They claimed some big scalps during 1993/94, including wins over eventual champions Manchester United and runners-up Blackburn Rovers. They were pushing hard for a European spot, and up until the final weeks of the campaign they looked good for it too. Only a 3–2 defeat against strugglers Everton scuppered Joe's dream, though his personal achievements had been recognised and he was later awarded the prestigious Managers' Manager of the Year award.

Sam was equally happy. At the close of the season he announced that the club would be returning to Merton, this time to a planned 25,000-capacity all-seater ground. It would mark another victory for the Crazy Gang and the dawning of a new era away from Selhurst Park. Outside the club, though, nobody was really holding their breath.

CHAPTER TEN

Despite Sam's promise of progress and stability, Fash was off, claiming he wanted a bigger challenge before his career came to an end. But Joe had his own theories as to how and why Fash signed for Ron Atkinson's title-chasing Aston Villa side in the summer of 1994.

Fash had been helping the Nigerian team during the World Cup finals in USA; he had also been filling his spare time by co-commentating for ITV. It was during his work there that Fash struck up a friendship with the charismatic Atkinson, a man who referred to himself affectionately as 'Mr Bojangles'. Joe believed that Fash had been tempted into a lucrative move to Villa Park.

Atkinson, though, had a slightly different take on the events that took Fash to Villa Park. He claimed he had been approached by Fash about the availability of the Nigerian striker Daniel Amokachi – a player Fash was representing along with a number of other notable Nigerian internationals, via his Blue Orchid agency. 'I told him I would be more interested in signing *him*,' Atkinson told reporters shortly after he had signed Fash, 'if he felt he could get away from Wimbledon. I thought his brand of aggression and competitiveness might just give us that little bit extra that we needed to perhaps make us the best … I am quite happy to call Fash my Rottweiler and put him up in the front line just to give my side a bit of snarl. He frightens defenders out of their skins.'

Joe and the club weighed up the pros and cons of Fash's move to Aston Villa. Wimbledon and their manager had come to rely on Fash as a leader who, along with Vinnie, defined Wimbledon's battling spirit. Nevertheless, Wimbledon's humble financial status suggested the club would have to sell one of their playing assets to balance the books: the accounts were littered with payment reminders from the bank, and the club was losing a reported £5,000 a week. According to press reports, the money being generated by ticket sales wasn't enough to cover the wages of half the team. Joe had never before considered selling Fash, such was his importance to the club. Like Vinnie, he was talismanic and hugely difficult to replace both on the pitch and in the dressing room. But Fash was adamant. He wanted to move on, and Joe knew he could get around a million in cash for him, which would also go some way to bringing in younger talent. He told Sam that Fash's sale would be controversial to the fans, but sensible for the club, particularly as Villa were actually offering £1.3 million.

For Sam, the decision was simple. The blossoming football market, where an increased popularity was being accompanied by uncontrollable wage demands, meant the club would have to sell one of their assets. Villa's cash would also go some way towards helping the still-proposed move from Selhurst Park (talk was now focusing on a move to the Wimbledon dog track). In addition, Sam figured that by getting £1.3 million for Fash in full and up front (an important part of the deal), he could put in a £2 million or even £3 million bid on a younger more impressive player and pay half of that transfer up front and the remainder the following year. For both Sam and Joe now felt that Wimbledon were a genuine force in the league. They weren't in the running for the title, but they did pose a serious threat in the cup competitions and could pick up a top-six spot and a place in Europe now that the post-Heysel ban on English clubs had been lifted. They were league underdogs no more.

Fash negotiated the details of the Villa transfer himself, such was his business acumen, but as he signed for Big Ron, former Wimbledon manager Bobby Gould issued a word of advice to his managerial counterpart regarding Fash's levels of commitment. 'He must watch the lad's training habits,' said Bobby. 'I know from my Wimbledon days how Fash would phone in saying he was stuck in traffic on Hammersmith Bridge while we were hard at it in training. I called him one day to talk about his lateness and, thinking of club fines, he said, "Here you are, boss, there's my chequebook and gold card. Give them back after training."'

The meaning was clear. According to Bobby, Fash was more interested in his business activities than football. But it wasn't just business reasons that had kept Fash away from training. He had, on occasions, appeared as a guest presenter on the holiday programme *Wish You Were Here* – in the middle of the season. When Peter Withe was sacked, for instance, Fash was sunning himself on a recording trip. Sam was furious that the club captain had been allowed to leave the country. Fash recalled, 'Sam called and said, "Hey, baby! Where are you?" I told him and he said, "You black bastard! We've sacked the manager, I need you back here. How can I appoint a new manager if my captain is on holiday?"' The subtext was clear: Fash had, at times, become occasionally distracted, with an eye for the high life, or 'The Fash

Lane' as he called it. But in the eyes of Big Ron – a man who owned three Shih-tzu dogs called Bella, Bambi and Bojangles, and who dripped in gold jewellery – Fash would fit in just fine.

Sam's dreams of a new ground were in tatters only days after Fash's move to Villa Park. Plans to sell Plough Lane for redevelopment were rejected by Merton Council, leaving the club in a financially precarious situation, despite the cash from Aston Villa. Defiantly, he vowed never to return to the borough. He felt cheated yet again and saw Wimbledon's future in another part of the capital, though he seemed unsure of exactly where that would be. When fans called Sam's office to voice their disaffection at the club's inability to move from Selhurst Park, he retorted, 'Merton Council are fucking me with the biggest dildo you've ever seen.'

Joe was having his own problems. The sale of Fash and later John Scales in a £3.5 million move to Liverpool alarmed a number of the Crazy Gang's membership. Senior players Warren Barton and Dean Holdsworth in particular seemed unsettled and made want-away noises, which was untimely. Joe responded by stripping Holdsworth of the captaincy and signing travelling veteran striker Mick Harford for £75,000 from Coventry City. On paper, this represented an odd deal: though Harford came with a fearsome reputation, he was old. Many wondered whether at 35 he could last the pace of a season with the Crazy Gang. Nevertheless, at previous club Luton Town he had busted heads with his aggressive aerial ability so regularly that even Vinnie rated his physical prowess. The press speculated that Harford would eschew the Wild West atmosphere of Wimbledon and that his attitude would cause plenty of trauma on and off the pitch, but they were wrong. Harford seemed to fit in just fine and was gently initiated on his arrival. During his first training session with the club, Joe organised short bursts of backward running. As Harford hit full speed, Holdsworth dropped to his hands and knees behind him, bundling him to the turf. Nobody gave a toss that their new striker was suffering from a strained back at the time.

Joe later upped the stakes by signing the Manchester-born Nigerian international Efan Ekoku for a cool million from Norwich City. This was a more positive purchase than the senior Harford. It was also one that could fill the huge gap left by Fash. Ekoku was a renowned striker who had helped win the African Nations Cup in 1994. He also held a record for being the first player to score four goals in a Premiership game, an achievement that was gilted: Ekoku, a Liverpool fan, had blasted four past Everton. The papers joked that, suddenly, Joe had gone 'international'. Ekoku came with a good reputation off the park too. He had previously been employed in double glazing and had played for non-league Sutton before signing for Bournemouth and later Norwich. Strangely, he'd been nicknamed the Chief after his father, a Nigerian tribe leader, arrived to meet him in Bournemouth dressed in traditional costume.

Ekoku was indeed just the sort of player the Crazy Gang needed, but he was walking into a club in crisis. With Sam's development plans in tatters and several high-profile ructions within the playing staff, Wimbledon were not running on full strength in 1994/95. The club captaincy fell to Vinnie, who responded typically by losing his cool, punching Coventry City's David Lowe on the first day of the season and claiming red card number one for the league campaign. The team picked up only five wins in their first fifteen games, losing to Manchester United, Spurs, Forest, Arsenal, Liverpool and Palace. The reason for the club's dip was plain to see: Joe's treatment room was suddenly packed, with Vinnie, Robbie Earle, Mick Harford and Dean Holdsworth all in regular attendance. He began blooding young players from the reserve team, for more new players seemed unlikely given the limited funds available to Sam and the money blown on Ekoku. Joe had earlier informed the press hacks that he couldn't afford to shop for new players in pricey stores (though given Ekoku's signing, this was disingenuous); Wimbledon would have to rely on the bargain basement from now on.

A snip deal arrived almost overnight. Shrewdly, Joe signed Norwegian international Oyvind Leonhardsen on a three-month loan from Rosenborg. A virtual unknown outside the Norwegian leagues, Leonhardsen was a 25-year-old midfielder who seemed something of an oddball to the football world. Sure, he had talent and dedication, having won three Norwegian championships with Rosenborg and a Norwegian Player of the Season award, but he carried none of the attitude or swagger of his English peers. Still, he seemed tireless: he'd just played fifteen months of football without a break or a moan, his spell comprising a Norwegian season and a World Cup tournament. In his country he was also renowned for being an honest individual with a passion for the game: when he signed for his first club Molde, he didn't ask for an extortionate amount of money, just enough to get him by on food and rent. Later, as he became established in the Norwegian game, he helped to produce a road safety video for kids.

'Players [in Norway] are encouraged to study or do something constructive when they are not playing football,' he explained. 'After training I used to go to schools with the police and I would put on this sketch which I would do to try and teach children. We took along a guy who was in a wheelchair – it was supposed to say, "OK, I'm a footballer, but this could happen to anybody."'

As a Premiership footballer, he was a godsend – not that the Crazy Gang treated him as such, however. During his first day at the office, Leo, as the players quickly nicknamed him, watched as his suit was cut to shreds. He laughed – he'd been made aware of Wimbledon's reputation before his arrival – but despite the mickey-taking and the light-hearted nature of his induction Leo's new team-mates seemed unsure of his suitability. Many felt he was too small to cope with their robust style of football (he was five foot ten, relatively short by the Crazy Gang's standards), Vinnie in particular. 'The manager's lost his mind,' he said with a laugh when Leo arrived. 'He's signed Jimmy Clitheroe.'

Vinnie wasn't smarting on Saturday, 9 November, when, on his debut, Leo popped up to score the winning goal in injury time to complete a 4–3 victory over Aston Villa. As he fired the ball into the back of the net he ran to the crowd and was swamped by the Wimbledon fans. Sam ran on to the pitch to hug him too. Joe knew there and then that he wanted to hand Leo a permanent contract. From that moment on the Crazy Gang and Leo fell in love. Norwegian wings of the Wimbledon supporters' club sprang up overnight, and within weeks Leo was teaching his new mates how to swear in his native language. When Scandinavian camera crews arrived to film him in training, a number of Wimbledon players shouted out their new vocabulary from behind a bush.

Leo's signing seemed to spark off a streak of form. After a couple of defeats against Manchester City and Blackburn, the club embarked on an eight-game unbeaten run, stamping on Coventry City, Ipswich Town and Everton among others. Suddenly, with the team in ascendance, Joe began to talk again about European qualification. 'Mmm, Wimbledon against Inter

Milan,' he mused. 'It's got a nice ring to it. Let's go and frighten the life out of a few foreigners.'

The press lapped this sort of thing up, and Joe loved feeding them quotes. He enjoyed frightening the life out of them too. On the training ground, as the sports reporters gathered for a story, Joe and Sam would order the first team to terrorise them. It was a simple hit-and-run affair as the players, usually led by Vinnie and disguised with balaclavas, would soak the press pack with buckets of ice-cold water, ruining their camera gear and drenching their notes. Sam would always lay the blame on the youth team. He promised the bedraggled writers that if anyone could be identified the culprits would be punished. Of course, nobody ever was.

Joe was now making his mark in training. He ordered the players to start playing the ball across the deck, hoping to shatter Wimbledon's stereotypical image as long-ball merchants. Like his predecessors, Joe was suffering from the age-old dilemma: a long ball played by any other team was a cultured pass, but a long ball played by Wimbledon was booted from football's dark ages. This time, however, Joe was determined to mix it up, and during matches quick passes were fired into areas where his team were renowned for getting results – in the box, to the wings – while in team talks his tactical knowledge would often expose Wimbledon's supposedly cultured opponents. As preparation for this, Joe would watch video after video. Once weaknesses were pinpointed – a dodgy full-back, an aerial shortcoming in central defence – he would order the players to assault them relentlessly. Despite the intelligent tactical masterstrokes and rapidly improving results, Joe's tactics were still greeted with derisory snorts from his peers. 'They're kicking the ball 50 yards instead of 60,' sniffed Norwich manager Mike Walker. 'We now play football as good as any side,' retorted Joe, though he knew that deep down nobody was ever going to give his team the credit they deserved.

But the snide remarks never smarted. Joe was hard nosed; he always had been, having endured a tough upbringing. His dad had died when Joe was seven, and he moved from his Dublin home to Watford with his mum and four sisters. He took on several part-time jobs to support the family, delivering papers and running errands, and later took up a trade in printing. When football came calling he signed for non-league St Albans, and then Spurs, where he served under Bill Nicholson and was immortalised in Hunter Davies's book *The Glory Game* as an imposing, smooth and confident player – 'very sociable and outgoing, with a smile for everyone'. He later moved to Brian Clough's Brighton but was forced out of the game following an injury to his cruciate ligaments. He was devastated, but he soon set out on a winding managerial road that took him first to Sharjah in Dubai and then to Doncaster, before joining Bobby Gould as reserve-team coach at Wimbledon. He fell in love with the club and Plough Lane almost immediately. The players would drink in the local pubs and eat full English breakfasts in a nearby café where the bacon sarnies were regularly accompanied by a dollop of fag ash from a chain-smoking chef, and when it came to matchdays his Portakabin office was flooded with the aroma of frying onions and chips from the nearby fast-food stall. The down-at-heel atmosphere suited him just fine.

Joe's success came as no surprise to those who knew him. He wasn't a disciplinarian like his predecessor Peter Withe, but he was hard. He allowed the players to fool around, but there was a limit to his patience. His players could enjoy themselves, provided they stuck to the club's code of conduct. If they got out of line, he would come down on them as hard as any of the game's notorious disciplinarians, his friend Alex Ferguson among them. He didn't believe in fines either, so long as the club wasn't being disregarded. If it was an internal matter, Joe would deal with it man to man; if it involved a shirking of duties – missed training, taking the piss out of the club – he would throw the book at them. By the same token, his door was always open to players with problems.

But if Wimbledon suited Joe to a tee, then he provided the perfect match for Wimbledon too, most notably when it came to defending the club's image. If his team was criticised or treated unfairly, he would hit back as hard as Vinnie or Mick Harford or Warren Barton. But Joe would always use his gob rather than his fists or feet. The authorities often came down on him with equal force as a result. After a 2–1 defeat at Norwich in January 1995, Joe was fined for hurling a wave of criticism at match referee Mike Reed. In early March he was dismissed from the touchline during the 1–0 defeat against Manchester United for protesting too enthusiastically at match officials. He called Mike Reed a 'little Hitler' after another game and claimed Paul Alcock comprised all cock and no balls. And when he told the Newcastle crowd at St James's Park to fuck off, he was overheard by a policeman and fined £20,000 by the FA.

From the stands, Sam loved every minute of Joe's chest-beating. 'Joe will be able to walk the Atlantic in a storm when he's done all he has to do for us,' he said. The fans loved Joe too. He'd marked their team with the same spirit as Harry and Bobby, but he'd injected some much-needed flair as well with the likes of Ekoku, who scored nine goals in 24 starts, and Leo, who was now a top-of-the-range cult hero. Wimbledon finished the season in a creditable ninth place; the failure to improve on the previous season's position was put down to another year dogged by injuries. Mick Harford, Vinnie Jones, Robbie Earle and Andy Thorn, who had returned to the club from Crystal Palace in October 1994, all endured stints on the treatment table. On the pitch, the only major reverse was a 7–1 defeat in February at the hands of Villa.

Some of Joe's players were beginning to receive international recognition too: Warren Barton was selected for England in the late winter of 1995. But eager to underplay Wimbledon's achievement, Sam would always greet such news with a practical joke. Most players called up for international duty had their tyres let down in the club car park. 'Yeah, but we got our own back,' said Barton. 'We'd always beat him at Trivial Pursuit for money.' Their overseas international, Leo, clearly loved the club too, especially once he'd signed from Rosenborg on a permanent basis for £700,000. In the summer of 1995 the cut clothes seemed a million years away, though he still couldn't believe how much the Crazy Gang loved getting drunk after games. He looked even more confused as he watched Sam parading an elephant around Selhurst Park following the final game of the season.

Just as fines and FA disciplinary meetings seemed to hit Joe's wallet and diary during 1994/95, Vinnie too was being reprimanded by officialdom at every turn. For some reason he just couldn't seem to stay out of the headlines. In November he was sent off for two yellow cards during a 3–2 win against table-toppers Newcastle. A media storm erupted around him, though according to his team-mates Vinnie wasn't the hellraiser of tabloid myth. Ekoku claimed that the press were blowing his reputation out of proportion, and that he was a 'nice chap' – though he was quick to point out that he did enjoy making his way into the limelight. But this, reflected Ekoku, was probably a good thing: Vinnie's enthusiasm and desire spurred on his team-mates.

But worse was to come in February when Vinnie was dispatched to Dublin by the *News of the World* to write a column on England's friendly against the Republic of Ireland. This game should have sparked a celebration for Wimbledon as Vinnie's team-mate Warren Barton was making his first full England appearance, but the game was abandoned when crowd trouble erupted in the stands. This was a minor detail in Vinnie's day, however. He'd already courted controversy after spotting Gary Lineker in the Jurys Hotel that morning. Demanding payback for the Ceefax jibe a couple of seasons ago, Vinnie hurled abuse and threw a slice of toast at the former England international turned TV pundit. To add insult to injury, he called Lineker 'big ears' too. The chaos continued when a crowd of journalists and pundits descended on the Jurys Hotel bar to collate their notes for the following day's press reports. Vinnie, now without a column to write after the game's abandonment, began drinking champagne. He wasn't drunk – a little oiled perhaps – but when *Daily Mirror* journalist Ted Oliver offended him with a gentle joke, he grabbed him in a headlock and sank his teeth into Oliver's nose. A kerfuffle exploded around him. One eyewitness later described the attack as leaving 'a hole' in Oliver's flesh. Vinnie desperately tried to apologise. 'It was a joke,' he explained, but his victim was unimpressed. 'Tell me what I can do to make it up to you,' pleaded Vinnie. 'I'll do anything, I swear on my boy's life.' Oliver retained his air of indifference; he was determined the story would be splashed all over the *Mirror* the following morning.

By the time Vinnie arrived at Stansted airport the next day the incident was national news. The press began to tail him from the car park as his wife Tanya called him tearfully on the phone. Apparently, journalists were camped outside the family home too, waiting for him to return. Ted Oliver's nose bled all over the cover of the *Daily Mirror*, and it was dripping all over the TV stations and radio waves too.

When he got home, Vinnie locked himself away. This was his darkest moment. As the paranoia and remorse oozed from his pores in a listless panic attack, he decided to blow his brains out with a twenty-bore shotgun. He chose his moment when Tanya went shopping at the local supermarket. Once she'd left the house, Vinnie walked to a small wooded area nearby in the wind, the rain and the dark. He sat down on an old oil drum he'd often used for a seat when he went pigeon shooting. He nursed the trigger, then suddenly spotted his Jack Russell dog Tessie playing in the garden. Watching her for ten minutes seemed to snap Vinnie out of his depression. He walked back to the house and put the gun away.

That night, he told Tanya everything.

He subsequently apologised to Sam and Joe for his behaviour, though he spared them the details of his trip to the woods. Both were sympathetic, but they explained he'd let the club down and would have to face up to his responsibilities. So Vinnie sat out the next game, against Liverpool. *News of the World* editor Piers Morgan was equally unhappy and ended up sacking him, though deep down he probably loved the thought of a correspondent tearing the nose off a rival hack with his teeth.

Elsewhere, things were looking bleak for another member of the Crazy Gang: while Vinnie contemplated blowing his brains out with a shotgun, Hans Segers was having his door kicked in by the police. The goalkeeper had somehow been implicated in a match-fixing scandal that was alleged to have connections with a corrupt betting ring in the Far East. Fash and Liverpool goalkeeper Bruce Grobbelaar had also been named and were receiving equally unpleasant visits at 6.30 a.m. before being hauled away for questioning. It looked like a bad deal. According to the investigators ransacking Segers's house for evidence, these arrests were taking place after an undercover reporter had exposed Grobbelaar during a newspaper sting. A former business associate of the goalkeeper, Malaysian entrepreneur Richard Lim, had fallen out with Grobbelaar over a cash dispute and had eagerly given details of his former partner's alleged business activities to the tabloid press. Another undercover reporter, during a bogus meeting with Grobbelaar, captured the finer details of the rigging process on a hidden microphone.

The press went into overdrive. Segers had been implicated, they claimed, because of a game involving Everton on the final day of the 1993/94 season. Wimbledon were swaggering at the end of their greatest ever performance in the League, while their opponents battled relegation and required a victory to ensure survival. This had looked unlikely after the Crazy Gang stormed into a 2–0 lead, but Everton picked up a quick reply, then an equaliser, then a winner. One of the goals was embarrassingly soft, a Graham Stuart strike that seemed to be a miscue and trickled past Segers's arm. At the time Joe was livid, and as the team trudged back to the dressing room he accused Segers of throwing the game for a bet, though deep down he didn't really mean it. The keeper claimed the ball had pinged off a divot and flipped over his outstretched arm, but in light of the Lim accusations the press were claiming foul play. As the news hit, Vinnie was offered £100,000 by a tabloid paper to put the finger on Fash and his involvement in the scheme, but he refused and gave his former team-mate the nod. Fash assured him that he had had nothing to do with a match-fixing scam. Vinnie was satisfied, though the police weren't. Segers, meanwhile, was released on bail, but Joe dropped him from the team. He would play only a handful of games in the next year. This was one stink Joe didn't need.

The scandal and subsequent investigations ran throughout the 1995/96 season, though Vinnie and Sam did their best to overshadow Segers in a typically forthright manner. Vinnie looked every bit the limelight grabber, with red cards against Liverpool, Nottingham Forest and Chelsea, the latter accompanied by assertions that the latest foreign influx to greet the Premiership that season – Gullit, Bergkamp, Zola et al. – often cried like 'pot-bellied pigs' when caught in a tackle. He appeared on the cover of a football magazine dressed as a referee while brandishing a red card, and later made a speech at Eton College, which included Prince William among its students. He even played in goal for 40 minutes during the October defeat against Newcastle after Paul Heald had been sent off, though it proved disastrous as Wimbledon lost 6–1. 'That was a laugh,' he proclaimed cheekily afterwards.

Sam, meanwhile, was still debating property and ownership matters. When the possibility arose of a sale to investors, he retorted that flogging Wimbledon would be akin to raping his own daughter, though another ground move was yet again very much on the cards. A Welsh businessman, Peter Thomas, claimed he'd been chatting to Sam about the possibility of a move to Cardiff, but these reports were soon dismissed by the club. Months later, as Wimbledon clawed their way to Premiership safety yet again after another disappointing league campaign (they finished the

1995/96 season in 14th place). Joe was shooting his mouth off. 'My players hate playing here [Selhurst Park],' he moaned after a 1–0 home win over Forest at the end of March 1996. 'It's like a morgue. The sooner we move to Dublin the better.'

The alarm bells began to ring even louder – the mention of Dublin was a new one on Wimbledon fans. Joe later withdrew the statement, apologising to supporters for any confusion he may have caused, but it was too late. The club, forever exploiting an endless loophole of squatter's rights, were obviously on the move again, and with the lease at Selhurst Park running out in 1997 the question was not only when, but where? Whispers began to circulate that a high-profile Irish consortium was preparing a takeover bid to whisk them away to Ireland, as Joe had indicated. The group was rumoured to involve the journalist and former Irish international Eamon Dunphy as well as U2 manager Paul McGuiness. A personal invitation to Wimbledon asking them to consider a move to Ireland from Jonathan Irwin of the Dublin International Sports Council only furthered the gossip. 'Of all the Premiership clubs, Wimbledon stick out like a sore thumb,' he said. 'They're homeless and they play to very small crowds. If they played in Dublin they'd play to full houses every week and people would get an opportunity to watch Premiership football in the flesh rather than on Sky. The city of Dublin deserves a Premiership club, and it has the means to acquire it.'

Wimbledon's fans felt they had hit rock bottom. Getting to Selhurst Park was troublesome enough, but Dublin? It would prove impossible. There was uproar in Ireland too. Local fans claimed the IRA would take action should Wimbledon and their Premiership rivals begin appearing in Dublin. The Irish FA began speculating whether Wimbledon's arrival would signal the end of their domestic leagues – after all, local clubs received smaller gates than Wimbledon. If Premiership super clubs began skipping across the Irish Sea with the likes of Zola, Klinsmann and Beckham in tow, what chance would they have to attract new fans? It was a deal nobody seemed to want, but Wimbledon's interest was understandable. If the consortium did take over with a rumoured £110 million bid, part of that money would be available to strengthen the squad.

The Premier League was dismissive, claiming that Sam would be forced to relinquish his League status if the club relocated to Ireland, while the media speculated on possible moves to Cardiff (a new ground to be shared with Cardiff City), Blackpool (a new ground to be shared with Blackpool), Wigan (another new ground, though this time to be shared with Wigan's rugby league club – 'Because they play a similar style of football,' quipped one fan), and the ever-present promise of a redeveloped Plough Lane or Wimbledon greyhound track. The fans had heard it all before, as had the players, who through all the talk were making tricky business of their day jobs. They only ensured survival two games from the end of the season. At least they were beginning to shake off their reputation as long-ball merchants. Now, with the ball being played intelligently on the deck at Joe's request, the Crazy Gang had to endure claims that they'd lost their bottle. It seemed to Joe that they just couldn't please anybody.

And if all that wasn't bad enough for the club, the Bosman ruling of 1995 and TV's gold rush moved the goalposts yet again. Expensive overseas players, the likes of whom were unaffordable to Wimbledon, were in vogue. Approximately 32 per cent of players in the Premiership at the start of the 1996/97 season were foreign. Homegrown footballers approaching contract expiry were allowed to walk away for free under the Bosman rule, and with restrictions lifted on the number of European players permitted per squad, cheap foreign staff were being signed instead of their more expensive British counterparts – the sort from whom Wimbledon made their money in the transfer market. To top it all, the Premier League was cutting the number of clubs in the division from 22 to 20. Sam finally sold Plough Lane, Wimbledon's home for 79 years, to supermarket chain Safeway for £9 million to put an end once and for all to the dream of a spiritual return there. With the odds stacked against them in the league and transfer market like never before, to Sam it seemed as if authority was trying to tear his dreams away while kicking the Crazy Gang back to non-league football.

Their Premiership peers seemed eager to kick them out of the league too, and when, on the opening day of the 1996/97 season, David Beckham curled a speculative shot from inside his own half over the head of goalkeeper Neil Sullivan (Segers had been released on a free transfer), the Crazy Gang seemed destined for whipping-boy status. The goal was later hailed as the strike of the season, and it helped propel Beckham towards superstardom. 'It was not funny, I can tell you,' Ekoku remarked. 'Neil Sullivan got a lot of stick from us for leaving his line, but who on earth could have imagined it would go in? It was one of those freak goals … you can't be too hard on him.'

The team was changing dramatically. The sale of Warren Barton to Newcastle for £4 million the previous season had weakened the defence, and a number of bit-part players had left on frees, leaving Joe only £2 million to blow on Millwall's tenacious full-back Ben Thatcher as his only major signing of the season. The lack of new additions didn't bother the Wimbledon squad, however. With a powerful front line of Marcus Gayle and Efan Ekoku, a midfield that boasted the international experience of Vinnie Jones (now playing for Wales) and Leo, and the Scottish goalkeeper Neil Sullivan impressing with every game, Wimbledon were chasing Europe for much of the season. There were some impressive youth players coming through the ranks too. During the 1995/96 season striker Jason Euell had marked his debut with an impressive scissors kick that screamed into the back of the net. Throughout the 1996/97 season he would regularly impress with substitute performances.

Wimbledon found themselves sitting in joint second place during the early stages of the season. Indeed, so impressive were their aggressive performances against more cultured opposition that the Danish coaching team visited Selhurst Park to watch them play. Wimbledon rampaged through a nineteen-game unbeaten streak, and a number of bigger, richer clubs eyed Joe enviously. Well, he had picked up the 1996 Sky Manager of the Year award after all. Suddenly ground attendances were up by 50 per cent as the club were in sole ownership of second place come December.

Good runs in both the FA and Coca-Cola Cup competitions debilitated fitness dramatically, however, and after falling from both tournaments at the semi-final stage a lack of squad strength pushed Wimbledon into a tailspin. Six games without a win during March and April effectively killed off their European hopes, but the team had enjoyed an impressive season, finishing in eighth place. Unbelievably, they'd also picked up the Fair Play award, which went some way towards diminishing their thuggish image – though Vinnie, as always, seemed to thrive on disharmony. He was fined £6,000 by Joe and Sam for slagging off his team-mates in a national newspaper. In private, the Crazy Gang laughed their heads off. He had described Leo as being 'terminally boring' after all. So, despite the rumours and scandals, authorities' attempts to price them out of the game and several personnel changes, yet again the Crazy Gang seemed stronger than ever.

CHAPTER ELEVEN

By the start of the 1997/98 season the Crazy Gang were undergoing a major facelift. For the first time since Sam's complete takeover in 1981, Wimbledon were being bankrolled by new major investors: Norwegian businessmen Kjell Inge Rokke – one of the five richest men in Europe – and Bjorn Rune Gjelsten, a duo who had made their money in oil, paper, fishing, ships and property. Unusually, they were fans of powerboat racing, the nautical equivalent of Formula One, and Gjelsten would later become a world champion in the sport in 1998. But football was a passion too, and the pair had been looking to invest money in an English club where profit appeared at a premium.

Certainly Rokke and Gjelsten made an impressive business team and possessed the clout to take on a challenge of Wimbledon's stature. They also owned Norwegian side Molde, having rescued the club from bankruptcy in 1992. According to legend, Rokke and Gjelsten had scribbled their plans on the back of an envelope while travelling to their first business meeting with the club's then owners. And when they finally took over at Molde, they responded to relegation in their first season by helping the team to immediate promotion and a Norwegian cup the following year. Within years, Molde were competing in the Champions League, drawing Real Madrid and entertaining Europe's greats in a brand-new stadium worth over £25 million. Rokke and Gjelsten claimed to have similar plans for the Crazy Gang. Admittedly, they'd initially looked at investing in Leeds United (Gjelsten was a fan), but later they'd been seduced by Wimbledon's romantic tales of triumph over adversity. They signed away a reported £28 million for an 80 per cent share in the summer of 1997. But Sam's bargain-driving meant the ownership of the club would remain in his control, despite a greatly diminished share. The Norwegians weren't too bothered. Sam had claimed that if Wimbledon moved to Dublin, as was still being mooted, they'd become Ireland's biggest team and Rokke and Gjelsten's investment could subsequently grow into a business worth £100 million. 'We came to Wimbledon because of Sam Hammam,' said Gjelsten. 'He was quite a character and we liked the underdog image of a small club fighting with the big guys. That's the way we grew up in Norway. We came from a small place and we built our business that way. The plan was always to work alongside him.'

For Wimbledon's fans, this was yet another confusing subplot in their club's skewed story. But Sam and Joe were pleased with the cash boost – after all, the club was losing £500 a day and both knew this financial situation could sour even further. Sure, the vulgar cash sums from Sky TV and other sponsorships flooding Premiership clubs meant that the standards within football's infrastructure were rising, but still Wimbledon weren't making enough money to compete with the big names.

Despite this, Joe was buying Premiership stars and Sam was paying top wages, while their team only attracted lower league attendances. It was a poor return. Meanwhile, the Bosman ruling had damaged Wimbledon on two fronts. Firstly, clubs were overlooking homegrown players – players from whom Wimbledon made their money in the transfer market – and buying cheaper, foreign imports. However, these foreign prices were still largely unaffordable to Wimbledon. Sam and Joe were competing at a huge loss and facing disaster. The appearance of Rokke and Gjelsten would provide some breathing space. With their money, Sam could attempt to halt the negative cash flow and force Wimbledon into Europe.

Regardless of their new benefactors, business carried on as usual behind the scenes. Sam and Joe still conducted many of their meetings in the local greasy spoon, where decisions and transfer deals were often contemplated over fry-ups and dirty coffee mugs. Rokke and Gjelsten liked this casual approach to office hours, and the pair were allowed to work away from the club. In the press Sam assured Wimbledon's fans that Rokke and Gjelsten were not 'sugar daddies' to the Crazy Gang. To the casual observer, then, nothing had changed.

Some of the players, though, were unimpressed with their new bosses. Leo wanted away, especially as Liverpool had shown an interest in his ability. He'd always been ambitious and was always up front with Joe and Sam about viewing Wimbledon as a stepping stone to bigger things, so naturally Anfield appealed to him. Joe wasn't going to stand in his way either – he was making £3.5 million from the deal. As with so many players before Leo, including Warren Barton, Fash and John Scales, the club had bought small and sold big. One magazine subsequently compared Joe to fictional antiques wheeler-dealer Lovejoy. 'We turn the unfinished article into polished gems,' Sam noted with a beaming smile.

But then Sam was pleased with any extra cash coming into

the club, for despite the Norwegians' involvement, financially things remained grey. The Football League seemed determined to litter the Crazy Gang's path with obstacles. Plans to create a European Super League, from which Wimbledon could undoubtedly expect exclusion – the league, claimed the rumour-mongers, would be for elite teams only – had received enthusiastic nods from several club chairmen. Simultaneously there were whispers of reducing the Premiership to sixteen teams – a change that could easily see Wimbledon dropping to the First Division, given an indifferent season. 'It's going to be more or less impossible for us to stay up if that happens,' said Joe. To survive, Wimbledon needed the Premiership's cash, and the sponsorship deals and TV money that accompanied its membership. Enlarging the drop zone would only increase their chances of relegation and financial ruin. Joe knew it was a rough deal. Again, he saw it as another example of football's sneering attitude towards his team. 'The richer clubs are going to get richer and richer,' he explained. 'Fuck everyone else. The top six are making noises about a European Super League, and where does that fucking leave everyone else? Two teams from London in the European League, and what are the rest of us going to do?'

At the same time the Premiership boom was moving into top gear, transfer fees and pay cheques spiralling out of control. Sam worried that his club would be unable to compete with the salaries paid at richer clubs, with or without the Norwegians' investment, and would suffer in the transfer market. The quality would simply be out of reach. If anyone was going to fall behind as the Premiership raced to opulence, it was going to be Wimbledon. Their time in the top flight seemed limited, and Sam warned fans in his programme notes that their club could soon be 'kicking the bucket' if they didn't act fast. It was a sad admission: English football's new-found exclusive status meant that any climb from the lower leagues to the top flight, similar to the one enjoyed by Sam over the last fifteen years or so, would be impossible without financing of gigantic proportions. Authority and greed, it seemed, had killed the small club's dream.

Wimbledon were facing an uphill struggle for survival in the top flight as the 1997/98 season got underway. Joe admitted that he began every league campaign a desperately worried man, given the limited resources at his disposal. Sam understood his predicament. Rather than simply ordering him to deal with it, the owner often lent a helping hand. 'He's unique in that he scouts with me,' said Joe. 'He'll tell me he's heard there's a good player at Grimsby, and we'll drive up there and have a look. I can't go and look at the top players because they wouldn't join us ... I'm envious when I see that [the then West Ham manager] Harry Redknapp has bought [midfielder and later, England International] Trevor Sinclair. I sit there and think, "Fucking hell, I wish I could get my hands on him." And [the then Chelsea manager] Gianluca Vialli ain't going to be thinking, "Have those kids [in the youth team] over there got a chance of making it in four or five years' time?" He'll be thinking, "I'll go to AC Milan next week and get so-and-so there." They're buying instant success.'

As the league campaign began, on the sidelines Sam was being battered at every turn. Despite protestations from the Football Association of Ireland, rumours of a move to Dublin were still rattling around the boardroom. Sam was hungry for it and did little to dispel the whispers, claiming that relocation to Ireland was a fantastic and 'sexy' move for the club. Joe was equally enthused by the idea, as was Irish prime minister

Bertie Ahern. But Wimbledon's fans were in uproar, and another protest group moved into action. Banners plastered with the catchphrase 'Dublin = Death' peppered Selhurst Park's terraces. Supporters' club leaders moved into political overdrive, staging protests and engaging the media with interviews and petitions. Joe became angry, arguing that the fans should spend more time supporting their team. Whether these demonstrations had any effect is unclear, though the sabre rattling was ultimately unnecessary. UEFA later waved aside the proposed Dublin switch, leaving Sam back at square one. Rokke and Gjelsten would not be overseeing Ireland's biggest club and a business worth £100 million; instead, they were going to be tenants at Selhurst Park for the foreseeable future, unless drastic action was taken.

Sympathy for the Norwegians was in short supply, however. In February 2002 in a speech at the launch of the Dons Trust – an organisation founded to help combat moves such as the one proposed for Wimbledon – Lord Faulkner of Worcester, a Wimbledon supporter, argued that Rokke and Gjelsten had been lazy in their assessment of the club. 'Most people are convinced that the prospect of opening up Premier League football in the Irish Republic was what persuaded the Norwegians to buy Wimbledon in the first place,' he said. 'What a pity that their financial advisers didn't bother to consult the Football Association of Ireland or UEFA or FIFA in advance. If they had, they would have realised that moving a club from one country to another would never find favour with the governing bodies.'

The only obvious way forward now was for Sam to eat humble pie and rely on Merton Council and a move back to Wimbledon, though journalists continued their speculation, this time on two planned moves: one to Gatwick and one to Hull, via a deal with Hull City chairman David Lloyd. Sam refused to comment on either.

On the park the 1997/98 season quickly became a struggle as the team capitulated under injury. Wimbledon managed just four victories in the opening sixteen Premiership games, their biggest losses coming against West Ham at the end of August (3–1) and Manchester United on 22 November (5–2). The wins had come against decent opposition – the likes of Newcastle, Aston Villa and Leeds – so Joe was at a loss to explain why his team were suffering.

In the dressing room Vinnie was contemplating his immediate future. He'd been tempted by an offer from Queens Park Rangers to join them as a player-coach. In March 1998 he decided to leave the Crazy Gang for the final time, having played over 250 games. 'At that point,' he said, 'the idea of management was all I wanted to do.' He then added that the move had 'left a lump in his throat'. Without Vinnie (and not for the first time), Wimbledon seemed drained of any fighting spirit, and they finished the season in fifteenth place. Joe's side had also lost the services of Dean Holdsworth, who had moved to Bolton for £3.5 million in October 1997.

And if the poor results weren't enough to give Joe and Sam a headache, yet another match-fixing scandal was dogging Wimbledon, though again they were involved only through bad luck. Fash, Segers and Grobbelaar had been acquitted of match-rigging charges in the summer of 1997, but when the floodlights popped during Wimbledon's game against Derby at Pride Park that same year, rumours of an elaborate swindle began to unravel in the papers. Initially, nobody was aware of an underhand plot when referee Uriah Rennie abandoned the game, even though Derby were at a loss as to why the power had failed. 'We had eleven maintenance people on duty, including six electricians,' said a club spokesman, 'but nobody has yet worked out why both generators failed. There was a bang of such strength that it fused them both.' A further match between West Ham and Crystal Palace was abandoned, and when the Selhurst Park floodlights failed yet again during the Crazy Gang's game against Arsenal, alarm bells began to sound. With only thirteen seconds on the clock, the ground was plunged into darkness. They were restarted nearly a quarter of an hour later, only to fuse again. Referee Dermot Gallagher abandoned the tie. 'This shouldn't be happening,' fumed Sam. 'Once was bad enough, the second wasn't pretty, and this is getting near a disaster. Unless we stop it, there will be shame on the game. We are all embarrassed by it.'

The police struggled to pinpoint any firm evidence of a malevolent plot, but four Malaysian men – part of another alleged betting syndicate – were later arrested after they'd been caught trying to break into Charlton's ground in an attempt to force an abandonment of a match. They'd planned to meddle with the floodlights and so fix the result. Security guard Roger Firth told police that he'd been offered £20,000 to allow the four men access to Charlton's floodlights.

Still, some positives could be taken from the season, despite the team's relentless battle against relegation. Debutant strikers Carl Cort and Carl Leaburn, both of whom were youngsters, had impressed. At six foot four inches Cort was a beanpole – he later drew comparisons to the Arsenal and Nigerian maverick Nwankwo Kanu – but he was no aerial powerhouse. Still, he'd thrived in front of goal with the Wimbledon youth teams. Former youth-team coach Terry Burton had noticed him when Cort was only fourteen; he reckoned he had an impressive touch for a player of his age. When he partnered Jason Euell up front in a youth-team game, Burton reckoned he had 'one hell of a partnership on his hands', even though Cort was raw. He was farmed out to Lincoln City on loan at the beginning of the 1997/98 season, and when Joe recalled him in September for the match against Newcastle at St James's Park, he scored within two minutes on his debut. He went on to score six goals in sixteen games that season, and claimed a handful of England U-21 appearances too, though as a shy kid he felt overwhelmed with the pressures of fame at Wimbledon. 'Even when I wasn't playing I had people coming up to me asking for autographs,' he said. 'The first time it happened it was really odd, because I was getting into my car and this bloke came up to me and asked me if I was that guy who played for Wimbledon. I didn't know what to do because I was so shocked. I just shook his hand and sort of said, "Er, yeah, I am." It happens when I go out for a drink too. If people in nightclubs and pubs recognise you they want to buy you a drink and shake your hand.'

There were other young players impressing on the pitch, and for spells of the season the starting line-up comprised a spine of homegrown players, including keeper Neil Sullivan, centre-back Chris Perry (a one-time Wimbledon fan nicknamed 'The Rash' because he was often found 'all over' his opponents when he marked them), Peter Fear, Neil Ardley, Stuart Castledine and Dean Blackwell. And sales had also allowed Joe to invest in some impressive mid-scale signings: he brought in Northern Ireland's international midfielder Michael Hughes from West Ham for £1.6 million and Mark Kennedy from Liverpool for £1.5 million. Both signings' cultured style of play forced pundits to speculate on whether this was the final nail in the coffin for the long-ball game. The Crazy Gang dismissed any thoughts of maturing by stripping Hughes on the training ground and dragging him through the mud. They also sliced the heels from his shoes and the collars and legs from his suit with a knife.

For Joe, these signings marked an encouraging change in fortunes. His team may have finished in the bottom quarter of the table in 1998, but for once he had been able to wave a chequebook around, thanks to the Norwegians. The League seemed eager to move the goalposts, but Wimbledon's new benefactors seemed determined to battle against elitism too. Joe even boasted that a £6 million bid for Emile Heskey had been considered. And the following season another transfer purchase proved a dramatic first not only for Joe but for Wimbledon: in January 1999, he splashed out £7.5 million on West Ham's Welsh striker John Hartson.

Everyone figured Joe had lost his marbles, but the Wimbledon manager believed he'd secured a good deal. 'As a manager you have to be a good judge of the player you want, and have a vision of the type of footballer you want and how you're going to survive,' Joe explained. 'I have never lost any sleep about buying players. I have looked at them and stalked them and then got them when they are available. Until Hartson became available, I didn't see anything that would help us. I knew the squad would be better than last year because we had so many injuries last season. I formed an opinion that we were good enough to stay in the league [in 1998/99].' Still, the sum lavished on Hartson raised eyebrows, mainly because it was such a huge figure for a relatively small club, representing a £5 million increase in their spending on any one player. Joe didn't care. The criticism went unremarked, and he remained convinced he'd been financially shrewd yet again. 'I've been here eight and a half years [as coach and manager],' he told *The Times*, 'and in those years until yesterday I have spent £12 million, and that is the same as [Manchester United paid for] Dwight Yorke. I have sold between £16 million and £18 million. I have always had to generate in the past. It has always been buy and sell, buy and sell. But now, all of a sudden, with all this money coming in from television, we are probably in the first season where we haven't had to sell.'

Typically, Joe was being disingenuous. Through Sam, he'd been given time to fashion a team in his own unique style. Yes, Wimbledon were a selling team, as he'd argued so regularly, but the club had never sold players unless they'd really wanted to. Wimbledon's transfers, under all of Sam's managers, had been consistently characterised by an increase on their initial expenditure (Fash, Barton, Scales, Winterburn – the list was lengthy), and deals had always been conducted at a time of their choosing. Joe, like Bobby and Harry, was rarely forced into rush deals at bargain prices to keep the debt collectors at bay. Hartson's signature marked a shift in power. Wimbledon, too, were calling the shots when it came to signing personnel.

Now Joe's team were mentally equipped to maintain the Crazy Gang spirit, in the most part because his players were outcasts, and deliberately so. Mark Kennedy and Michael Hughes had been offloaded by clubs who had viewed them as unnecessary surpluses. Chris Perry, despite his impressive performances, was never going to fit into Kevin Keegan's England plans – he was such an unfashionable choice. Even Joe's younger players, Carl Leaburn and Kenny Cunningham, had previously been youth players with top-flight clubs, later bombed out and sold to lower league sides before Wimbledon's bargain-basement scouting policy sprang into action. If Joe had until now been working on a limited budget, his research was reaping a generous harvest. More importantly, the players that had grown up through the youth ranks had been schooled by the Crazy Gang's original protagonists – Vinnie, Fash, Bobby, Sanch – and were well versed in the art of intimidation and high jinks. Under Bobby, pranks were regularly extended to the youth team. Ritual beatings were handed out to players from the moment they signed for the club at sixteen, and the scraps continued into the youth team and the reserves. The idea was that these rites of passage would ensure a legacy of mayhem for generations to come.

John Hartson was the biggest outcast of the lot. Even at 23 years of age he'd already secured a notorious reputation. Prior to signing for Wimbledon he'd been dismissed as a thug after kicking West Ham team-mate Eyal Berkovic's skull into orbit during a training-ground bust-up in October 1998. People still wince when recalling the incident. The touch-paper was lit during a practice match when Berkovic slammed a late tackle into Hartson. As Berkovic rose to his feet, the Welshman retaliated by powering a boot into his assailant's chin. That the assault took place in full view of fans filming the session with hand-held video cameras only quickened Hartson's controversial ascent. The incident was all over the news wires in minutes. West Ham panicked as reactions to Hartson's kung fu chop were plastered over national telly that evening, though no TV company would actually show the incident as it was considered 'too horrific'. Eyewitnesses later claimed the kick could have killed Berkovic.

Clearly, Hartson was always going to be surplus to requirements at Upton Park after that little stunt. It would also be a brave manager who signed him, but, spotting a bargain, Joe grabbed his signature. Immediately, Wimbledon fans raised concerns that Hartson was a liability. He was also habitually unfit, they argued, and many reckoned Joe had gone too far. Yet, reckless outbursts of violence aside, Hartson had enjoyed a fruitful career.

At his first club, Luton Town, he'd netted eleven goals in 54 matches before becoming Britain's most expensive teenager when he signed for Arsenal in January 1995 for £2.5 million. He then scored fourteen in 52 games for Arsenal, though for the most part he was playing second fiddle to the prolific Ian Wright and Dutch maestro Dennis Bergkamp. West Ham swooped with a £3.3 million bid in February 1997, and Hartson was on the move yet again. Under manager Harry Redknapp he became a first-team regular.

It was easy to see why he represented an asset for any team. As a striker, Hartson was a pretty handy package: strong on the ground, even stronger in the air. He was also built like a brick shithouse. When asked for an opinion on his ability, Fash ventured that Hartson was a unique player simply because of his strength. When he went in for a tackle, Fash warned, Hartson would either win the ball or break your legs.

In his first full season with West Ham he became the Premiership's leading scorer with 24 goals, but between the net-busters there were scraps – lots of them. In April 1998, Redknapp claimed that Hartson's temperament had cost West Ham a place in Europe. The striker had been sent off for punching Croatian international Igor Stimac in the face and was suspended for four weeks; Redknapp's argument was that had Hartson stayed on the pitch that day and avoided suspension, the Hammers would have been strong enough to qualify for a UEFA Cup spot. There were punch-ups off the pitch too, mainly because Hartson stood out from the crowd with his Honey Monster physique and shock of red hair. As his fame grew, he quickly became a target for drunken revellers as he relaxed away from football. 'I get it all the time,' he said. 'I used to walk into pubs and get abused by people I'd never even seen before. I've been called a scumbag by people I haven't even met. I was in a packed boozer a while ago and I was getting abused to my face for two hours when all I wanted was a drink with my mates. What do you do? I just lamped the geezer and suddenly I'm all over the papers just because I'm John Hartson.'

Joe, more than anyone, was aware that Hartson would need a change in attitude if he was to justify his price tag. He was also aware from Vinnie's personal experiences that Hartson was a handful. Once, after a civilised meal with girlfriends, the pair became tangled in a fight with a group of lads. The mob had verbally abused them as they left the restaurant, Hartson and Vinnie had given some stick back, and they were set upon. According to Vinnie, a punch-up in the street ensued, though urban myth claimed that they'd really enjoyed a scrap among themselves over 'who was the hardest'.

As the press and media descended on Wimbledon's training ground, the Crazy Gang greeted their new team-mate with typical venom. Hartson was stripped and his flashy tracksuit set ablaze in front of shocked journalists. Later, when he returned home after a long day chatting to TV reporters, Hartson discovered that a piece of paper emblazoned with the word 'bollocks' had been stuck to his back. Within days, then, he was a fully signed-up member of the Crazy Gang, and Hartson was excited by his move to Wimbledon. He was impressed with Joe and seemed eager to follow in the footsteps of Fash, Beasant, Vinnie and Sanch. 'It showed you how much the club had progressed,' said Sanch, who approved of the signing of this talented handful. 'For a player like that to join Wimbledon showed you how much they had grown.' Sam claimed that this signing signified Wimbledon's progression into the Premiership's 'Big Four'. Only Manchester United, Liverpool and Arsenal were bigger than Wimbledon, he said, and Joe agreed with him. 'Do you know that if you add the points we've won since the Premiership started, only Arsenal, Manchester United and Liverpool have more?' he pointed out. 'That's some achievement.' Secretly, the club also believed Hartson's signing could push them into a Champions League qualification spot. Given the money Sam had convinced the Norwegians to part with, it was a big, big gamble.

Joe believed that Hartson would provide enough goals to keep the doubters quiet, though the striker seemed keen to prove him wrong. Hartson marked his first appearance for the club, on 16 January 1999, with a yellow card after carving a savage tackle into Spurs midfielder Andy Sinton. It was business as usual. Despite his attempts to restrict the hot-headed outbursts and wild fists, Hartson was aware that his personality had a wide reckless streak. 'It's a part of my game,' he said. 'But you've got to realise that there are times when you can get stuck in and there are times when you just can't punch players in the face … But no one else can change your mistakes but yourself. I can go and get sent off every week if I wanted to. Obviously it's something that's in you. But I don't go on the pitch and think, "Right, I'm going to hurt someone and get a red card this afternoon." I fucking hate getting sent off. My missus goes mad. I'll get home, she would have heard about it, and before I'm through the door she'll be having a go at me.'

Prior to Hartson's arrival, Wimbledon had been on the up, beating Spurs, West Ham, Sheffield Wednesday and Forest in the run-up to Christmas. They were making good headway in both the FA and Worthington Cups too, though they'd be knocked out by Spurs in both tournaments (in the fourth round of the FA Cup and the semis of the Worthington Cup); with replays, Wimbledon would play the North London side a total of six times in 1998/99. The cup runs eventually took their toll: the Crazy Gang dropped to ninth place and Joe was left to rue his failure to secure a game at Wembley.

Whether this had any outward effect on his health is unclear, but by early March he was out of the game. During the warm-up to Wimbledon's game against Sheffield Wednesday at Hillsborough he suffered a near-fatal heart attack. At the time, his players were out and about in the ground, inspecting the pitch. As Joe walked down the tunnel to return to the dressing room for his team talk, he was struck by a sensation of nausea. He'd felt unwell on the team coach, too: as the squad had travelled to the ground he'd sweated to such an extent that a club physio asked him if he was feeling all right. Joe blamed indigestion and swallowed a couple of pills, but now his throat had tightened, his lungs burned and a dull buzz tingled up and down his left arm. 'The pain was excruciating,' he said. 'I've never known pain like it. Until you experience it you have no idea how it feels.'

Wimbledon physio Steve Allen rushed to his side. He reckoned Joe was experiencing a heart attack and called an ambulance. Syringes were plunged into his arms, an oxygen mask was strapped to his face and he was laid out on a stretcher. An ambulance duly arrived, and it rushed Joe to Northern General Hospital to a specialist unit where he was subjected to a series of tests. It was the worst moment of his life. 'With the blue lights flashing and the sirens blaring I did think I was dying as I lay there in the ambulance that was taking me to hospital,' said

Joe. 'It was the longest journey of my life, which honestly did flash before me.'

As Joe battled for his life, the Crazy Gang were doing the same on the pitch. They somehow beat Wednesday, and the win pushed them up to fifth in the League. The game was won for Joe, claimed Robbie Earle. Days later he was still recovering in hospital. The doctors blamed diet rather than stress, and it was easy to see why. A life on the road with Wimbledon had forced him into a routine of late-night meals – fish and chips after away games, mainly. He was prone to lavish meals in fancy restaurants too. Although the food was good quality, his weight had ballooned to over sixteen stone. A healthy change was in order.

Despite the rumours that filled the papers, Joe didn't intend to quit football. In an interview with the *Daily Express* he even joked that he'd be back in time for the game against Manchester United a couple of weeks later. Typically, Joe was showing the same dogged spirit that had propelled him to success during his playing career. 'I love football too much to be without it,' he said. 'I know I have to take stock of my life, but it is one that has always revolved around football. I have never had a break from it. It has been my whole life. I can't see myself ever switching off. This puts everything in perspective and now I'll have time to reflect. But, God willing, I'm told I should make a complete recovery in six weeks. It's right when people say football is a drug some people can't do without. I'm an example.'

Sam knew his friend was a football madman who was desperate to get back on the training ground with his team, but he didn't want him to rush back and he handed the reins over to Mick Harford and Dave Kemp – temporarily. Both were coaches at the club, and suddenly they'd been handed the task of forcing the Crazy Gang into Europe. John Hartson was expected to deliver too, though an injury was dogging his performances. He managed only two goals in twelve appearances. Without Joe, the club lost its impetus. Wimbledon didn't win a game for the rest of the season and slumped from European hopefuls into sixteenth place. 'We lost sight of what we were about,' admitted Robbie Earle. 'It wasn't Wimbledon in the [last months] of the season; those traits like the fighting spirit, the camaraderie, the fact that we're normally difficult to beat, weren't obvious. Maybe because Joe wasn't there the message wasn't getting through. Maybe as a club we got a little bit complacent.' Sam called it a disaster.

Joe, though, was bearing up nicely. He gave up the booze and shifted over a stone and a half in weight. A fitness trainer ensured he did the right amounts of daily exercise, and Joe took an aspirin every day, as well as the drugs prescribed by his doctor. He dropped out of the Crazy Gang too. At the season's close, Joe told Sam he wanted him to give the job to someone else, somebody who could take Wimbledon into Europe. Joe was terrified his illness would hinder their chances; he also figured he could manage a bigger club when he was fit enough. Sam begged him to reconsider, but Joe's mind was made up. He wanted out. 'I was heartbroken when he dropped the bombshell that he wanted to leave,' said Sam. 'Joe was more than my manager, he was my greatest pal – not in the game, but in my whole life.' Not that the papers believed him: when the decision was announced, journalists speculated whether Sam had actually given Joe the bullet. 'That was unfair on Sam,' said Joe. 'I called all the shots over my going.'

Which was fair enough. Because when it came to picking his successor, Sam called all the shots.

CHAPTER TWELVE

In the summer of 1999, the club was seeking someone who possessed Joe's football acumen and verve as well as a wild streak capable of coping in the jungle warfare of the Crazy Gang's day-to-day to existence. Perhaps still influenced by the arrival of Rokke and Gjelsten, Sam snapped up former Valerenga manager and Norwegian national coach Egil Olsen to lead his club's charge for the 1999/2000 season.

Olsen carried all the right attributes. He had taken Norway into the 1994 World Cup finals, having elbowed England out of the way during the qualification stages, and later to the 1998 finals, where they defeated Brazil in the group stage of the competition. More impressively, he had achieved this success with a Wimbledon-style vigour. With Norway Olsen relied on grit and determination from his players rather than style and swagger. His side included few international superstars, especially when compared to the giants of the world game. 'Brazil obviously had superior players,' he said, 'but Norway had a Wimbledon-style game to beat them.' Norway took 47 wins from 89 games under him, which was considered by many to be one of the more impressive runs in the international game at that time. He had also been capped sixteen times as a player, and had secured the nickname 'Drillo', or dribbler, for his mazy style of play. Rokke and Gjelsten were enthused by Sam's choice. 'Egil was hired for the right reasons,' said Gjelsten. 'His results, historically, spoke for themselves. He took the Norwegian side into the top ten teams [in the world] and there were all the right intentions when we first made the move. Also, he believed in the way Wimbledon were built.'

But it was off the pitch that Olsen really attracted attention. The media marked him out as a football freakshow who stood apart from everyone in the game, even the Crazy Gang. By his own admission, Olsen was 'a little bit crazy'. He looked like Ronnie Corbett, while politically he was opposed to the very culture of professional football, having been a member of Norway's Marxist Red Front Party as a student in the 1960s. Typically, his views on the wages afforded to his players were very forthright. 'I came from a very working-class background,' he explained, 'and it was natural to believe in that philosophy. I don't like all the money in football but there is little I can do about it. I would be reluctant to sign a player if too much money was involved and I think players are paid too much. No wonder some clubs have financial trouble.'

It was an ominous warning for the Crazy Gang, but nobody in the press was listening – they were too busy gawping at his feet. By way of protecting his toes against arthritis, Olsen had taken to wearing a pair of wellies during training sessions, which he then paraded before cameras on his arrival. Many speculated how long it would take before the boots were reduced to a smouldering, bubbling blob at the Wimbledon training ground, but Olsen just laughed. 'I am prepared for whatever they do,' he said. 'I will take it in the spirit it is intended. Anyway, I have bought two pairs just in case. But I don't like my feet to get wet. Two days ago I walked to training [at Wimbledon]. It took me 35 minutes. It was sunny so I wore my training shoes. But when I was going home it rained, so I put my wellies on. I always take them with me because I don't like to take chances.' Cue frantic headline writing and mickey-taking think pieces in the tabloid press. And the howls of derision clearly audible from Wimbledon's Premiership peers didn't end there. Olsen loved ice cream and dog walking. It was revealed that both he and his assistant coach Lars Tjernaa would ride to work on bicycles in an environmentally conscious break from the normal car journey. Olsen also had a pig named after him living in Glasgow Zoo: when the manager had criticised the Scots during their 1998 World Cup campaign, keepers at the zoo decided to name a newborn swine after him. Later, he revealed he was a geography nerd. 'It started out as a competition,' he admitted. 'I was about ten in Norway when my friends and I began to learn the population of every capital in the world, the size of each country and the biggest mountain.' His interviewer then proceeded to ask Olsen whether he knew England's physical size, and the name of Russia's biggest mountain. 'Easy.' Olsen beamed, then announced Russia's tallest peak to be Mount Elbrus, the highest mountain in Europe at 5,633 metres. Apparently, England was the world's ninth biggest island.

The players remained confident that their new manager wouldn't tinker too drastically with their effective formulaic style, though they were aware a cultural learning process would have to take place. 'He is going to have to learn about us and the Wimbledon ways, and we are going to have to learn about him,' said Robbie Earle. 'I have always said that the way we are gives us an extra ten points a season. It's important that he retains that.

Originally the Crazy Gang used to be John Fashanu, Lawrie Sanchez, Vinnie Jones and Alan Cork. Despite players leaving we have maintained that spirit. It will be different under Egil Olsen. It might be that we are all wearing Wellington boots, or playing in them. Who knows?' Chris Perry wasn't convinced. The Rash had seen the wellies, heard about Olsen's ice-cream obsession, and sat through a pre-season tactical briefing before deciding he'd be better off playing elsewhere. The jokes and enthusiasm that had accompanied Joe's team talks had disappeared. Olsen had his own ways of motivating his players, and fooling around wasn't one of them. Perry was transferred to Spurs for £4 million the next day. Elsewhere, Andy Clarke moved to Peterborough, Peter Fear headed to Oxford, and Mark Kennedy was signed for Manchester City for £1 million. In came Tore Petersen from Eintracht Frankfurt on a free transfer, Walid Badir from Israeli club Hapoel Tivkah, and Luton players Kelvin Davis and Chris Wilmott for £1 million. Wimbledon's squad percentage of foreign players rocketed to three per cent. It was hardly enough to excite the fans.

Despite the protestations and pleas from the Crazy Gang's senior players, Olsen was indeed changing their trademark style of play. In pre-season training he introduced the previously eschewed concept of zonal marking, a tactic in which each player becomes responsible for defending a designated area of the pitch when their opponents are in possession. He even began playing his staff in unfamiliar positions – putting centre-forward Carl Cort out on the wing, for example. 'I've been picked to do a job,' said Cort, 'so the boss obviously thinks I'm up to it. But he's a bit of an unpredictable manager.' During pre-season it worked, and Wimbledon turned over Bournemouth, Millwall and Plymouth in friendlies. They secured victory in the opening game of the season as well, beating Watford 3–2, but just when Wimbledon looked likely to settle into a playing routine, they hit the skids, conceding sixteen goals in the next seven games as they fell to Everton and Chelsea and drew with Coventry, Newcastle, Middlesbrough and Derby, and Cardiff in the Worthington Cup.

The press were after Olsen's blood. He lacked the charm of Joe Kinnear and many felt he was diluting the spirit of the Crazy Gang with his European signings, new-found techniques – introducing computer analysis to enhance fitness and performance, in particular – and dour personality. He was also eager to use a 4–5–1 formation, a system completely at odds with the ones most British players were used to and one that also stood against the Premiership's frantic pace. Most of the play in British games took place in the final third of the field; with only one Wimbledon player working in this area, it was proving difficult to maintain control of the game. Long gone were the days when the ball was fired into the danger zone to feed the likes of Fash, Vinnie and Sanch.

The players were confused. Olsen didn't participate in training; he merely picked his squad by watching videos of the team playing. He seemed aloof and clinically detached. Certainly, as the performances became increasingly disappointing, the shouting and hollering that had accompanied Joe's team talks were a long-forgotten memory. According to Robbie Earle, Joe was in your face; under the new management team, the players were often greeted with mumbled instructions. The cracks were beginning to show. 'When we played badly or [got] beaten, you might not get a reaction, so you don't know what he's thinking,' revealed Carl Cort. 'He's the opposite of Joe Kinnear, who used to come in and give us absolute bollockings, name names and throw things – but at least you knew where you stood.' Somehow, in mid-September they managed to claim a 1–1 draw against Manchester United at Old Trafford and a 3–2 win against Bradford City, but then at the beginning of October Wimbledon were humiliated 5–1 by Sheffield Wednesday. Under Olsen, it seemed, the Crazy Gang had developed a split personality.

Olsen brought in more Scandinavian players in an attempt to stem the bleeding: Trond Andersen (£2.5 million) and Andreas Lund (£2.5 million) from Molde, Martin Andersen from Stabaek (£1.8 million), and Hermann Hreidarsson from Brentford (£2.5 million). Statistics now showed that over the past ten years Wimbledon had been one of the Premiership's biggest spenders, blowing over £16 million on players. Worryingly, however, their biggest signing remained in the stands having undergone a knee operation. Alongside Hartson, Robbie Earle, Ben Thatcher and Kenny Cunningham – all vital players – were also sidelined through injury. Thatcher's injury came in January 2000 during a 1–0 win against Sunderland. He made a run down the left wing before clattering into Sunderland's Nicky Summerbee. As he moved past his opponent he slammed an elbow into his face before firing in the pass that led to the winning goal. Anyone screaming for Thatcher's head that night as the gruesome pictures were splashed across the TV would have felt vindicated the following morning, when news broke that he had broken his ankle during the game and would be out of action until the tail end of the season.

Morale in the new millennium was at an all-time low. Players talked openly of relegation, and Wimbledon's Norwegian owners discussed stemming the unstoppable negative cash flow at the club by selling their biggest stars. Olsen, for once, was in uproar, opposed to this move to sell key members of his squad. Rokke wasn't listening though, and Hartson was on his way to

Spurs until he failed a fitness test. For the papers it became open season: Carl Cort, Jason Euell, Neil Sullivan and Ben Thatcher were all tipped for moves away from Wimbledon. Several players believed they were bigger than the club; others had simply accepted the prospect of relegation. The fight had gone out of them. 'Egil Olsen has taken the players who were the heartbeat of Wimbledon and either chopped them, changed them or axed them,' Joe Kinnear sneered. It was indeed the death of a riotous party.

How the hell had it come to this? Sam wondered. His club was in disarray, slumped in the bottom half of the table. The Crazy Gang was a shadow of its former self. This is what Wimbledon had been reduced to: a squad peppered with petulant kids – chancers who wanted to jump ship at the first sniff of relegation – and a board of Norwegian bean-counters who were seemingly intent on dragging his legacy into mediocrity by offloading their greatest assets.

Unhappy at the seemingly endless cash haemorrhage and Wimbledon's failure to move to Dublin, in December 1999 Rokke had employed a Norwegian financial troubleshooter called Svein Bakke to rifle through the club's books. Sam feared he would order the sale of some of Wimbledon's biggest stars, which would probably mean relegation, and resisted the move. He called Bakke a 'small-time operator' and claimed Rokke had no love for his club. As if that wasn't enough, Sam also accused the Norwegians of trying to kill the Crazy Gang's dream of success. 'Bakke is an inexperienced man,' he argued. 'I will vigorously resist him having anything more to do than making his study [of the club's finances]. Maybe they can send him every few months to make another study – he can suit himself. But he is not coming to stay here. [Rokke] lives in the aura of accountants and advisers and all that. He is a special man and I have tried to get him to love the club before, but I never see him. He can only see things on a balance sheet, but I must get him to love this club.' The financial implications of life in the First Division, Sam knew, were huge. He estimated that the club would lose between £7 million and £11 million in TV revenue, sponsorship and the other earners that accompanied Premiership status. Wimbledon would never claw their way back into the top flight if that happened. The gulf would be just too huge. Secretly, Sam loved the idea of buying his club back, but his wife Nada was strictly opposed to the idea. 'In the Middle East,' Sam explained, 'the wives obey, but ever since my wife came to the West, first in the US and then in England, she has had her own views. She has been hounding me for years or more because she can see the effect [the club] has on my emotions when things are not going right.'

Despite Sam's protestations, Bakke arrived at Wimbledon promising to investigate the club's financial situation and deliver his report at the end of the season. As he took up his role as chief executive, the *Sun* newspaper, forever Sam's supporter, organised a Save Our Sam campaign and rallied the Crazy Gang's old guard. John Scales was one of the first to sign up. Bobby Gould also promised to stand by Sam and claimed he was a fighter of courage and great spirit. 'He weathered the financial storm on his own,' said Bobby. 'Wimbledon is his love and passion.' Even Vinnie, by now a full-time actor having starred in the British movie *Lock, Stock and Two Smoking Barrels*, weighed in with his opinion. 'If Sam goes,' he said, 'you'll rip the heart out of the club. It will be the final nail in the coffin of the Crazy Gang. Sam has been holding the lid open on his own for all these years;

now it looks as if it might finally close down. It will be a real, real sad day. I've seen it all happen [at Wimbledon]. I saw Fash go, Wisey go, I went. Now this. It will make me very, very sad.'

Sam was determined to fight back, as he had done with the FA, with referees, with his fellow chairmen. He reckoned on forcing Rokke and Gjelsten into a love tryst with the club. And if that didn't work, he figured he could force the Norwegians out of the club, in spite of their superior ownership stake. Sure, the duo legally had the run of the club, but without the backing of Sam, the board and the fans – who, Sam believed, would rally against the Norwegians at every turn – Wimbledon's new owners would find life in southwest London very tricky indeed. Sam, like Vinnie, Fash, Harry, Bobby and so many others in his teams, was showing little sign of shirking from the bloody battle ahead. 'When I was born,' he said, 'God did not give me a towel so there is nothing for me to throw in. Wimbledon can win things and still balance the books [Bakke had found that Wimbledon were £3 million in debt despite the Norwegians' cash injections and losing more money at an alarming rate], but there is absolutely no value in treating Wimbledon like a business. When you die, you don't have engraved on your tombstone what your bank balance was when you popped off. It's about what you achieve as a person while there is still the last breath in your body. This situation is not about me, it's about Wimbledon and its future. The Wimbledon dream is all about the small man coming good and winning in the end. If Wimbledon slip away then there is no room for your dreams.'

According to Sam, romance was not in force on the Norwegians' side of the fence. In a press conference he accused them of trying to teach him how to suck eggs. The duo took the insults very badly. 'It was quite frustrating for us to come to the training ground and have people pointing fingers at us,' said Gjelsten. 'They were saying, "You guys are ruining the club."' He also claimed they'd worked as a passive ownership, sending Sam upwards of £19 million in cheques from Norway during a twelve-month period without ever questioning his spending. 'We got only shit in the media we didn't deserve,' moaned Gjelsten.

Despite his fighting talk, by February 2000 Sam was tired. He decided to sell up and leave the club that had been his life since 1977. According to reports, he received £1.2 million for his final slice of Wimbledon, but Sam still felt 'shafted'. He put his resignation down to the growing tension with Gjelsten and Rokke: as he'd predicted, by February they'd announced their intention to sell players to ease the £3 million overdraft. Sam managed to block the move and, despite his wife's concerns, offered to pay back the debt from his own resources. He argued that the Norwegians should do the same, but the idea was swept away. A favourable bank loan was offered to Wimbledon, but Rokke and Gjelsten rejected it. The money was later loaned by the Norwegians at a higher rate of interest. Sam was angry and described the bickering as 'a cancer eating into the club'.

Fighting back the tears, he announced his departure at a press conference on 13 February. 'For a relatively small consideration, I have sold my shares to Bjorn and lost my power and privileges,' he said. His 20 per cent of shares went to Gjelsten and South African businessman Charles Koppel. When it was over, he was mobbed by the Wimbledon players and dragged through the mud at their training ground. The high jinks had turned full circle, and the following morning the press gleefully splashed their back pages with pictures of a bedraggled Sam standing ankle deep in a huge puddle. Everybody was taking revenge for the pranks and beatings of previous seasons. Vinnie was heartbroken. 'Wimbledon can never be the same now that Sam has decided to get out,' he said. 'And I for one am glad he has walked away. Something inside him must have died, because I feel as if something inside of me has been ripped out. You can only take so many bricks out of a wall before it crumbles, and Sam is the brick whose removal could see them collapse. John Fashanu went, then Dennis Wise, and this season manager Joe Kinnear. No one realised at the time just how big a bearing that would have. Well, now we have all found out that Joe was the final nail in the coffin. All those names have fled, and now Sam has as well. I'm glad he's out of that place. It's like the kids leaving home and the old man decides to pull the shutters down and walk away while the house gathers dust. Wouldn't it be ironic if Wimbledon got relegated? The man who has held it together for so long has decided to walk away. That's it. I'm not interested in Wimbledon any more. I'll look for their results, but I won't get the same sort of arseache when they lose. I'll probably never go to the club again. How could I when Sam's not there?' Harry Bassett agreed with Vinnie, saying, 'Sam is the Crazy Gang. This is a very sad day.'

Robbie Earle put Sam's work into perspective: 'It's like saying [non-league team] Rushden and Diamonds will do the same in ten years' time, although Wimbledon had none of the backing that Rushden now do. That was the scale of Sam's achievement.'

Across London, like some horrible symbolic ruin, Plough Lane was a crumbling wreck. As a result of arguments over planning permission, Safeway's bulldozers had failed to clear away the terraces and pitch, and Wimbledon's former ground had simply collapsed into a rubble-strewn tombstone. The stands were smothered in weeds, the pitch was caked in dog shit, and Harry Bassett's old office stank of piss. Graffiti smothered every wall. One newspaper invited Fash to walk around the ground and deliver his opinion. He was heartbroken. 'Honestly, this has stunned me,' he said as he walked gingerly through the rubble. 'The best years of my life were here, helping to build up this club. Plough Lane was my second home, and the supporters of the club will be shocked to see this. How could it be left to end up like this? This place has real history. Myself, Vinnie Jones and Dennis Wise had the best moments of our lives here. There are so many memories ... now look at it. Why would people just trash the place like this? It hurts me because this was once our beautiful Wimbledon.'

And in some small way, football had lost out too. Throughout his career, Sam had fulfilled the fantasy of every small-time club owner across the country. On a shoestring budget he'd taken a football club right through the divisions of the Football League and secured an FA Cup victory. Only UEFA's bureaucracy prevented the Crazy Gang from blazing a trail of long-ball passes across Europe too. He'd also chiselled Wimbledon into an impressive club. They had won Fair Play trophies and manager of the year awards and secured international transfers. They'd also competed in top-flight football for over a decade, played their part in the Premiership's inaugural year and been offered £10 million for one of their players (though nobody at the club would reveal who it was). Meanwhile, surveys proclaimed them as having the most intelligent fans in the country (upwards of 40 per cent of them were university graduates) and their team to be the most efficient: on a relative pittance, a small fan base and a loaned ground they had maintained their Premiership status while mounting serious challenges within the cup competitions. Now the money men, of a type infiltrating football at every level, had torn Wimbledon's fantasy existence apart, and driven away their spiritual leader.

Sam Hammam, it was reported, walked away with a total of £37 million after his sales to Rokke and Gjelsten, twinned with the Plough Lane deal. But this was scant consolation. When a drenched Sam left Wimbledon's public park training ground for the last time, the Crazy Gang was officially disbanded, and First Division football was unavoidable. By April, Wimbledon were involved in a relegation scrap. They had conceded 67 goals, sharing the Premiership's worst defensive record with Watford. On 1 May, in a desperate attempt to squeeze their way out of the bottom three, the board sacked Egil Olsen and installed newly promoted assistant manager Terry Burton to the role of manager. 'I have never been able to implement my style of football,' moaned Olsen as he departed from the club. 'In England they are more interested in fighting spirit than real knowledge about football.' Gjelsten was sympathetic to his complaints. 'A change was needed,' he said. 'I am sorry Olsen has been relieved as manager. It is tough for him and it was a tough call for us, because we brought him on board. I would like to thank Egil for doing his best. That is all we can ask from the man. He cares a lot for the club. But I think from the club's side and Egil's side, we underestimated the cultural differences in a tough league.'

Terry Burton's task was an unenviable one, but at least he was aware of how the Crazy Gang had worked in the past. He'd been at the club for twelve years, having worked as academy director, reserve-team coach and assistant manager after joining Wimbledon from Arsenal in 1988. Sure, he was no Harry, Joe or Bobby, but he carried a damn sight more respect than Egil Olsen. But with only two games to save Wimbledon from relegation, the odds were stacked heavily against him. He tried to instil a sense of fear into the players, talking about the embarrassment of relegation, the legacy of the club and the financial implications of life in Division One, for both Wimbledon and its staff. At first it seemed to work: Wimbledon scraped a 2–2 draw against Aston Villa on 2 May, a John Hartson equaliser in the final seconds keeping their hopes alive. All they had to do to ensure Premiership survival was to match the result of fellow strugglers Bradford the following week. But, according to Terry Burton, Wimbledon 'bottled it', and his team went down 2–0 to Southampton. Bradford won. As Sam had predicted, the dream was over.

CHAPTER THIRTEEN

In a last-ditch attempt to resurrect the Crazy Gang spirit, Fash offered his leadership services to the club via a press report. That he had little coaching or managerial experience didn't seem to matter; he was eager to encourage the battling qualities the team so desperately needed to escape from Division One with a minimum of fuss. 'I'm interested,' he said. 'And I think that any Wimbledon player from Alan Cork to Vinnie Jones, Dennis Wise – anybody who has their heart in Wimbledon has to be interested in a job like that. I think if we don't bounce straight up again, there's going to be problems, because once you stay in there too long it is very difficult, if not impossible, to get out of there. The Norwegians have got to get back the confidence of the Wimbledon supporters and they have a very short period of time in which to do it.' Despite Fash's verbal application, Terry Burton was promoted as full time manager.

More to the point, the club had to rekindle the faith of the players. Confidence had struck an all-time low, and the team spirit – formerly sky high under Harry, Bobby and Joe – was now missing. According to senior players who had grown with the club – Jason Euell in particular – morale had been crushed by a combination of Olsen's managerial techniques, the disappointment of relegation and newspaper speculation about the club's financial situation. In Euell's opinion, the team had been a few players short of European contention under Joe; now they were facing a year in Division One at the very least.

Despite Burton's permanent appointment and the Norwegians' vow to ensure a Premiership return within the next twelve months, fan frustration soon began to creep in. This was understandable to outsiders. Rokke and Gjelsten's methodology appeared confused. They took the players on a pre-season training trip to Molde and moved their practice sessions to the salubrious Bank of England sports ground in South London. This represented a positive move, but the summer of 2000 was punctuated with transfer deals as Wimbledon cleared all vestiges of quality from the club's ranks in a desperate attempt to slash the wage bill. John Hartson was flogged to Celtic, Neil Sullivan and Ben Thatcher moved to Spurs, and Robbie Earle decided to retire; Andy Roberts and Michael Hughes were loaned out. Over the 2000/01 season, Carl Cort, Marcus Gayle, Carl Leaburn, Kevin Cooper, Hermann Hreidarsson, Andreas Lund and Walid Badir would leave the club. The sales were valued at around £25 million. The fans viewed these transactions as unnecessary. After all, Rokke and Gjelsten, it was estimated, were among the richest men in Europe. They were even richer than Harrods owner Mohammed Al Fayed. 'What I don't understand is that the people who took on the club are billionaires, not millionaires,' said Lawrie Sanchez, 'yet they seem to be worried about running the club on a £10 million deficit. You don't take on Wimbledon in order to balance the books, do you?'

The clearances weren't enough to do that however, and newspaper reports estimated that Wimbledon were set to lose £8 million during their first year away from the Premiership. It was also reported that the club was bleeding £20,000 a week in general costs, while gates for home matches were dropping to the 5,000 mark – the smallest in the First Division. With the likes of Manchester United and Arsenal visiting Selhurst Park, Wimbledon had been able to expect healthy gates of around 20,000 to 25,000 to counteract the sub-7,000 attendances; in Division One, the likes of Watford and Wolves were a less enticing draw. Worse, the club would be receiving £5 million less from TV revenue. Sky's money was in abundance if you'd been invited to their Premiership party, but if you weren't a member of the Beautiful People, their elite clientele, the perks were slashed significantly. Added to that, Wimbledon were still paying Premiership wages to their players: according to football contracts, a drop in division didn't justify a drop in pay. It was also reported that, by not owning their own ground, Wimbledon were losing out on an estimated £3 million in income a year.

The vultures began to circle, but Rokke and Gjelsten remained defiant. The duo made attempts to move forward and splashed out £6 million on a plot of land estimated at 48 acres to house a brand-new training ground. They were also hoping to open a club shop in Wimbledon High Street. They'd previously tasted relegation with Molde and had transformed the team into Champions League qualifiers playing in a £25 million stadium, and they reckoned on the same career path for Wimbledon. 'Relegation made us even more determined to succeed,' said Rokke. 'We don't take defeat for an answer. It is the same with relegation. Relegation has not changed our vision for the club. That Sunday in Southampton [the last game of 1999/2000] was one of my worst ever days. It was very tough to see the supporters and I felt very guilty. But if we can learn from it as we did at Molde then we can become stronger. We have set ourselves a target of three years to get back into the Premiership and to build a new stadium.'

Rokke and Gjelsten were whistling in the dark, and the fans seemed confused by their mixed messages: they were losing money and had to sell players, but there were proclamations about new training facilities, high-street shops and a stadium. And three years for promotion? It was hardly the fighting spirit Wimbledon fans had been used to in the past. But then the Crazy Gang spirit had been laid to rest. According to Terry Burton, the image of previous Wimbledon teams was something the club had decided to actively distance themselves from. The new manager believed that the moniker had disguised a lot of the positive achievements Wimbledon had secured in the past and, that it was associated with chaos and indiscipline rather than football success. The message was clear: under the new management, Wimbledon's approach to games would be considered and practical, rather than the headless-chicken enthusiasm of the past.

Meanwhile, Charles Koppel – the South African businessman who bought the final 20% of the club's shares – had been chosen to fill the gap left by Sam. It was rumoured he'd previously been a powerboating associate of the Norwegians and he shared a similar dream of football success, he claimed. On the opening day of the 2000/01 season he was introduced to the Wimbledon crowd at Selhurst Park where he announced that the club would be quickly returning to Premiership football. It didn't match the cautious estimate of three years offered by Rokke, but then over the coming years contradictions would fly across Wimbledon like Dave Beasant's goal-kicks.

Behind the scenes, plans were being put in place to relocate the team in their own stadium away from Crystal Palace in an attempt to recoup the money blown under Sam's reign. It marked the beginning of a full-scale war between the club and its fans. During pre-season Gjelsten had admitted that the club required a new stadium to survive. Wimbledon needed to make more money from tickets, and this was an impossible dream so long as they remained at Selhurst Park. He'd also admitted that his vision for a new stadium in the capital was fraught with difficulties. London, he figured – and particularly Wimbledon – was short on land space big enough to cope with a new football ground development, as Sam had discovered. The land that was available was also too expensive. Then, of course, there was the potential cost of building a ground that would be capable of holding upwards of 30,000 spectators. Gjelsten reckoned it would set them back somewhere between £30 million and £60 million, which would have to be funded in the most part by the Norwegians, though they would also require the investment of other benefactors. Presumably Koppel was one of them.

But as the 2000/01 season got underway, the dream of a new home twisted into a dark nightmare. Rumours that the club had agreed a deal to relocate to Milton Keynes began to leak into the newspapers, but then there had also been rumours of moves to Glasgow, Wigan and Basingstoke. This time, though, the conspiracy theories were gathering weight. In January 2001 it was revealed that Wimbledon *were* seeking to relocate to a proposed 45,000-seater stadium in Milton Keynes's North Denbigh area. The development would cost £50 million, and adjoining buildings would include offices, a supermarket and a hotel. The man behind the scheme was Pete Winkelman, a music producer and leader of the Milton Keynes Stadium Consortium. Winkelman also revealed that talks had been staged with Palace,

Luton Town and Barnet over a proposed move to his development, but Wimbledon was the team that appealed to him the most. An official statement, one of many that would fizz across the press wires over the coming years, was drafted by Wimbledon's board. 'In response to media speculation surrounding the relocation of Wimbledon Football Club,' read the letter, 'it is a well-documented fact that the club has for some time been actively seeking an appropriate location to develop a new stadium. In this regard, the club are evaluating various opportunities and in the event any of those opportunities should appear to be appropriate for the club then a statement will be made.' Gjelsten moved to defend the club's actions, claiming once again that Wimbledon had to move or die. Life as a tenant at Selhurst was a road to extinction, while the land options in the capital were limited. Wimbledon had to move out of town.

The fans were up in arms. 'We are a southwest London club and belong in Merton, not 50 miles away in Milton Keynes,' argued Kris Stewart, then chairman of the Wimbledon Independent Supporters Association. 'If you take the club away from south London it will not be Wimbledon. It will be the end of Wimbledon FC.' The mood continued to blacken, especially when Winkelman claimed on Radio Five Live that Wimbledon's move to Milton Keynes was 'a probability not a possibility'.

Reports then filtered to the press that the club was planning to merge with Queens Park Rangers. Charles Koppel even confirmed that talks had taken place with Rangers, who were sinking in an £11 million debt, though he admitted nothing would be done until the fans had given their blessing. The potential deal was also transparent: Wimbledon were offering to merge as a cheap way of securing QPR's ready-built Loftus Road ground in London as well as establishing a partnership. As with the proposed merger between Palace and Wimbledon a decade earlier, fans moved into action to prevent the union. 'QPR fans will fight to retain the identity of our club,' said Libby Magrill, spokesperson for QPR 1st, the QPR Supporters Association. 'We know that Wimbledon fans will do the same.' QPR were quick to calm a rapidly spreading panic. In an official statement, the owners of the club, Loftus Road plc, said: 'It is not helpful that the news has been leaked as we were intent on exploring the opportunity in a sensible and controlled manner. That included sending a letter to all season ticket-holders, club members and shareholders, asking them of their opinion and whether the proposal is worth pursuing. Should these discussions continue, the questionnaires will be distributed in the near future and we welcome honest and constructive feedback. The talks with Wimbledon will only continue if there is general approval from our supporter base. Our initial view is that, in the current financial environment for football outside the Premier League, the idea could have merit and may be worth exploring further.' Koppell, too, promised that the Wimbledon management would be meeting with the fans to discuss their plans for the team's future. A venue and date was even arranged – 1 July 2001 at the Wimbledon Theatre – but neither the Norwegians nor Koppel arrived. Instead, on 2 August a letter was sent to season-ticket holders informing them that Wimbledon would be upping sticks and moving to Milton Keynes in the near future.

When Sam arrived in a pub to discuss matters with the fans the following day, the mob turned on him, blaming him for the sorry mess. They reckoned he'd sold them out to Norwegian businessmen eager for cash profit rather than football success. 'He shafted the club,' said Kris Stewart. 'He sold our ground and took the money. He may not have understood that Plough Lane could have been redeveloped properly. But the one thing he did do was sell the ground and not replace it, which we'll never forgive him for. The biggest problem that faces football is that the game, particularly in London, relies on large pieces of land that would make for lucrative property developments. That affects everybody at every level of football. If we had a ground then the move to Milton Keynes would never have come up. Having said that, we had a lot of fun times when Sam was around too.'

The Football League was not enthused by Wimbledon's relocation and claimed they would block any move away from South London. A nine man panel later voted unanimously against the move. 'After a long and detailed discussion the Board has concluded that the proposed move by Wimbledon Football Club to Milton Keynes cannot be sanctioned,' said Football League chief executive David Burns. 'League rules clearly state that clubs should play in the conurbation from which they derive their name or are traditionally associated unless given the approval to do otherwise by the board.' Koppel claimed their decision was unlawful, demanded an appeal and promised to press ahead with the appeal. Anyone looking for confirmation as to where the club's future lay should have logged on to the internet where Pete Winkelman had registered a website entitled www.mkdons.co.uk.

Somehow, through all the arguments, football continued to be played – not that anyone really cared. In 2000/01 Wimbledon crawled their way to eighth place. The 2001/02 season looked equally bleak as the club – without a training ground to call their own (the Bank of England sports ground was not their property), without a stadium, with a team stripped of class and reliant on homegrown talent, and with sub-5,000 crowds – was in turmoil. Rokke was now threatening to leave the club unless it was relocated to Milton Keynes. Insiders at the club also revealed that Terry Burton was under increasing pressure to meet the financial restrictions imposed by the board. As the new campaign got underway in August 2001 he was forced to blood ten youngsters in the first team because of the huge numbers of established professionals he'd been asked to sell over the past twelve months. Promotion to the top flight looked like a distant fantasy, with or without the move to Milton Keynes.

The small-scale war against the proposed relocation continued to rage. The Wimbledon Independent Supporters Association went on the offensive, organising meetings, demonstrations and mechandise boycotts, and drawing up petitions and press statements. During the first game of the 2001/02 season, against Birmingham City at Selhurst Park, hundreds of black balloons were released into the air. They even published the English game's first unofficial matchday programme, entitled *Yellow and Blue*. Produced in the office of qualified journalist Niall Couper and bankrolled by friends and fans, it was distributed outside the ground. The fans didn't want to move from Wimbledon, the fanzine bellowed. *Yellow and Blue* outsold the official matchday programme by 66 per cent.

The fans had high-profile allies too. Mayor of London Ken Livingstone leapt to their defence, warning the club of the dangers of alienating their fan base. 'A move to Milton Keynes would mean most of the supporters would not be able to see their team play,' he warned. Leader of Merton Council Andrew Judge was also opposed to the move. 'I don't believe this move is in the interests of the fans or the club. It will be completely alienated by such a move. The fans will now have to make a considerable journey to see their club play. It was less than a month ago that Mr Koppel, in front of fans' representatives, agreed to work with the council and supporters to look at neighbouring boroughs to investigate if there was a suitable place for a stadium.'

However, the wheels to move away from London were clearly still in motion. Despite the Football League's ruling on Wimbledon's proposed move and without a legal appeal in sight, the club made applications to relocate in time for the 2002/03 season. To Charles Koppel, the benefits of such a move were clear. Milton Keynes would give Wimbledon a home and a previously untapped fan base. According to Winkelman, it was the largest urban area in Europe without a football club: Milton Keynes was double the size of Ipswich yet had no representative in the Football League. 'What is the point of us playing every match away from home and having to carry it on year after year?' Koppel argued of their tenancy at Selhurst. 'If we had our own home at least the club could then begin to generate its own resources. As it is, we are playing in front of small crowds in a big ground already miles away from Merton.' He had a point, but Koppel had failed to take into account the crippling loss of identity that would accompany the move. The fans had more questions. Was this, as evidence suggested, a football franchise – where the history and identity of a community's club was being bought up by another town? Would the club keep its name? And more importantly, what was the point in having a stadium in Milton Keynes when it was suggested the club would maintain their youth and training facilities in southwest London?

The complaints gathered pace. During the Liberal Democrats' political conference in September 2001 MP Alex Foulkes made a stand against franchising in football, putting forward Wimbledon as well as a number of other clubs as examples of its negative effects. Foulkes was a champion of seemingly impossible causes, however. He'd previously suggested that cannabis should be decriminalised and that the monarchy should be abolished. Later, there was a Fans United Day when supporters from clubs across the country joined in the protest against Wimbledon's move to Milton Keynes. During one match the fans held up signs with the words 'Back to Plough Lane' written across them. A supporters' fund, The Dons Trust, was even founded to help aid the fans' protests. Ex-player Carl Leaburn arrived at the launch party held in the Wimbledon Theatre.

When Terry Burton publicly criticised the club's inability to find a new ground, the fans' support seemed complete. They had a voice in authority. Better still, he was managing the team. On the final day of the 2001/02 season, Wimbledon's board responded by sacking Burton, claiming that another season without promotion had cost him his job. Burton argued that the controversy surrounding Milton Keynes had been a major distraction.

As the fans' discontent grew louder, Wimbledon publicly announced that they were hoping to move to Milton Keynes's 18,000-capacity hockey stadium as they waited for Winkelman's dream ground to be developed. If they didn't, argued Koppel, the club would die. Clearly, in the eyes of the board at least, it was Milton Keynes or bust. But the move to the hockey stadium for the start of the 2002/03 season was blocked because it didn't reach the criteria set for Football League grounds. Wimbledon would have to play at Selhurst for at least another year.

The disasters piled up. The parachute payment – a sum of £5.5 million handed out to clubs relegated to the Football League from the Premiership as a means of easing the financial burden – had expired. Meanwhile, the promised £3 million a year in TV revenue to lower division clubs from ITV Digital had also disappeared: the company had gone bust. For Charles Koppel and the Norwegian investors, Wimbledon had turned into a financial catastrophe. They'd lost £8 million (nearly £20,000 a day) during the season, and in the process the Football League's battle against their relocation had racked up a £500,000 legal bill. Everyone was losing money over Wimbledon.

The fans made their feelings clear yet again, and when 3,400 season-ticket renewal forms were sent out, the numbers of applicants were underwhelming (only 150). Koppel announced that he was going to cut the wage bill from £10.5 million to £2 million, though the only way of doing this would be to sell the last remaining top-end professionals – Neal Ardley and Gareth Ainsworth among them – and rely solely on newly signed players who had progressed through the youth ranks, though the majority of these would be under twenty years of age. For newly appointed manager Stuart Murdoch, things looked bleak indeed.

At least Koppel was happy (although he was receiving violent threats and was under police protection). After months of campaigning he got his wish when the Football League set up a three-man commission to re-evaluate his case for a move to Milton Keynes. To the horror of the fans, they voted two to one in favour of the move on 28 May 2002. An application to develop a 12,000-seater stadium in the Milton Keynes Bowl was quickly delivered, and after months of speculation it was announced the club were finally leaving Selhurst Park. 'If we had not got permission to go to Milton Keynes, the club would have closed in the summer,' insisted Koppel. 'It would not have gone into administration, it would have closed. In order to go into administration you can park your historic debt, but you have to be able to meet your day-to-day obligations. We're still losing money, but the difference is that it's going into something that has a viable future. We'll have a £30 million stadium, an asset, with other facilities, and we'll be able to generate revenues that we've never been able to at Selhurst Park.'

Fans were in tears. Some taped their shirts to Selhurst Park's gates; others simply turned their back on the club forever. Author Niall Couper collated the despair of numerous supporters. One fan registered his disbelief that Charles Koppel, a man who claimed he was in charge of Wimbledon because of his wealth but had never been to a game of football before 2000 (Wimbledon against Manchester United), could take away a club that had been his life. He also argued that Koppel had destroyed over a hundred years of football heritage. Fans took to referring to the chairman as 'Club Killer'; others referred to him as Dr Evil. Koppel understood why the fans hated him – he wasn't stupid. He had ripped the soul from their team by taking them to Milton Keynes, though he felt aggrieved that the blame was laid solely at his door. He tried to explain that bad financial decisions over the past three decades had caused the club's woes, but nobody listened.

For most supporters, not just those who followed Wimbledon, the relocation to Milton Keynes represented the death of a football club. Not that anyone else was really made aware of the fact. The morning after Wimbledon died, the papers were dominated by World Cup hysteria. England were due to fly to South Korea and Japan for pre-World Cup finals preparation. A broken bone – David Beckham's metatarsal – and Roy Keane's decision to quit the Republic of Ireland squad dominated the tabloid's back pages. The FA's controversial decision, like Wimbledon, had been buried. By moving from their home, the team had become the first franchise in football history. 'Some bastard nicked our football club,' complained WISA's Kris Stewart. 'An investor came along and bought Milton Keynes a place in the Football League. There is no way of making sense of this story without figuring that someone, somewhere, was making huge wads of cash out of the move.' It was the end of an incredible era.

By November 2002 even Rokke had tired of the Wimbledon soap opera. Some £23 million of his personal investment had been scattered to the winds, with a further £17 million being spent on loans. The club was still languishing in Division One and he was a publicly disliked figure. Sam had never mentioned these pressures when he'd signed him up for the job. Frustrated, he sold his shares to Gjelsten for a quid. For another pound, Gjelsten bought out his loans, and later invested £4.5 million in the club. Cash seemed to be disappearing down the plughole at an alarming rate.

As were the fans. During one game, a midweek fixture against Rotherham, the club drew just 849 supporters. An incredible 21 turned up for an away fixture against Grimbsy Town. One national newspaper even named every one of those travelling fans, pointing out that a number of them were related to the players. On average, Wimbledon's attendance figures had dropped by 60 per cent. The fans were boycotting the club. 'You say Wimbledon fans are boycotting the club,' said Koppel, 'but they are no longer Wimbledon fans. The Wimbledon fans we have turned up at this game. [The rest] are former fans of the club who decided they don't want to be part of the club's future. If we had a hundred or 3,000 fans, they are the Wimbledon fans, and they are the ones I have to look after. We are now losing less money than we were last year, and last year we were losing £20,000 a day.'

Bizarrely, of the original Crazy Gang, only Vinnie was happy that the club was moving to Milton Keynes. 'It's got to be done,' he said. 'It's the only way the club can save itself. I had my time with Wimbledon, so did all of us from the Crazy Gang days, but it's not the same any more. The club has got no home. It has not had one for years. And if I'm being truthful, I hated every day I went to Crystal Palace. That was never the true Wimbledon home, so what are they giving up? Selhurst Park is a bloody awful place to get to. I gave up trying to drive there in the end and always went by train and got a cab to the ground on matchdays. So I don't see how Wimbledon people can get nostalgic about that. It's good riddance and a chance to start anew with a home of their own at Milton Keynes.' Clearly Vinnie had missed the point. Leaving Selhurst was what the fans had always hoped for, but only if a local alternative was provided. If Vinnie felt aggrieved at travelling to Selhurst by cab on a matchday, then how were Wimbledon's supporters going to cope when travelling to Milton Keynes by public transport?

Worse news was to come. The low gates took their toll, and by June 2003 the club was in administration with debts of an estimated £20 million. In addition, at the end of the 2003/04 season dwindling levels of quality within the playing staff forced the club into League One (the old Division Two), though by then they had completed their move to the Milton Keynes National Hockey Stadium (a move that proved unpopular with other football clubs as well as the fans: both Spurs and Charlton boycotted pre-season friendlies at the ground). Finally, by 2004 the club had been taken over by a Milton Keynes consortium headed by Pete Winkelman and renamed themselves as Milton Keynes Dons. Outsiders wondered out loud what the hell was happening. Supporters began referring to the club as Franchise FC, and by April 2004 the club logo had been changed. The College of Arms had informed the Wimbledon board that their

THE CRAZY GANG

crest included arms granted to the borough of Wimbledon, and given that the club were now located in Milton Keynes it was therefore illegal to retain the crest. The new badge, an updated take on the eagle that was emblazoned on the team's shirt, was described by Koppel as a symbol of the team moving forward. Fans described it as 'bloody awful'.

In the stands, the Wimbledon faithful were voting with their feet yet again. 'The promised football frenzy in Milton Keynes has failed to materialise,' said Nicole Hammond, new chair of the Wimbledon Independent Supporters Association. 'The people behind the move said that the club would get bigger crowds in Milton Keynes, yet the gates there are much lower than they were in London before the move was announced. This has now translated into results on the field, since the club has had to sell most of its best players in order to meet its running costs. The move was always morally wrong, as it totally conflicts with the guiding principle of football – that a club should remain within its community … [The] move has been an unmitigated commercial disaster.' Hammond also argued that the reason Wimbledon's new Milton Keynes stadium had been given the go-ahead by planning officers was because it was announced that the deal was linked to the Asda/Walmart chain. 'They were desperate to build an out-of-town superstore which otherwise would have flouted planning regulations,' she said. 'However, by including a stadium in the plans, it was able to get round the rules. A football team was needed to justify building the stadium, so a deal was struck with Wimbledon's then owners – but only after several other clubs, including QPR and Luton, had been cynically approached. There again, there have been empty boasts. Wimbledon FC was supposed to own the new stadium in Milton Keynes. But it seems likely the real owner will be Pete

Winkelman, through his own company Inter MK ... it appears the club will not actually own the stadium it plays in.' If Hammond was right, Wimbledon's fans had been sold down the river.

But the fans had already found another outlet for their disaffection. Rather than protesting and voicing their disgust as they had done on so many occasions, a group of supporters decided to go it alone and start their own football club – and like Harry's team they planned to do business in the lower leagues. The idea had been developed in 2002, when Koppel was given permission by the FA to move away from South London. The club was to be led by Kris Stewart, accountant and one-time chair of WISA, and local factory owner Ivor Heller, and bankrolled by The Dons Trust and WISA. Heller became commercial director, Stewart took on the role of chairman, and the pair immediately began discussing names such as Real Wimbledon and Anti Franchise FC with supporters. Realising that the London FA probably wouldn't sanction those titles, they plumped for AFC Wimbledon and employed former Wimbledon player Terry Eames as manager.

'We got together a hundred people in a pub on the night of the news the club had decided to move to Milton Keynes, and I started work on AFC Wimbledon the next day,' Stewart explained. 'That's how it started. We knew it had to be done. I had a bit of spare time so I threw myself into it. Then we had to get non-league status, but we had a few knockbacks. To get into a semi-professional league you have to be the senior club in your area according to the county, but by definition you're only the senior club if you're the senior club. That seems to be the strange definition of it: if you are, you are; if you're not, you're not. It's as subjective as that. Initially we applied to the Ryman League Division Two, and to get in we needed 95 per cent of votes from the other members of the league at their AGM, but we only got 87 per cent. One of the secretaries from the league rang us up that night and said that there was another league that might take us, and that was the Seagrave Haulage Combined Counties League. They eventually voted us in.'

Life at AFC Wimbledon gathered pace, and in under twelve months they were holding trials and capturing the best in local amateur talent. 'They were held on Wimbledon Common on the day of the [2002] World Cup third-place match,' Stewart continued. 'A lot of people came down on the day and Terry Burton was kind enough to give us a helping hand. Yes, there were a few chancers there who came along simply to say they'd had trials, but we picked up some pretty good talent too. We soon started whittling down the crop of players into a good squad.'

They later organised a groundshare deal with Kingstonian (which competed in the Ryman League), sold 2,500 replica shirts, hawked 1,500 season tickets, and scored the biggest sponsorship deal outside the Football League and the Premiership, with computer game *Championship Manager*. 'Getting the ground was the first step, and we were very lucky,' said Stewart. 'A lot of people wanted to help us out because they didn't like what had happened to the supporters of Wimbledon. The club had also built up some excellent contacts in the lower leagues through our time before Wimbledon attained league status in the 1970s. We'd also played a lot of friendlies with non-league sides during pre-seasons. Kingstonian were kind enough to let us play there, which was great because it was a nice ground and it was fairly local.'

In their first season together they cruised to third place in the Seagrave Haulage Combined Counties League, notching up 35 victories from 45 games in the process. Their first game, a friendly against Sutton United at Garden Green Lane, drew a crowd of 4,500. Their first league match, an away fixture against Sandhurst Town at Bottom Meadow, drew 2,449 fans, smashing the attendance record. 'The first season we had sell-outs on the first and last days,' said Stewart. 'But we were getting gates of 4,500 people. Later we attracted around 2,800, but they're going up all the time. There are also a lot of new fans at AFC Wimbledon. People believe that this is the true lineage of the club and they want to follow us. There's a real passionate support. The great thing is seeing the young faces at the ground. We've kept the prices down deliberately for the kids and they were probably too young to have been regular supporters in the past. Saying that, one of the first season-ticket applications we received was from a guy who first saw Wimbledon at Plough Lane in 1919 and stopped going when the club moved to Selhurst Park. Now he wants to see us play. There's a really nice atmosphere because people see us as the real Wimbledon.'

AFC Wimbledon's average gates settled at around the 3,000 mark, and it was announced that this was higher than their former incarnation, the Milton Keynes Dons, in League One. AFC Wimbledon are only six divisions below Milton Keynes Dons and hoping to catch up fast. Many fans hinted that a dramatic overlap could take place. Said Lord Faulkner of Worcester, a Wimbledon supporter, during a speech at the launch of The Dons Trust in February 2002: 'AFC Wimbledon, the non-league club set up by former fans, and which embodies the true soul of Wimbledon, is attracting huge crowds in non-league terms, and hopes to win promotion this season. Meanwhile, Wimbledon FC [MK Dons], the club that fought its way to the pinnacle of English football on the passion and commitment of fans and players alike, is now spiralling downwards, thanks to the greed of businessmen who have no love for the game.'

During 2003/04, as Milton Keynes Dons were on their way to relegation, AFC Wimbledon were smashing records. They went an entire season unbeaten, winning 42 games and drawing four as they steamed to their first title victory and won promotion to the Ryman League (formerly the Isthmian League), where Harry Bassett had started his run 40 years earlier. That unbeaten run was eventually extended to 78 games. AFC Wimbledon had a goal difference of plus 148, and picked up the Premier Challenge Cup along the way, beating North Greenford United 4–1 in the final. They later won the 2005 Surrey Senior Cup, a trophy they'd previously secured in 1955. The real Wimbledon were back on the map. 'The lineage of the club starts with us,' said Lawrie Sanchez. 'It continued with the team that went to Selhurst and then the team that became AFC Wimbledon, whether Milton Keynes Dons like it or not.'

Today, however, the club remains aware of the challenge ahead. Harry's dream and Sam's ambitions remain a distant fantasy. The gulf in money between divisions today is bigger than ever. A rise from the lower leagues to football's pinnacle is an unlikely jump, though it remains the club's ultimate ambition. 'Yes, getting the team to the [Premier League] is a dream,' says Kris Stewart, 'but you'd be mad not to recognise the financial differences in football these days. With money ruling football at every level, it is a lot, lot harder for us today. At the same time, in 1975 nobody would have believed that Wimbledon would get to the First Division and win the FA Cup. So we have to be as ambitious as we can and aim to win every game we can. You have to remember that football is about dreams, and if some of those dreams are bloody crazy, well, that's even better.'

BIBLIOGRAPHY

Barrett, Norman, *The Daily Telegraph Football Chronicles* (Colour Library Direct, 1999)

Bassett, Dave, *Settling the Score* (John Blake, 2002)

Butler, Bryon, *100 Seasons of League Football* (Queen Anne Press, 1998)

Couper, Niall, *The Spirit of Wimbledon: The Living Memories of the Dons from 1922 to 2003* (Cherry Red Books, 2003)

Crabtree, Stephen, *Wimbledon: The Premiership Years* (Desert Island Books, 2000)

Davies, Hunter, *The Glory Game* (new edition; Mainstream Publishing, 1996)

Fry, Barry, *Big Fry: The Autobiography* (CollinsWillow, 2000)

Gascoigne, Paul, with Hunter Davies, *Gazza: My Story* (Headline, 2004)

Gray, Andy, with Jim Drewett, *Flat Back Four: The Tactical Game* (Boxtree, 1998)

Hall, Eric, *Monster!: True Tales From A Show Biz Life* (Boxtree, 1998)

Hall, Stuart, *Heaven and Hall: A Prodigal Life* (BBC Worldwide Limited, 2000)

Hoddle, Glenn, with Harry Harris, *Spurred to Success: The Autobiography of Glenn Hoddle* (Macdonald Queen Anne Press, 1987)

Hugman, Barry J., *The PFA Premier and Football League Players Records 1946–1998* (Queen Anne Press, 1998)

Jones, Vinnie, *Vinnie: The Autobiography* (Headline, 1998)

Kinnear, Joe, with Hunter Davies, *Still Crazy: The Authorized Biography* (Andre Deutsch, 2000)

Leatherdale, Clive, *Wimbledon: From Southern League to Premiership* (Desert Island Books, 1995)

Moore, Brian, *Brian Moore: The Autobiography of the Voice of Football* (Coronet, 1999)

Orakwue, Stella, *Pitch Invaders: The Modern Black Football Revolution* (Vista, 1998)

Redknapp, Harry, with Derek McGovern, *'Arry: The Autobiography of Harry Redknapp* (CollinsWillow, 1998)

The Rough Guide to Cult Football (Rough Guides, 2003)

Segers, Hans, with Mel Goldberg and Alan Thatcher, *The Final Score: The Inside Story of Soccer's Trial of the Century* (Robson Books, 1998)

Sheringham, Teddy, with Mel Webb, *My Autobiography* (Little Brown, 1998)

Thomas, David, *Foul Play: The Inside Story of the Biggest Corruption Trial in British Sporting History* (Bantam Press, 2003)

Thompson, Phil, *Do That Again, Son, And I'll Break Your Legs* (Virgin Publishing,1996)

Tibballs, Geoff, *Do I Not Like That* (Virgin Publishing, 1999)

Varley, Nick, *Parklife: A Search for the Heart of Football* (Penguin Books, 2000)

NEWSPAPERS

Daily Express; Daily Mail; Daily Mirror; Daily Telegraph; Evening Standard; Guardian; Metro; Mail on Sunday; New Nation; News of the World; Observer; South London Press; Sun Sunday Express; Sunday Mirror; The Sunday Times; The Times

MAGAZINES

90 Minutes; Arena; Empire; Esquire; Esquire Sports Quarterly; FHM; FourFourTwo; GQ; Loaded; Match; Nuts; Observer Sports Monthly; Shoot; Total Film; Total Football; Total Sport When Saturday Comes; World Soccer; ZOO

INDEX